# KURSK

# KURSK

## *Russia's*
## *Lost Pride*

## Peter Truscott

**SIMON & SCHUSTER**

London . New York . Sydney . Tokyo . Singapore . Toronto . Dublin

**A VIACOM COMPANY**

First published in Great Britain by Simon & Schuster UK Ltd in 2002
A Viacom company

PICTURE CREDITS
1, 2, 5, 7, 8, 14–21: PA Photos
3, 4, 6: reproduced by kind permission of Valeria and Ludmilla Milyutina
10: Popperfoto; 9, 11–13: courtesy of MoD, Crown copyright
22: Peter Truscott

1 3 5 7 9 10 8 6 4 2

Simon & Schuster UK Ltd
Africa House
64–78 Kingsway
London WC2B 6AH

Simon & Schuster Australia
Sydney

www.simonsays.co.uk

A CIP catalogue for this book is available
from the British Library.

ISBN: 0-7432-3072-8

Map by Neil Hyslop

Typeset in Goudy by M Rules
Printed and bound in Great Britain by
Butler & Tanner Ltd, Frome and London

This book is dedicated to the crew of the *Kursk,*
and to the families who survive them.

# Contents

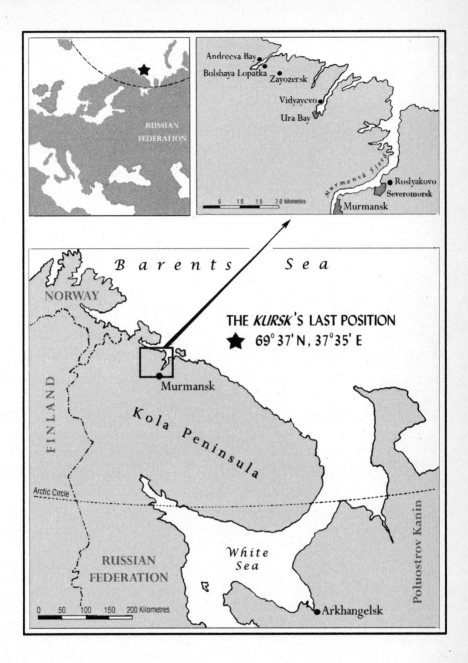

THE *KURSK*'S LAST POSITION
69°37'N, 37°35'E

'There is no fleet in the world where there is such sacrifice. You leave shabby Vidyayevo and sail in a submarine to defend a country which exists more as an ideal than in reality.'

—Russian Orthodox priest, Vidyayevo, August 2000

# Preface

I was at my wife's family *dacha* outside St Petersburg in Russia when I saw the *Kursk* tragedy unfold on television in August 2000. Watching the media coverage day by day, I was appalled at what I was witnessing. As the Russian rescue teams struggled with their patently obsolete mini-subs operating from rusting old ships, I – along with the rest of the world – watched in growing frustration and anger as it became increasingly apparent that any survivors aboard the stricken submarine had little or no chance of escaping. Anybody who might have survived the explosions aboard the *Kursk* was doomed due to the incompetence, arrogance, indifference and tardiness of Russia's rescue efforts. Like many people, I thought any survivors still alive at the bottom of the Barents Sea would have stood a much better chance of escaping from their iron coffin if Western rescue teams had been invited to help a lot sooner.

A few months later I decided to try to write a full and accurate account of what had happened aboard the *Kursk*, why it had happened, and what that meant for modern Russia. Almost all of what follows in the book is documented fact, which I have cross-referenced with media accounts, official statements and my own interviews to try to eliminate errors. The Russian media is notoriously sensationalist and cavalier with the facts, while the state media often repeats official disinformation, so I have been very cautious about including any facts based solely on these accounts. Similarly, I have been careful not to repeat Western media stories or Internet accounts verbatim. All facts have been checked as far as humanly possible, often with those directly or indirectly involved, and with the appropriate experts.

The re-creation of events aboard the *Kursk* itself at the time of the accident is based on known emergency procedures and the layout of the submarine, as told to me by senior Russian submariners who have served aboard a similar Oscar II-class sub from the Kola Peninsula, and other senior officers who have served aboard other types of modern nuclear submarines. Russian submariners have also provided me with details of commands, operational procedures, likely dialogue and conditions aboard the *Kursk*. The crew's relatives have provided other information about life on the submarine, and the time leading up to the disaster. The subsequent official Russian inquiries and investigations, particularly by the prosecutor-general's office, have provided further information about what happened to the sub and its ill-fated crew. Experts in the UK and Russia, including escape-training instructors, divers, rescue teams, military officers, submariners, torpedo specialists and seismologists, have helped me put together a complete picture of what occurred aboard the *Kursk* on 12 August 2000. However, it must be stressed that this part of the book is a reconstruction based on the known facts; I have filled in some gaps in our knowledge – of details that will forever remain unknowable – in the interests of creating a strong and plausible narrative.

I have worked in and on Russia for the last decade, but spent over a year researching the *Kursk* tragedy. Not everyone I met and talked to wanted to be quoted or acknowledged. This applies to people in the defence and intelligence fields, but also to some of the relatives of the *Kursk*'s crew. Many experts freely gave of their time and knowledge. I am deeply grateful to them all, some of whom allowed me to interview them several times. Any conclusions and mistakes, of course, remain my own.

The British Ministry of Defence (MoD) was most co-operative. I would like to thank the Secretary of State for Defence, the Rt Hon. Geoff Hoon MP, and his staff for responding to my queries. The same applies to the Rt Hon. John Spellar MP and his staff. At the time of the *Kursk* crisis John Spellar was Minister of State for the Armed Forces and the man responsible for co-ordinating the government's response to the tragedy. Commander Mike Finney, Staff Officer to the Navy's Director of Corporate Communications, was most helpful, as was his successor, Commander David Heley. I would also like to thank Laurie Manton of the Warship Support Agency, Lorraine Coulton of the Defence Press Office, South West, and her colleague Wendy Shaw. For showing me around the Trafalgar-class nuclear attack submarine HMS *Talent*, based in Devonport, Plymouth, I am grateful to Lieutenant Commander Jim Perks, the boat's Executive Officer, who showed great patience in answering my many questions.

Visiting the Submarine Escape Training Tank (SETT) at Fort Blockhouse, Gosport, Hampshire, I was lucky to be briefed by expert training instructor Brian Wood and Lieutenant Aaron Whild. Commander Jeff Tall, a former Polaris nuclear submarine commander and director of the UK's Submarine Museum, kindly gave me the benefit of his vast experience. Les Stickland BEM, a survivor from the British submarine HMS *Truculent*, provided me with a horrendous inside account of a survivor's experiences after a submarine goes down. I also received help from Bob Morby, Chairman of the UK's Submariners' Association, and enjoyed many conversations with veteran submariners.

The LR5 mini-sub rescue team were very generous with their time and expertise. Commander Alan Hoskins and his wife Jean invited me into their Cumbrian home to recount Alan's experiences. Following a visit to Rumic, the company that operates LR5, and the UK's Submarine Rescue Service HQ in Renfrew, Scotland, I would like to thank Allan Meads, Martin Bulley, Tom Heron, Eric Wrightson and Ben Sharples. Commodore David Russell, formerly based at the MoD's Permanent Joint Headquarters in Northwood, added invaluable information on the British rescue effort.

On torpedoes, I would like to thank Dr John Walker, technical leader, torpedoes and acoustics at DSTL, and John Wade, site director for Qinetiq at Bincleaves, the former Defence Evaluation Research Agency site in Weymouth. Dr Walker and his colleagues made me very welcome in Weymouth and taught me a lot about torpedo technology. Specialists in Russia also provided me with insights into Russian torpedo technology. Other scientists I would like to thank are Dr David Bowers and Dr Peter Marshall OBE, head of the Atomic Weapons Establishment Blacknest Seismological Centre, Aldermarston. My Blacknest visit gave me a vital insight into the scientific evidence surrounding the two explosions aboard the *Kursk*. Dr Frode Ringdal, Scientific Director of NORSAR, the Norwegian Seismic Research Centre, kindly supplied me with details of NORSAR's analysis.

As former Vice-President of the European Parliament's Security Committee and a member of the delegation for relations with the Russian Federation, I have met many members of the Russian political and military establishment, which has provided an invaluable background to this book. I have met hundreds of senior Russian figures from politics, business, academia and the armed forces, including former Soviet President Mikhail Gorbachev; former Prime Ministers Victor Chernomyrdin, Yevgeny Primakov and Sergei Stepashin; Deputy Prime Minister Valentina Matviyenko; Moscow Mayor Yury Luzhkov; St Petersburg Governor Vladimir Yakovlev, and former St Petersburg Mayor and old Putin boss the late Anatoly Sobchak; communist party leader Gennady Zyuganov; Grigory Yavlinsky; Vladimir Zhirinovsky; Duma Speaker Gennady Selezynev and Federation Council Speaker Yegor Stroyev; ex-US Ambassador Vladimir Lukin; and Emergency Minister Sergei Shoigu. I was privileged to be a European Parliament international observer for the 1995 Russian Duma elections and the subsequent 1996 presidential election, and in 1999 I worked on behalf of the Organisation for Co-operation and Security in Europe (OSCE) to cover that year's Duma elections.

As part of the EU's TACIS democracy programme, I have delivered lectures to senior Russian military officers at Coventry University, giving me an insight into the Russian military psyche. My late lamented father-in-law, Colonel Professor Nicolai Chernikov, also helped me achieve a detailed understanding of Russian military perceptions.

His Excellency Grigory B. Karasin, Russian Federation Ambassador in London, met me at the Russian Embassy in Kensington Palace Gardens and provided his country's perspective on the *Kursk* crisis. Vladimir Andreyev, Counsellor at the Russian Embassy, filled me in on the initial reaction to the tragedy. In Russia, Academician Dr Igor Spassky, General Designer and head of the state-owned Rubin Central Design Bureau for Marine Engineering in St Petersburg (which designed the *Kursk*), kindly responded to my enquiries. Captain First Rank Igor Kozyr, International Secretary of the St Petersburg Submariners' Club, was extremely helpful and generous with his time. I also met Captain Igor Kurdin, chairman of the St Petersburg Submariners' Club, who impressed me with his tireless world travel in support of the club.

Although meeting relatives of the *Kursk* crew was a harrowing and delicate task, I would like to publicly record my thanks and condolences to some of those I met. Vladimir Mityayev, Valeria Milyutina, Natalia Tileka and Ludmilla Milyutina were generous and unstinting with their help in very difficult circumstances. Liza Alekseeva and Nicolai Chernikov were kind enough to facilitate a number of meetings in St Petersburg. Of the Russian submariners I spoke to, I would like to thank Captain First Rank Arkady Yefanov, former commander of the *Smolensk*, an Oscar II nuclear submarine like the *Kursk*; and also Ruslan Yudichev, a former Assistant Commander on a modern Delta IV nuclear ballistic-missile submarine and previously an officer in charge of a nuclear sub's torpedo compartment. Both men provided an essential insight into the layout, working practices and procedures aboard modern Russian nuclear submarines. Igor Kuznetsov, a veteran submariner, regaled me with stories of life aboard older Soviet submarines. While in St Petersburg I was lucky to meet Simon Lister, Britain's Naval Attaché in Moscow and someone who had been closely involved in the *Kursk* disaster in the Barents Sea. The British staff in the UK's defence section in the Moscow Embassy proved very co-operative.

Although I am an avid watcher and reader of the Russian media, I must thank my mother-in-law, Svetlana Ivanovna Chernikova, for monitoring the Russian media on my behalf when I was in the UK, and for providing me with relevant videos, books and newspapers. I am especially grateful for copies of those Russian newspaper articles and books not available on the Internet which covered the *Kursk* crisis and appeared when I was working in London.

On the Norwegian side, I am very grateful to Rear-Admiral Einar Skorgen, who was Norway's COMNON (Commander Armed Forces North Norway) during the *Kursk* tragedy, and was intimately involved in the Anglo-Norwegian response to the crisis. Rear-Admiral Skorgen showed extreme courtesy, frankness and patience on the several occasions I contacted him. I would also like to thank the Royal Norwegian Embassy's Defence Attaché, Captain Jan Hagga, for his assistance. In my dealings with the United States, I found a ready willingness to help. Captain Stewart R. Barnett III, Navy and Defense Attaché in London, and Lieutenant Commander Dave Waterman, Director of the Navy Office of Information in New York, provided very useful information. Vice-Admiral John J. Grossenbacher, US Commander Submarine Force, Atlantic, gave me the definitive US Navy response to the *Kursk* disaster.

As background to my politico-military analysis, I must acknowledge the influence of previous meetings in the US with the Hon. David Oliver, Principal Deputy Under-Secretary for Defense in the Pentagon; Dr John Hamre, President and CEO of the Center for Strategic and International Studies and former Deputy Under-Secretary of Defense; Dr Bill Schneider, former Under-Secretary of State; and Robin Beard, former NATO Assistant Secretary-General. Field Marshal Lord Vincent and General Sir Rupert Smith, NATO's Deputy Supreme Allied Commander Europe (DSACEUR) have also been kind enough to previously meet me, the latter at SHAPE headquarters in Mons.

That this project came to fruition at all is down to Andrew Gordon, non-fiction Editorial Director at Simon & Schuster UK. Andrew has been terrifically supportive and thoroughly professional throughout, and I owe him my heartfelt thanks. My good friends, Professor Alistair Cole and Caroline Ancely, were very generous with their hospitality during the course of my research. Last, but by no means least, I would

like to thank my wife Svetlana, a native of St Petersburg, for reading
or listening to my drafts so patiently, and for working with me on the
huge mound of Russian material. *Ogromnoye spasebo*!

Peter Truscott
Artillery Mansions, London
June 2002

# KURSK

# Prologue

In 1596 the explorer Willem Barents set off from Amsterdam on his third attempt to find a north-east passage to eastern Asia. On this third voyage he became the first European to discover Bear Island and Spitsbergen (now Svalbard), and his desire to forge a path through had by now become an obsession. Barents' two ships agreed to separate, hoping to find each other later, but on rounding the north of the island of Novaya Zemlya, half-way between the Russian mainland and the North Pole, his vessel became trapped in the encroaching pack ice. Wintering in the freezing north, with the long nights closing in, Barents and his sixteen crew survived scurvy and polar bear attacks as well as the hostile elements. He and his men were the first West Europeans to survive a winter on Novaya Zemlyà. After building a large wooden house in Ice Haven Bay from driftwood carried from distant Siberian forests, Barents' expedition remained stranded and ice-bound until early 1597. Later that year they decided to make a 1,600-mile dash for freedom, with Barents and his colleagues trying to escape in two small open sailing boats, leaving their ship still marooned in the ice.

Most of the crew made it, but two weeks after their break for salvation on 13 June Barents died in the attempt. In 1871, almost three hundred years later, the house in which Barents and his men spent the winter was discovered, a testament to their tenacity and will to survive. Four years later part of his journal was found. Both the journal and a number of artefacts from Barents' last epic voyage are preserved at The Hague in the Netherlands. Barents' exploits were also faithfully recorded by a surviving member of his last and fateful expedition. Only with the benefit of steam-driven ships, three centuries later, would explorers finally surpass Willem Barents' discoveries and find a north-east passage to Asia.

Barents' courage and determination, combined with his accurate charts and meteorological findings, mark him out as one of the most important early Arctic explorers. He was undoubtedly the greatest ice-pilot of his time. The wild and inhospitable Barents Sea, which claimed him as one of its many victims, was named in his honour.

Formerly known to the Vikings and medieval Russians as the Murmean Sea, the Barents Sea is known to the Norwegians as *Barentshavet*, and the Russians as the *Barentsevo More*. The Barents is an outlying portion of the Arctic Ocean. Bounded by Svalbard and Franz Joseph Land in the north, Novaya Zemlya in the east, the Greenland Sea in the west, and the Russian and Norwegian mainland in the south, it is 800 miles long and 650 miles wide and covers 542,000 square miles.

The Barents is a rich fishing ground. Microscopic phytoplankton feed deep-sea invertebrates, bivalves, sponges and small shrimp-like crustaceans. These in turn feed abundant cod, herring, plaice, salmon and catfish. The Arctic conditions support a surprising variety of wildlife, including whales, seals, polar bears, Arctic foxes, sea gulls, and sometimes even ducks and geese. The climate here is subarctic, with winter temperatures averaging minus 25°C and in the summer rising to an average 10°C. Because of the vastness of the region, temperatures in the north and south can vary by twenty degrees. Navigation in the north is hampered by pack ice, but the North Atlantic Drift is just warm enough to keep the southern coasts clear of ice.

The Barents Sea has an average depth of 750 feet, falling to 2,000

feet in the Bear Island Trench. The continental shelf below the
Barents is quite shallow compared to many of the oceans' depths
extending from the Eurasian landmass. The seabed of sand and silt is
bisected from east to west by the major Bear Island Trench, and the
smaller South Cape, Northern and North-Eastern trenches. The western mainland coast is dotted with fjords, while east of the Kola
Peninsula the coast is low-lying. The coasts of the northern islands are
high and steep, with glaciers creeping out to sea. The fjords of the Kola
Peninsula provide shelter for the Northern Fleet's nuclear-powered
ships and submarines, located at the five Russian naval bases of
Zapadnya Litsa, Vidyayevo, Gadzhievo, Severomorsk and Gremikha.
Severomorsk is the Northern Fleet's main base and administrative
centre. Between them, the bases are home to 100,000 naval personnel
and their families.

Ice-free ports are found at Murmansk and Teribyorka in Russia,
and Vardo in Norway. With a population of 412,000 people,
Murmansk is the world's largest city north of the Arctic Circle. Sitting
on a flat treeless plain on the Kola inlet, Murmansk's main industries
are shipbuilding, fishing and, to a lesser extent, supporting the country's Northern Fleet. Sixteen and a half miles north-west of Murmansk,
nestling on the eastern side of the Ura Bay, lies the closed naval town
of Vidyayevo, a garrison of Russia's Northern Fleet and home to the
crew of the *Kursk* submarine.

# 1

# Disaster in the Barents Sea

On Saturday, 12 August 2000, at exactly 7:28 A.M. Greenwich Mean Time, 11:28 A.M. local time, the Norwegian seismological group NORSAR recorded a disturbance in the Barents Sea. This first 'seismic event' measured around 1.5 on the Richter scale.

Two minutes and fifteen seconds later, it was followed by a much larger event, measuring 3.5 on the Richter scale. The second disturbance was picked up by seismometers in Finland, Scotland, Alaska and the Central African Republic. Because it was the weekend, no one was working at NORSAR, and the significance of the seismic signals from the Barents Sea only became apparent later.

The day before the mysterious readings, Friday 11 August, the Russian Northern Fleet began its annual military exercise in the Barents Sea. The manoeuvres were the largest naval training operation for ten years, the largest in fact since the days of the old Soviet Union. Over thirty warships and 7,800 naval personnel took part, including cruisers, anti-submarine ships, three nuclear submarines, auxiliary vessels, ten shore-based army units, two airborne armies and elements of the Ukrainian air force. The training exercise was led by

Admiral Vyacheslav Popov, the popular Commander of the Northern Fleet. Popov hoped for promotion if the exercises went well, and was looking forward to being transferred to a senior job in Moscow, possibly replacing Admiral Vladimir Kuroyedov as Commander-in-Chief of the Russian Navy. Among the gathered flotilla was the redoubtable state-of-the-art *Kursk* K-141, a Project 949A Antei-class (NATO designation 'Oscar II') guided-missile nuclear submarine. Described as the most effective multi-purpose submarine in the world, the *Kursk* had been commissioned in 1994 at a cost of $1 billion. The boat could dive to a depth of 600 metres and run at a maximum speed of 30 knots on the surface, 28 knots submerged. One of twelve Oscar II submarines built, the *Kursk*'s primary mission was to operate against aircraft-carriers and their battle groups close to Russian waters.

The *Kursk* and its 118 crew, comprising 86 commissioned and warrant officers, 31 non-commissioned officers and sailors, and 1 civilian, had set off to join the exercises the previous Thursday. The *Kursk* was due to take part in the manoeuvres for four days, returning before Tuesday 15 August. The submarine's home base was the Bolshaya Lopatka naval facility, part of the giant Zapadnya Litsa naval base situated on the Litsa fjord twenty-eight miles from the Norwegian border. Zapadnya Litsa is Russia's most important submarine base, and is home to the Northern Fleet's most modern nuclear submarines. After loading up with torpedoes and missiles at Bolshaya Lopatka using two rusty cranes, the *Kursk* headed for Vidyayevo, on the eastern shores of the Ura Bay, some twelve miles to the south-east, where most of the crew lived. Vidyayevo, a closed or 'secret' garrison town, was also a naval base in its own right. As the torpedoes were lowered into the first compartment in the boat's bow at Bolshaya Lopatka, they were carefully checked and accounted for. Stories later circulated among relatives that some of the crew had said they would be test-firing an old torpedo which had had its battery or warhead modified. In any event, both the officers loading and receiving them on board had to certify the munitions were fit for use. The *Kursk* was armed with eighteen torpedoes and twenty-three Granit (NATO designation 'Shipwreck') cruise missiles, affording it fearsome firepower.

After taking on board its full crew the *Kursk* set off to join the military exercise in the Barents Sea. Heading out from Vidyayevo the *Kursk* was an impressive sight, slicing through the Ura Bay on the surface. At 18 metres wide, 154 metres long, five storeys high and 18,000 tons, the vessel was the size of two jumbo jets laid end-to-end. The sun was shining and the water in the bay was as smooth as oil as the *Kursk's* massive twin seven-blade propellers came to life. While some submariners watched her leave the pier, the wives did not. They felt it was tempting fate to watch their husbands disappear into the distance on their beloved *Kursk*, and preferred to say goodbye at home. Superstitious submariners (and that meant most of them) would sit on their kit bags before leaving, the idea being that this would help ensure their safe return.

As usual, the Russians' Barents Sea exercises were being closely watched by NATO. In fact both the United States and Britain had been spying on Russian military movements in the Barents Sea since the 1950s, and particularly Russia's naval bases on the Kola Peninsula. Every 'boomer' or Soviet nuclear ballistic-missile submarine leaving its base had its shadow, usually an American nuclear sub. The underwater game of hide and seek had become a semi-official exercise in blind man's bluff. The mutual watching, or spying – whether from a US Los Angeles-class boat or a Soviet trawler – became an accepted part of the process. The US had even tapped Soviet communications cables in the Barents Sea, and had sown a network of sensitive hydrophonic eavesdropping devices across the oceans to trace the Soviet boomers. Known as SOSUS (sound surveillance system), the technology effectively enabled the US to tap large parts of the Atlantic and Pacific oceans. Combined with air and satellite intelligence, and the use of acoustic sonar buoys, the US had been able to keep a reasonably accurate track of the Soviet Union's underwater nuclear threat.

Watching the Barents Sea exercises in August 2000 were the usual collection of NATO spooks. These included the US surveillance vessel the USNS *Loyal*, the American Los Angeles-class attack submarines USS *Memphis* and *Toledo* (both of which carried cruise missiles), and the Norwegian reconnaissance ship *Marjata*. The *Marjata*, nominally a science vessel but in fact part of the intelligence section of the Norwegian Navy, was moored twelve miles outside the 249-square-mile exercise area. The *Loyal*, technically an oceanographic surveillance vessel, was about 200 miles away from the exercise area. In addition, the Americans had their network of secret underwater hydrophones scattered throughout the Barents Sea, and were as usual tracking the Russian manoeuvres by satellite and radar. Meanwhile, the Norwegians were monitoring the exercises from their navy's northern division headquarters in Bodo, commanded by Rear-Admiral Einar Skorgen. Skorgen himself was following the exercises from the Reitan command centre, buried deep in an Arctic mountain. As COMNON, Commander Armed Forces North Norway, Skorgen commanded all four services, including the coast guard.

By Friday 11 August the *Kursk* was already in the exercise area in the Barents Sea. The crew, under Captain First Rank Gennady Petrovich Lyachin, successfully test-fired a Granit cruise missile with a dummy warhead. A big man, weighing almost sixteen and a half stone, Lyachin looked older than his forty-five years. A strict but fair commander, he had served in the Northern Fleet for twenty-two years and was both respected and slightly feared by his crew. Affectionately called 'Batya' (father) by his men, he was nevertheless known as a fanatical workaholic who always put the *Kursk* first. This mission was going to be Lyachin's last trip, and by way of an old seamen's tradition, he was preparing to throw his slippers overboard on the way home.

Having completed the first part of their mission, Lyachin ordered the *Kursk* to proceed full ahead to a point 69° 37'N, 37° 35'E, north-east of Fisherman's Island, about eighty-five miles east of Severomorsk and Russia's Arctic coast. Here, he and the *Kursk* were to wait until they were provided with an opportunity to test-fire their massive 'Fat' practice torpedo (so-called because of its 650 mm diameter), carrying a dummy warhead. Torpedoes with live warheads were never used in exercises. They were too expensive and too dangerous – an experimental torpedo needed to be studied, not blown up. Instead, the *Kursk* would fire its dummy torpedo at a battle group of ships led by the nuclear-powered Kirov-class heavy cruiser *Pyotr Veliky* ('Peter the Great'), making sure that the torpedo sped safely underneath its 'target'. The torpedo would be collected from the seabed later. Even a basic torpedo cost 'as much as a good jeep', according to one insider, and would not therefore be left to rot at the bottom of the Barents Sea. The torpedo the *Kursk* was about to fire had been recycled many times in the past, and was over twenty-five years old. Unlike the British Royal Navy, the Russians still used the highly volatile hydrogen-peroxide fluid as an oxidant for propellant fuel for some of its torpedoes. The British had abandoned the high-test hydrogen-peroxide (HTP) torpedo following the June 1955 explosion and sinking of the submarine HMS *Sidon* in Portland harbour, with the loss of thirteen lives. The experimental torpedo's casing had exploded while it was being loaded.

Saturday 12 August was a clear and calm day in the Barents Sea, with the waves taking on the appearance of cold slabs of grey slate stretching across the distant horizon. That morning, the *Kursk* watched and waited. At 8:51 A.M. the *Kursk* made its last radio contact with the Northern Fleet's headquarters in Severomorsk, confirming its current position and its intention to launch a torpedo in a mock attack on the Northern Fleet. It received the reply 'Dobro', good. The test-firing was scheduled for around 11:30 A.M., local and Moscow time. At about 11 A.M. the *Kursk* made sonar contact with the *Pyotr Veliky* and its battle group, the submarine's intended target, about thirty miles to the north. Admiral Popov, ensconced aboard the *Pyotr Veliky*, was busily monitoring another Russian nuclear submarine. Popov stood by, awaiting further contact from the *Kursk*.

In the *Kursk*'s Central Command Post (CCP), set just forward of the conning tower in the second compartment, Captain Lyachin was flanked by Captain First Rank Vladimir Bagryantsev, Chief of Staff of the Northern Fleet's 7th Submarine Division, of whose 1st Submarine Flotilla the *Kursk* was a part. Bagryantsev, aged forty-two, was the most senior ranking officer on board. Alongside him was the boat's *Starpom* or Executive Officer, Captain Second Rank Sergei Dudko. Before leaving home, 31-year-old Dudko had sat on his kit bag in silence with his wife, Oksana, to bring him luck. With around thirty-six submariners in the CCP, the place felt like a traditional Russian *banya* or steam bath, despite the best efforts of the air-conditioning system.

The CCP was an oval-shaped room, quite spacious but at the same time efficiently designed, with everyone having their own space. The helmsman sat in the right-hand corner, his hands gripping a wheel the size of a dinner plate which controlled the boat's aft stabilisers. Next to him sat the planesmen, who controlled the sub's hydroplanes, which 'steered' the boat up and down when submerged or enabled it to stay at the depth the captain had ordered. They all sat in front of a bank of computer screens and gauges, showing depth, speed and course. Next to them was the sonar officer, watching a screen showing a flickering cascade of sound. Around the compartment there were consoles for radar, weapons, electronic countermeasures and damage control, all manned by specialists. In the centre of the CCP stood the captain's raised black chair with a soft head-cushion, from where he could survey all the officers and crew at their posts. The command post was particularly crowded today. In addition to the regular 111 crew members, the *Kursk* had five captains from the seventh submarine division on board and two torpedo-design engineers from the Dagdiesel plant in Dagestan, one of whom was a civilian.

Captain Lyachin wanted a visual confirmation of his target, picked up on the sonar and identified by the acoustics. Lyachin ordered the *Kursk* to rise to periscope depth. Getting up from his chair, Lyachin gave the necessary orders.

'Helm, surface to periscope depth.'

'*Yest, capitan*' came the reply – the standard Russian response to a military command.

'Engine turns for fifteen knots.'

Captain-Lieutenant Maxim Safonov, navigation commander, reported: 'Initial course three one zero, captain.'

The *Kursk* began to rise, driven by its two steam turbines and the hydrodynamic action of her diving planes. Lyachin glanced at the boat's chronometer. It was now time. He turned to his *Starpom*, Sergei Dudko. 'Sound battle stations. Prepare for torpedo attack.'

'*Slushayus!* I hear you, sir!'

The Executive Officer picked up a *kashtan* microphone.

'Battle stations! Battle stations! Prepare torpedo attack!'

Captain Lyachin was preparing to have a look around and receive his final orders to launch a practice torpedo. Regulations stated he must have permission before firing in an exercise area.

'Raise periscope and power up the ESM mast.'

A special antenna rose from the boat's fin, heading for the surface. The antenna was designed to sniff out electronic signals from any snooping subs or ships.

The radar officer reported, 'My display is clear, captain. No signals present.'

The periscope rose like a mottled green hooded cobra's head, with a glass eye peering out from white wake as the boat cut through the waves at speed. As Captain Lyachin grabbed the periscope rising from its well, he swivelled the two handles around to face north. Ever cautious, he first scanned the whole horizon quickly from his search periscope, which featured infra-red detection, a camera facility and satellite communications capability. No foreign vessels were within sight. But there, sure enough, he could make out the distant silhouette of the *Pyotr Veliky* and its attendant anti-submarine warships.

The order came: 'Torpedo attack, prepare tube number one!'

Senior Lieutenant Alexei Ivanov-Pavlov, sitting in the Central Command Post, passed on the order to the torpedo section in the first compartment. Ivanov-Pavlov, aged twenty-three, was the commander of the torpedo combat unit and in charge of the launch operation. He had passed out of naval college with distinction, and had been thrilled to be sent to the *Kursk*, which he said was the 'best sub in the world'. Although he had the rank of senior lieutenant, he acted as a captain second rank on the *Kursk*, and his friends were convinced he would become an admiral some day.

Each of the ten compartments in the sub had three or four decks. Running sequentially from fore to aft, the compartments were numbered one to nine, with 5 and 5-bis containing the reactors. The fourth compartment comprised the sleeping quarters, canteen and recreational areas. Senior officers had their own cabins, junior officers shared two to a cabin, and other ranks slept in bunks. The recreation rooms on the second and third decks contained a sauna, solarium and six-metre pool. Another contained a space to watch videos and play chess, along with an aquarium, aviary and potted plants. The crew could sit on rocking chairs in the rest area changing digital images on the wall from snowscapes to pictures of beaches or pine forests. They could even bring cats aboard if they had no one to look after their pets when they were away at sea. All this luxury was a far cry from the cramped Soviet subs of old.

Next to the CCP was the first or torpedo compartment. The compartment was huge, the size of a basketball pitch, and contained four 533 mm and two 650 mm-calibre torpedo tubes, plus the torpedo and missile magazine. The eighteen torpedoes were stacked in three rows suspended over the crew's heads like giant cigars. The torpedoes themselves were conveyed along a hydraulic tracking system to the tubes in the boat's bow. Apart from the old 650 mm-calibre practice torpedo, the *Kursk* carried a variety of other weapons on board, and could fire either torpedoes or shorter-range anti-ship missiles from its six tubes. These included the 533 mm VA-111, TEST 68/71/96 and the USET-80/ET 80 electrically powered torpedoes, and the 650 mm SS-N-16A (Stallion) missile, 110-RU Veder or Type-40 Veder torpedo. Most of these 'warshot' torpedoes and missiles have warheads of between 200 and 300 kilograms. Designed in 1978, the Stallion is programmed to be fired as a missile from a torpedo tube, flying up into the air and then dropping its torpedo payload near the target area, which then sets off in a search and tracking pattern.

There were five crew members and two engineers from the Dagdiesel torpedo plant in the torpedo compartment on Saturday 12 August. Leading the crew was *Mitchman* or Senior Warrant Officer Abdulkadyr Ildarov, a forty-year-old veteran from the Caucasus. Ildarov was the father of two teenage girls with another child on the way. With him were another Warrant Officer, two torpedomen and a bilge mechanic. One of the torpedomen, Maxim Borzhov, at nineteen one of the youngest on board, had written excitedly to his parents earlier that month: 'Dear mother and father, I'm proud I've become a real seaman. I'm happy I'm on such a sub. This is the best sub in our fleet and we have the best commander in the world. I like it here very much. Be happy for me!'

With the crew in the torpedo compartment were Captain-Lieutenant Arnold Borisov and Mamed Gadjiev, both engineers and torpedo specialists from the Dagdiesel factory in Dagestan, on the border with Chechnya. Borisov had not expected to be on the *Kursk* at all: his boss, Captain Second Rank Lohmatov, was meant to have gone on the trip, but dropped out at the last moment. Instead Borisov, due to be married that autumn, found himself roped in to do the job. Gadjiev, a Dagestani civilian engineer at the same plant as Borisov, was easily persuaded to join his friend on the short training exercise to oversee the firing of the 'Fat' practice torpedo. Gadjiev had not wanted to miss going on one of the navy's most modern nuclear submarines, and couldn't wait to tell his daughters about his adventure.

Both Borisov and Gadjiev were engaged on a fairly routine practice test-firing of a modified torpedo. The 650 mm torpedo itself was an old design, of 1953 vintage. The idea was to supply the old torpedo with a new battery. The propellant used to fuel the torpedo was hydrogen peroxide, which the Russian Navy has used since 1957. The relatively low-level representation from Dagdiesel, and the few military top brass aboard the *Kursk*, attested to the minor importance of the impending test-firing. If this had been a test of a major new system then many senior officials would have wanted to be present. Attendance at a major test-firing always looked good on a military CV, and was usually accompanied by a generous apportionment of medals.

As the order to prepare the torpedo for launching came through from Lt Ivanov-Pavlov in the CCP, Warrant Officer Ildarov supervised the laborious loading of the 'Fat' torpedo. Ten metres long and weighing over two tons, the torpedo was moved slowly along its tracking into position in front of torpedo tube 1. Ivanov-Pavlov was still calculating the attack co-ordinates as the torpedo slid into its firing tube. But before the tube's inner door could be closed, disaster struck. While the two torpedomen were moving the weapon into launch position inside the tube, it exploded in their faces.

Hydrogen peroxide is odourless and colourless, and cannot explode even if exposed to a natural flame. However, it does react violently when mixed with certain chemicals or metals, like silver (often used in this type of torpedo), copper and brass, or even if it comes into contact with an oily rag. A mechanical breakdown inside the old torpedo, probably due to a faulty component like an 'O' ring or sealant, led to an internal leak. The inside of the torpedo became a volatile mixture of superheated water, pure oxygen, kerosene and hydrogen peroxide. A physico-chemical reaction ensued, resulting in increased pressure and temperature. As the pressurised hydrogen peroxide had nowhere else to go, it expanded in volume 5,000 times. The torpedo's casing exploded like a balloon, creating a massive fireball in the first compartment, reaching a temperature of over 8,000°C. Everyone in the torpedo compartment would have died instantly from the conflagration. The torpedo tube's door was blown straight through into the second compartment.

Russian nuclear submariners had developed a rather sloppy practice when it came to firing torpedoes. Although naval regulations state that the hatch between the torpedo compartment and the adjoining command post should be securely shut when launching a torpedo, this was rarely the case. In order to lower the tremendous pressure in the torpedo compartment at the time of firing, and to protect their eardrums, the torpedomen usually left the hatch between compartments one and two open. The officers in the CCP turned a blind eye to this practice, which was widespread on Russian submarines. The result was that the fireball created by the explosion of the torpedo casing and the volatile hydrogen peroxide went right through the first compartment into the heart of the Central Command Post. A single *boom* sent the massive ball of flame racing throughout the length of the torpedo magazine and spewing out of the connecting hatch. In an instant, before anyone had time to react, the CCP and its occupants were either incinerated, knocked over by the force of the blast, rendered unconscious or engulfed in the ensuing thick choking smoke and toxic gases. There was no time even to hit the emergency alarm, let alone get off a distress signal. Captain Lyachin, his *Starpom* Sergei Dudko, Captain Bagryantsev and the other senior officers died where they stood. It all happened so quickly, no one in the CCP had a chance to put on their emergency breathing-masks.

Flames licked into the third compartment, where twenty-four crew members worked on navigation, sonar, communications and chemical control. Blue sparks filled the air, followed by brown acrid smoke. Captain-Lieutenant Dmitri Repnikov, compartment commander, did not need to be told what was happening. Like the other survivors, he had heard the explosion in the bow and felt the whole boat shudder and momentarily stop in its tracks. The full force of the conflagration had been felt in the first and second compartments and the third had so far escaped major fire and smoke damage. Men had been sent off-balance by the shock of the blast, knocking their heads on machinery on the way down. But they were alive, nursing only bruises and light fractures. Amid general mayhem, the crew in section three put their emergency drill training into effect. There was shouting and cursing, but no screaming or blind panic as the training took over. Like automatons, the crew donned their facemasks and plugged their air hoses into the boat's central oxygen supply. The fear was there, near the surface, but for now it remained suppressed.

All the crew had red emergency breathing-apparatus canisters hitched to their belts, containing a rubber mask and a hose which could be plugged into the boat's central manifold. They could also breathe independently for fifteen minutes from their OBA canister. Dmitri Repnikov would have bellowed into the intercom to make himself understood in the compartment, no doubt hoping against hope for orders from the CCP, but fearing everyone there was already dead. His comrades next door would not even have had time to hit the emergency alarm, which blasts between twenty-five and thirty times and turns every submariner's stomach. Repnikov probably activated the alarm himself. By now the heat was intense and smoke was rapidly filling up the third compartment. His men clanged shut the hatch isolating the compartment from the second section and closed down the ventilation systems to prevent the spread of smoke and fire, making the area watertight. Repnikov ordered a check of the compartment for damage and injuries. It was now extremely difficult to see more than a few feet ahead in the billowing toxic smoke, even when the dim red emergency lights came on. The automatic chemical-fume alarm sounded throughout the boat. As conditions quickly deteriorated in the third compartment, Repnikov ordered the other twenty-three officers and men to retreat to the fourth compartment.

The scene in the third compartment was replicated throughout the largely intact compartments to the stern of the boat. In the fourth compartment's canteen, Sergei Vitchenko was given a nasty shock when he felt the sub jolt violently backwards. A junior cook and conscript, twenty-year-old Sergei had recently written to his parents, proudly announcing that he had been awarded his submariner's certificate: 'Everything is fine with me; they finally accepted me to work in the ship's Mess . . . The cooks are a privileged class on the boat – we are allowed to wash every day and we get to sleep twelve hours at night . . . Bye, I love you, I miss you.' With his cutlery and dishes scattered all around him, Sergei crouched on the floor of the galley in his mask, braced, and waited in the flickering red light.

The reactors in compartments 5 and 5-bis were protected by the strongest bulkheads in the boat. It would take a truly awesome explosion to threaten the reactors. The job of the sixteen officers and men in these compartments was to protect the integrity of the reactors, keeping them running until a decision was taken to shut them down. That would be done automatically if the sub was in extreme danger, or it could be done manually from inside the compartments, or from the control panel in the adjacent sixth compartment. As the alarm continued ringing, Captain-Lieutenant Rashid Aryapov and Senior Lieutenant Alexei Mityayev, a 23-year-old engineer, watched the reactor control panel anxiously in the sixth compartment. If the reactors were damaged they would all certainly die. In the seventh and eighth compartments, Captain-Lieutenant Dmitri Kolesnikov and Captain-Lieutenant Sergei Sadilenko and their men were doing all they could to keep the turbines running. At the moment, their priority was to keep the sub from sinking, and, if possible, to get her to the surface where she could reach assistance.

The first explosion had struck at periscope depth, around 16–18 metres below the surface, at exactly 11:28 A.M. Moscow time. Despite the efforts of Kolesnikov and Sadilenko, the sub started gliding down. In these circumstances, the usual emergency routine was to 'blow and go', blowing all the ballast tanks to rise to the surface. Compressed air at 3,000 pounds per square inch would hiss into the tanks as the valves opened, enabling the *Kursk*'s bow to start rising. With the CCP taken out and on fire, thick with impenetrable smoke, this was impossible. The inferno was raging so fiercely that Repnikov and his men, next to the Command Post, were fighting to contain the smoke and fire in their own section. They were in no position to venture into the wrecked CCP. Besides, despite Repnikov's repeated efforts to raise the CCP on the intercom, it was pretty clear there was no one left in the second compartment. In the eighth compartment, things went from bad to worse as it became impossible to release the emergency distress buoy. This was normally activated either in the CCP or by pulling a lever in the eighth compartment; or, in an emergency, the buoy would be automatically released and float to the surface. However, unknown to the crew, the restraints on the buoy topside of the hull had not been removed after leaving the factory. These would have to be removed manually, from the outside, before the buoy could become operable. Due to a disastrous oversight, this was not done before the *Kursk* set out to sea. Neither were the emergency antennae in working order. The crew found themselves facing a dire emergency without being able to signal for help or release the distress buoy to indicate their position.

Two and a quarter minutes later the second, catastrophic explosion struck. This explosion was one hundred times greater than the first, measuring 3.5 on the Richter scale – equivalent to an explosive force of around five tons of TNT. The submarine had by now descended to about 100 metres below the surface. The fire and intense heat in the confined torpedo magazine had 'cooked off' several of the torpedo warheads, which could tolerate that sort of heat for only a short time. This second explosion sounded the death-knell for the *Kursk*. Compartments one to four were completely obliterated. The bow section was blown into more than fifteen separate fragments. All those still alive up to the fifth reactor compartment were killed instantly. Three of the reinforced bulkheads were completely blown in by the massive explosion, which was accompanied by a flash-fire of intense heat, reaching almost a third of the length of the boat.

The force of the blast destroyed all in its path. Machinery from the first and second compartments was blown as far as the fourth compartment. Only the reactors' protective bulkhead, twenty times stronger than the others, held, containing not only the tremendous force of the explosion but also the fire and the flooding seawater which followed not far behind. The emergency lights on the devastated boat flickered, then went out. The explosion was followed by a *whoosh* as seawater displaced air from the forward torpedo compartment. In sections three and four the watertight hatches blew in with the force of the initial blast, and over thirty crew members were caught in the corridor of the fourth compartment, where some had retreated from the third section.

The second explosion had violently shunted the *Kursk* into reverse, then caused it to plunge headlong into a brief freefall dive as thousands of gallons of seawater engulfed the four sections of the boat now exposed to the Barents Sea. As water gushed through the gaping hole in the bow at a pressure of 100 pounds per square inch, the *Kursk* was sinking at an angle of 5–7 degrees bow down and listing 25 degrees to the port side. At that angle, everything not nailed down slid towards the port side of the boat, including tools, books, bedding, charts, cups, magazines and people.

Miraculously, the Granit cruise missiles, contained in their specially-strengthened individual launch silos, did not explode. The SS-N-19 Granits have a range of 340 miles, weigh over seven tons, and are ten metres long. A long-range supersonic missile, it has a velocity of Mach 1.5. The power of each top-secret warhead is equivalent to 618 kilograms of TNT, and has a destructive radius of 1,200 metres. On the *Kursk*, the missiles were located between compartments two and five, and fired from tubes at an angle of 40 degrees. The tubes are arranged in two rows of twelve, covered by six hatches on both sides of the fin, with each hatch covering a pair of tubes. The launchers are placed between the reinforced inner pressure hull and the boat's outer hydrodynamic hull. The Granit missiles can also carry nuclear warheads, although there were no nuclear weapons aboard the *Kursk*. Nevertheless, if the conventional Granit warheads had exploded, the whole submarine would have completely disintegrated. As it was, containers holding six missiles nearer the bow were badly deformed, and some on the starboard side filled with water.

In compartment 5-bis, which contained one of the two nuclear reactors, Senior Lieutenant Vitaly Kuznetsov, aged twenty-four, was Reactor Officer in charge of his section of four men. No one could leave or enter his compartment as it was sealed off from the rest of the boat to protect the reactor. He had been blown off his feet by the second explosion, striking the deck with a thud. Now he was pinned down by some machinery as the submarine went into its dive. Lying at an acute angle, Kuznetsov gripped a cooling pipe to prevent himself slamming against the forward hatch. The Reactor Officer was desperately sucking oxygen out of his OBA canister as it was impossible to plug his breathing apparatus into the overhead air supply, even if it was still functioning. As the boat plummeted it picked up speed. The lights had momentarily gone off but now the emergency battle lanterns came on, giving the compartment some dim visibility. The main power systems had gone, but the emergency batteries were still operating. The status of the twin nuclear reactors remained uncertain.

As Kuznetsov looked around him, his familiar surroundings had taken on the appearance of Dante's inferno. Water was spurting out of overhead piping, wires were hanging down and short-circuiting, giving off dense white smoke as the electrics came into contact with water. Smoke billowed up from the bilges, cables smouldered, and some sort of gas was coming through the air vents. Around him, he could see through his mask contorted and bloodied faces etched with terror as the crew in his compartment waited to hit the bottom. Kuznetsov must have thought he was probably going to die. The one positive thing was that the reactors still seemed in one piece, still secure in their special lead-lined sarcophagus. He may drown, burn or choke to death, but at least Kuznetsov knew he wouldn't be killed by his own reactors.

The *Kursk* didn't have far to sink. The Barents Sea was relatively shallow at this point, with the seabed lying at just 108 metres or 354 feet. But even at a depth of 200 feet, enough water could be forced by sea pressure through a one-inch hole to overwhelm and sink a sub. With the *Kursk*, the hole was over seventy metres across. The double-hull of the submarine had been ripped apart, exposing the interior of the boat to the sea. The Oscar II-class sub was designed to withstand a direct hit from a conventional enemy torpedo. The distance between the inner pressure hull and outer hydrodynamic hulls varies between one and two metres. The outer hydrodynamic hull is made up of 8 mm

steel plates, and covered by 80 mm of rubber to muffle sounds and provide added reserve buoyancy. The stronger inner pressure hull is made
up of 50 mm-thick steel plates. However, the *Kursk* was not designed
to cope with a massive *internal* explosion.

Compartments six, seven, eight and nine included the turbines,
stern control panel, electric propeller motors, additional machinery
and systems. Six compartments had survived the two explosions with
varying degrees of damage, and those nearest the stern were the least
badly affected. In each separate half-lit compartment, secured for the
time being by their watertight hatches, each man waited for the submarine to reach the bottom. Some men would have shouted in terror,
while others cursed or prayed. Most just braced themselves for the
inevitable impact. Of the crew of 118 men, fewer than 40 had survived
the second cataclysmic explosion.

At a depth of 300 feet air compresses so much that a single lungful
contains about ten times the surface amount of oxygen and nitrogen.
At these concentrations, oxygen becomes poisonous and nitrogen has
a drug- or alcohol-like effect. The result is nitrogen narcosis, and an
increasing inability to think straight or exert yourself. The surviving
crew also faced carbon monoxide poisoning. When a confined space is
flooded, with both water and air being compressed, for every additional atmosphere of pressure the concentration of the exhaled carbon
dioxide is doubled. A level of 25 per cent is regarded as lethal, but
even at lower concentrations the excessive $CO_2$ affects the normal
functions of the brain and can induce unconsciousness. As the sub
went down, every two feet added another pound of pressure per square
inch. By the time the boat hit the bottom, the pressure in the remaining watertight compartments would be twice that on the surface, and
would increase as the compartments continued to flood. The remaining crew would be dependent on existing oxygen supplies, emergency
OBA canisters, and carbon dioxide absorption equipment.

The *Kursk* struck the bottom of the Barents Sea with a reverberat-
ing thud at 7:32 GMT, 11:32 Moscow time. Four minutes had elapsed
since the first explosion. The impact of hitting the bottom would
have been greater but for the fact that the seabed here was largely
made up of soft mud and sand. But the whole submarine was not lying

at the bottom. Stranded at a depth of 108 metres, the angle of the boat remained at 5–7 degrees bow down, listing heavily to port. The air and buoyancy in the stern of the sub meant that the aft section of the vessel (containing the rear escape hatch) floated above the seabed, while what was left of the bow was stuck in sand and silt. As the *Kursk* continued to flood, the boat would gradually settle on the sea bottom, the increasing weight in the stern of the submarine dragging it down to rest. Outside, at a depth of 100 metres, the water temperature was about 2°C, while nearer the surface it reached 8–10°C.

The explosions aboard the *Kursk* were picked up by the US subs *Memphis* and *Toledo*, the surveillance ship USNS *Loyal* and the Norwegian intelligence ship *Marjata*. In the sky above, NATO's P3 Orion planes monitored the explosions from signals relayed by air-dropped radio buoys. The first sounded like a distant boom, the second more like a violent volcanic eruption. Aboard the *Pyotr Veliky*, Admiral Popov, Northern Fleet commander, was horrified to receive reports from his sonar operators of two explosions in the vicinity of the last known position of the *Kursk*, followed by obvious flooding noises. Popov, with his ginger eyebrows, walrus moustache and puffy red sea-blown face, was distraught. His first thoughts were '*Chyort!* Those poor boys!' He had little doubt that disaster had struck the *Kursk*. Normal practice was for the sub to call in immediately with the torpedo test-fire results. Such explosions, especially the second one, meant the *Kursk* must have blown up and flooded. It would be a miracle if anyone had survived and Popov didn't believe in miracles. He didn't know how it had happened, but he knew it was not just a horrible tragedy for the crew and their families. As Commander of the Northern Fleet, with overall responsibility for the manoeuvres, he would be blamed whatever the reason.

Popov had been trained and groomed under the Soviet system. He knew the two golden rules were never take or admit responsibility for failure; and never be the one to give bad news to your military or political bosses. Life still wasn't that different nine years after the collapse of communism. So, confronted with what seemed like evidence of a huge disaster, Popov did what a long line of senior officers and politicians had done before and after him. He did nothing. It had been the same in the days immediately after Chernobyl in 1986. It was the Soviet way, and it came naturally.

Now in his mid-fifties, Popov had been born in Lugar, a small town outside Leningrad, in 1946. His father had been an artillery officer but Popov himself had spent all his career in the Northern Fleet. A submariner, he had been on twenty-five missions, fifteen as commander, and had spent a cumulative total of eight years underwater. Both his younger brothers Vladimir and Alexei were also nuclear sub commanders. Popov's crowning moment in his career had been when the Patriarch of all Russia anointed him Commander of the Northern Fleet. With his background, he could imagine only too well what sort of hell the *Kursk* and its crew might have gone through, indeed might still be going through. But Admiral Popov also knew enough about submarines and survival rates to know that the crew of the *Kursk* had little chance of surviving such devastation. He half-convinced himself that there might be other reasons why the *Kursk* had not called in. Perhaps they were not in position to fire; maybe they hadn't found the target; or perhaps there was some fault with the practice torpedo which had delayed the launch.

There was no reason to believe, he must have justified to himself, that the absence of the test-firing, the lack of communication from the *Kursk*, and the explosions and sounds of flooding were definitely linked. It could even be a foreign sub in trouble. But Popov was delaying the inevitable: the acknowledgement that the unsinkable *Kursk*, the billion-dollar pride of the Northern Fleet – not to mention 118 men – were clearly in the gravest jeopardy.

There was another reason why Admiral Popov would want to avoid facing the terrible possibility that the *Kursk* had sunk. If that were the case, Popov knew better than anyone else that he did not have the resources to rescue any submariners who might, against the odds, still be alive. The navy's rescue service had been drastically reduced over the last fifteen years, with savage cuts starting under President Mikhail Gorbachev. Effectively, the Russian Navy no longer had a deep-sea rescue capability to speak of. Russian naval divers in Soviet times were trained to go below 100 metres. By August 2000, not a single military Russian diver was trained to go below 100 metres. The Northern

Fleet did not have any functioning diving bells. Two deep-sea mini-subs, Mir 1 and 2, which could reach 1,500 metres and had been used in the 1989 *Komsomolets* submarine rescue mission, took no part in the *Kursk* operation. Reportedly the mini-subs were earning the Russian Defence Ministry, or someone in it, hard currency by taking rich tourists down to see the wreck of the *Titanic* in the North Atlantic. Mir 1 and 2 only reappeared in time for the salvage operation. The Northern Fleet rescue service, under the immediate command of Captain First Rank Alexander Teslenko, only had two old mini-subs at their disposal, both of 1970s vintage and designed originally to operate from a Lenok-class (NATO code 'India') mother sub. The Northern Fleet's two mini-subs, *Priz* and *Bester*, had originally been based on one of two India-class subs which operated the Deep Submergence Rescue Vehicles (DSRVs).

The two India-class subs were launched in 1975 and 1979. Designed for rescue work, the subs each carried two twelve-metre DSRVs placed on the boat's after-casing. The mini-subs operated directly from the mother sub. Both mini-subs had an operating depth of 2,000 metres which was reduced to 600–700 metres in actual rescue conditions. One India-class sub went to the Pacific Fleet, the other to the Northern Fleet. However, due to budgetary cuts, the Northern Fleet's mother sub was axed. Only the red and white- and orange and white-striped DSRVs, *Priz* and *Bester*, were retained. Instead of being launched from a mother sub, they were now based on the *Mikhail Rudnitsky*, a rust-boat and former civilian floating crane, used to lower the mini-subs into the water. The problem with this arrangement was that to prevent the mini-subs smashing into the side of the *Mikhail Rudnitsky*, the crane operators needed paranormal concentration and a sea as flat as a mill-pond to operate. No one even knew if these preparations would actually work in practice, as the ramshackle rescue system had not been properly tested.

Admiral Popov was in a state of denial, assuring himself that he was right to wait and see. If the sub really was down, the best chance for the crew was to get out through the escape capsule in the fin in the second chamber, if it was undamaged. In his heart, given the state of the Northern Fleet's rescue service, Popov knew he could offer no effective help to any survivors on the *Kursk*. In any event, he needed to double- or triple-check before proceeding. Lack of communication from the *Kursk* was worrying but not necessarily a problem. It could be keeping quiet until Captain Lyachin sent his pre-arranged message, scheduled for 2300 hours, that the submarine was 'surfaced and leaving the exercise area'. For twelve hours after the sinking of the *Kursk*, picked up by *Pyotr Veliky*'s own hydro-acoustics, Admiral Vyacheslav Popov refused to declare an emergency. In his mind, the emergency would only become real when the *Kursk* failed to make contact at 11 P.M. Only then would he accept that his own worst fears had been realised and announce the start of the rescue mission. During the day, the Northern Fleet tried continually to communicate with the *Kursk*, to no avail.

While Admiral Popov agonised, but did little else, the situation on the *Kursk* was deteriorating. The commanders of the sixth, seventh, eighth and ninth compartments were communicating with each other via the intercom system, but had lost contact with the 5 and 5-bis reactor compartments. The hatch of the fifth compartment nearest the bow had been badly damaged by the second explosion, but remained jammed shut. All the other hatches were securely battened down. The fifteen men in the two reactor compartments had effectively sealed themselves in to help protect the reactors. With the communications down, they stayed put, gradually succumbing to the build-up of toxic gases, rising pressure and nitrogen narcosis. One by one, they fell unconscious, falling into a long and deep sleep from which they would never awake. Captains Third Rank Dmitri Murachyov and Nicolai Belozyorov and their men obeyed naval regulations in letter and spirit. In such an emergency, their orders were to secure the reactor compartments and wait for further orders or external rescue. That's exactly what they did, and that's where they died.

Water was starting to flood the sixth compartment. Frantically discussing the situation among themselves on the intercom telephones, Captain-Lieutenants Aryapov, Kolesnikov, Sergei Sadilenko and Senior Lieutenant Brazhkin of the sixth, seventh, eight and ninth compartments respectively, decided upon a plan of action. Dmitri

Kolesnikov emerged as the natural leader. They agreed a plan to secure the stern of the sub and retreat to the ninth compartment, which was the least damaged and where there was the boat's only other escape hatch. The escape hatch in the torpedo compartment was clearly impossible to reach (if it still existed), as was the escape module in the conning tower, which was designed to get the whole crew out. As the sub filled with water from the bow, the ninth would be the last compartment to flood. They would move back together, taking any injured with them, carrying them if necessary, and collecting emergency food supplies of condensed milk, cream, sugar and water, breathing apparatuses, spare oxygen regeneration plates, spare masks and any waterproof emergency suits. Each compartment should contain enough emergency food and water to last at least three days, providing the officer in charge of provisions had done his job. Sometimes, for short exercises, they didn't bother taking emergency provisions on board at all, because it was too complicated for the captain to return them afterwards. The bureaucracy and paperwork was a nightmare.

Rashid Aryapov and Senior Lieutenant Alexei Mityayev manually closed down the nuclear reactors from their control panel in the sixth compartment. These should shut down automatically as the cooling waters of the twin reactors became restricted, but Aryapov and Mityayev were taking no chances. Already, there were no signs of life in the two reactor compartments. Aryapov assumed the worst, and came to the conclusion it would be too risky to try to enter the compartments to check on the reactors. As fumes and water started flooding into the sixth compartment through breached pipework and ventilation trunking, Aryapov evacuated his men. Electrical wiring hung down from the inside of the hull, short-circuiting and providing some dull light to the terrified submariners, who were left scrambling in the semi-dark. The men groped their way out of the compartment, along the sloping hull, hauling themselves up the incline, still listing heavily to the port side, grabbing on to pipes and machinery, hand over hand. It was as if their submarine world had been torn apart and turned on its side. They stopped to help each other, pulling each other along and crawling over each other's bodies. Some had fractured limbs or burst eardrums from the second explosion.

Rashid Aryapov and his four men joined Dmitri Kolesnikov and the eight other submariners in the seventh compartment. Dmitri and Rashid, aged twenty-seven and twenty-nine respectively, knew each other very well and were good friends. They had a lot in common: both had attended the same naval college and now held the rank of Captain-Lieutenant, commanding their own compartment. Rashid was born in Samarkand, the exotic city on the old Silk Route, now part of independent Uzbekistan. Dmitri jokingly called Aryapov 'Sayeed, son of the desert', reflecting his dark southern looks. Rashid had married his wife Khalima (who was now pregnant) on the same day Dmitri married his spouse, Olga. Dmitri, called Mitya by his family, was tall (almost 6 foot 5 inches), weighed about sixteen stone and had ginger-red hair. A keen wrestler and athlete, Dmitri was known as *solnyshko* or *zolotoy malchik*, 'sunny' or 'golden boy', because of his hair and general sense of optimism. He had celebrated his twenty-seventh birthday in Vidyayevo on 10 August, two days before the *Kursk* sank.

Dmitri Kolesnikov came from a submariners' family, like many of the officers on the *Kursk*. His father, Roman, had served on nuclear subs in the 1960s as a Captain First Rank. Following in their father's footsteps, both Dmitri and his younger brother Alexander joined the Northern Fleet's 'Silent Service', serving on nuclear submarines. Dmitri had attended the prestigious Admiralteiski Naval College in St Petersburg, graduating with distinction in 1995. He joined the *Kursk* within two months as a junior engineer, and was later promoted to head the seventh, turbine, compartment. Concerned about his bachelor lifestyle and a bout of heavy drinking, his mother Irina introduced him to a fellow teacher at her school in St Petersburg. Olga Borisova was a beautiful auburn-haired biology teacher, who had been married before, and was slightly older than Dmitri. Olga described her first impression of the man who would become her husband: 'Tall, big, red-haired, trousers too short, jacket too small. Impossible to fall in love with from first or even second sight.' But fall in love she did. The couple were married on 28 April 2000, and had their photo taken beside the statue of Peter the Great overlooking the Neva river in St Petersburg, like many newlyweds do in that city. Later, Dmitri showed Olga around the

*Kursk*, together with another friend, Captain-Lieutenant Sergei Lubushkin and his wife. Lubushkin was a senior officer in the fifth compartment. Looking over the huge sub, including Dmitri's own seventh compartment, Olga was overwhelmed by the technology, and told her Mitya she would now love him 'twice as much'.

Dmitri Kolesnikov also had another side to his character which he kept hidden from his crewmates. A romantic at heart, Dmitri liked writing poetry. He had proposed to Olga near the spot where Pushkin had fought his fateful duel in St Petersburg. Before he went to sea that August, he wrote Olga an unsettling poem which she received on 12 August, the day the boat went down: 'When the hour to die will come, although I try not to think about it, I would like to have time to say, my darling I love you.'

Dmitri, Olga thought, had had a premonition of his own death.

By the time the crew reached the ninth compartment, there were twenty-three submariners from the four stern sections huddled together in a space about eight metres long by three metres wide. Here the men sat or crouched on the steeply listing floor, bunched together in between propeller motors, the stern control panel and other machinery. Normally there were just three crew members in this part of the boat. The survivors could hear the hull straining and groaning under the weight of the sea and its own twisted frame. The temperature was dropping. Since the storage batteries were located in the bilge in the first compartment, the *Kursk* had no power supply. By now the emergency lighting had failed completely, and the few available flashlights or emergency battle lanterns had packed up. The men were sitting in the dark.

Dmitri Kolesnikov took it upon himself to assume command. Aryapov and Sadilenko, both also Captain-Lieutenants, must have been partly relieved Kolesnikov took control of the situation. Although nominally Russian Orthodox, Olga always said Dmitri believed in himself more than God. Kolesnikov's calm authority comforted Aryapov, Sadilenko and the others. With the oxygen regeneration unit, Dmitri believed the survivors could last out for days if necessary.

Around 1 P.M., Kolesnikov decided to hold a roll-call. As he sat in the dark, he asked around the men if anyone had a piece of paper. One submariner, sitting hunched up against the hull, had found a small notebook lying nearby, and feeling in the dark for the Captain-Lieutenant's hand, passed it over. Kolesnikov began to write, aided only by the light from the hands of his luminous watch: 'All personnel from sections six, seven and eight have moved to section nine. There are 23 of us here. We have made this decision because none of us can escape . . . I am writing blind.'

Calling out names and ranks one by one, Kolesnikov put a tick against each name. He dated and timed the note, 12.08.2000, 1315 hours. Almost two hours had elapsed since the first explosion. Kolesnikov, good officer that he was, was keeping a record for the benefit of his senior officers and the investigation that he knew would follow. But more than that, he wanted to show that he and his men had kept their discipline and cool in the most difficult of circumstances. Kolesnikov was aware that according to the letter of the navy's regulations, the men should have stayed in their own compartments. His note makes the point that this was an exceptional emergency, and that they had made a rational decision to retreat to the ninth compartment. Dmitri also makes it clear that some of the crew had already tried to escape through the escape hatch, but had come to the conclusion that this escape route was hopeless.

Dmitri and the twenty-two other survivors then made a devastating discovery. For anyone who has looked at the design plans of the escape hatch in the ninth compartment (as this author has), it is quickly apparent that it was not actually designed to enable men to escape from inside the submarine. There was no mechanism to flood up the inner chamber, to allow the pressure to be equalised so the outer hatch would open and allow an escape. The crew would have to open the outer hatch manually, which was impossible given the huge pressure of the sea outside. The escape chamber's inner hatch was even difficult to access from inside the sub, as it was placed two metres from the floor, making it difficult to climb into. Once inside the inner chamber, there were no valves either internally or externally to allow the chamber to flood-up. The so-called 'escape chamber' was purely designed as a sluice chamber, and was not an 'escape tower' of the type used on British and NATO submarines.

On British submarines, the escape tower or chamber is designed in such a way that it can be entered and flooded up from the inside by those escaping. On the *Kursk*, the escape chamber was designed solely to link up with a rescue submersible. A submersible would mate with the outer hatch, which would then be opened from the inside by the crew, allowing access to the submarine via the inner hatch. The Russian crew were trained to escape in the escape module in the conning tower (which was essentially a mini-sub within a sub), or even through the torpedo tubes if necessary, but they were not expected or trained to escape individually through the escape hatches in sections one or nine. If the escape capsule was out of action, they were expected to sit and await rescue. Later Russian excuses that the escape chamber must have been damaged to prevent individuals from escaping were disingenuous at best. They were never designed for individual escape, and the Russian Navy's High Command knew it.

Nor did the Russian crew have any training in 'free ascent', 'tower escape' or 'rush escape', the escape methods taught at the UK's Submarine Escape Training Tank (SETT) at Fort Blockhouse in Gosport, Hampshire. Visiting SETT, it is hard not to be impressed with the quality of training offered to British submariners. Young submariner recruits are taught to escape from an escape hatch using a tank of water 100 feet deep. In the 'tower escape' technique a submariner escapes individually in a controlled evacuation from the stricken sub wearing an emergency suit, shooting up to the surface once he has passed through the escape tower or chamber in a 'free ascent'. It takes each man about two minutes to escape through the escape tower, helped by a colleague. In a 'rush escape', used as a last resort, the submariners flood-up their compartment within the submarine. As the pressure inside the sub equalises with the pressure outside, the outer escape hatch opens and each submariner quickly passes one by one though the tower to the surface. The 'rush escape' is particularly dangerous because of the danger of making mistakes in the dark and hostile environment inside the sub, the difficulty of passing through the escape hatch in bulky suits, and the likelihood of panic.

One of the most important things taught at SETT is to breathe out on the way up, to prevent the lungs from bursting like a balloon as they expand. Divers like SETT instructor Brian Wood have themselves 'escaped' in training from submarines between 500 and 600 feet down, much deeper than the *Kursk*'s depth of 350 feet. There is no doubt that if the *Kursk*'s escape chamber had been of a similar design to those used in British submarines, and if the Russian crew had received training in free ascent, tower and rush escape, many if not all of those who were not killed in the explosions would have survived. The threat of the 'bends', the severe effects of decompression sickness, could be overcome if escapees were swiftly put in a decompression chamber.

There was a danger, however, that even if Kolesnikov and the others had been able to escape from the *Kursk*, they might have died of exposure in the Barents Sea before they were picked up. This was certainly the case with the British sub HMS *Truculent*, which collided with the 643-tonne Swedish tanker *Davina* in the Thames Estuary on 12 January 1950. Although sixty-seven submariners successfully escaped from the sunken sub forty-two feet down, only ten survived after the others drowned or died of exposure. Some, like survivor Engine Room Artificer First Class Leslie Stickland, had to wait up to one and a half hours to be rescued in the dark. The surface water temperature was about 3°C. Some lasted only a few minutes in water that cold. Relating his story to the author, Les, who was later awarded the British Empire Medal, put his survival down to his generous body fat. If men had been able to escape from the *Kursk*, they would have needed ships close by to pick them out of the water quickly if they were to survive. As the *Kursk*'s location was broadly known, and the Northern Fleet's ships were within thirty miles at the time of the first explosion, this should not have been a major problem. As part of the UK's modern rescue service, SETT supplies a Submarine Parachute Assistance Group (SPAG), a group of officers and escape instructors specially trained to drop in to the sea to offer immediate assistance and first aid to submariners who have escaped from a sub. Russia has no such group.

Dmitri Kolesnikov knew he and the rest of the survivors had no way of getting out of the *Kursk* by themselves. They had to pray that somehow their own run-down navy would get them out. They would not have been overly optimistic. Kolesnikov knew enough about the Northern Fleet's rescue service, based in Severomorsk, not to place too much faith in it. It was, he knew, abysmal. A submariner always believes that his chances of survival are very slight if there is a major accident and the sub goes down. It is not for nothing that submariners all over the world refer to their boats as 'iron coffins'. Rather like a plane crash, one instead prays that a serious incident never happens. Dmitri knew they needed a miracle to survive.

As the temperature in the ninth compartment fell to 2°C, and hypothermia became a real danger, Kolesnikov prepared to take another roll-call. Before he did so, he wrote a note to his wife Olga. Writing in the pitch dark, Dmitri's second note is more difficult to read than the first, as his brain slows and the air pressure and carbon dioxide levels rise. The effect of nitrogen narcosis leaves Dmitri feeling drunk. Composing the note, written on a type of log-sheet, is a huge effort.

> Olechka!
> I love you.
> Don't be too upset.
> G.V. [Galina Vasilyevna, his mother-in-law] hello. Hello all my lot.
> Mitya

> 15.15
> It's too dark to write here, but I'll try [to write] blind!
> It looks like we have no chance, 10–20%.
> Will hope,
> That someone will read this.
> Here is the list of those present from the compartments who are now in the 9th & will try to escape.
> Hello to everybody,
> don't despair,
> Kolesnikov

Around him, some of his friends and colleagues also wrote notes to their loved ones, saying goodbye. Senior Warrant Officer Andrei Borisov, a veteran technician from the eighth compartment, addressed a personal letter to his family, sealing it in an empty mineral water bottle. He hoped that at least it might be found later.

On Saturday afternoon, President Vladimir Putin was in the Kremlin getting ready to take his annual holiday at the Black Sea resort of Sochi. Sochi was one of the last Russian resorts on the Black Sea, following the break-up of the Soviet Union. Yalta and the Crimea, so beloved by Stalin and the Tsars, were unfortunately now part of the Ukraine. Like Yeltsin before him, President Putin would have to make do with the presidential villa overlooking the azure sea and palm trees of Sochi, on Russia's own Riviera. The only trouble was that half of Russia would be in Sochi as well, so the place resembled Nice, Cannes and St-Tropez rolled into one, with its grand whitewashed buildings fronting broad promenades, and packed beaches. Most wealthy Russians preferred the French Riviera, Spain or Florida, mainly to get away from their fellow countrymen and because going abroad was now far more chic. As he departed for Sochi Putin had no idea the *Kursk* had sunk. Nor was Admiral Popov or the Northern Fleet in a hurry to tell him.

After a meeting with Duma Speaker Gennady Seleznyov at 1 P.M., President Putin sped out of the Kremlin's Spassky Tower Gate. Seated in his black armour-plated Zil limousine, the president was on his way to Moscow's Sheremetyevo airport and his summer vacation. The day was warm, bright and cloudless, with the afternoon sun dancing off the golden crosses of the Kremlin's Cathedral of the Annunciation. As the presidential motorcade crossed the tourist-filled Red Square, passing Lenin's tomb on the left and the onion domes of St Basil's Cathedral on the right, the pride of the Russian Navy lay stricken helpless on the bottom of the Barents Sea.

# 2

# The Cover-Up Begins

### Saturday 12–Sunday 13 August

'We didn't lose a single minute,' Admiral Popov later defensively told the journalist and writer Nicolai Cherkashin. At 4:30 A.M. on Sunday morning the *Pyotr Veliky*'s sonar identified the *Kursk*'s exact location, 69° 37'N, 37° 35'E. Reported initially as an 'anomaly on the seabed', the submarine was lying at a depth of 108 metres, 85 miles off Severomorsk. Just over sixteen hours had elapsed since the *Kursk* had exploded, and it was five hours since Popov had belatedly given the order to begin the rescue mission. The only problem was that by that time there was already nobody aboard the doomed submarine left to rescue.

The end, when it came for Kolesnikov and the other twenty-two submariners left alive on the *Kursk*, was mercifully quick. As carbon dioxide and carbon monoxide levels rose to dangerous levels in the ninth compartment early on Saturday evening, the men decided to change the regeneration plates on the sub's oxygen regeneration unit. By this time, the compartment was dark, freezing and gradually filling up with water. While recharging the double-decker regeneration unit with the plates, they came into contact with water and oil. Possibly one of the drowsy crew members dropped one of the plates in the slowly flooding compartment. In theory, the plates should only be changed using rubber gloves, on a mat, in a vertical position and preferably in a dry environment. In practice, they are therefore wholly unsuited for use in a sunken and partly flooded submarine, precisely when they are most needed. A single drop of oil can be enough to cause a chemical reaction and fire. Reacting with the oil and water, the plates sparked a spontaneous and short-lived flash-fire, which reached about 300°C.

Three crew members tried to shield their crewmates from the fire, badly burning their upper torsos. They suffered fatal chemical and thermal burns. One man's breathing mask melted on his face. Sealing the fate of the other submariners, the fire sucked the remaining oxygen out of the compartment, the survivors swiftly falling unconscious, overcome by carbon-monoxide poisoning. Most didn't have time to put on their masks. After postmortems Russian doctors put the time of death at between 7 and 8 P.M. on Saturday 12 August.

Dmitri Kolesnikov, one of those who tried to shield the others from the fire, died with his right hand covering his pocket above his heart, protecting his note to his wife, Olga. When they removed his body from the submarine on 25 October that year, his hand was still in the same position. The note was his final testament.

With agonising slowness the Russian rescue operation began to get under way. The *Mikhail Rudnitsky* left Severomorsk at 8 P.M. on Saturday evening, carrying two deep submergence rescue vehicles (DSRVs) with her. It took the ship over twelve hours to reach the accident site. Over twenty ships and about 3,000 sailors of the Northern Fleet would eventually take part in the rescue operation. At 7 A.M. on Sunday 13 August, Russian Defence Minister Marshal Igor Sergeyev put through a phone call to his president on vacation in Sochi. Sergeyev, then aged sixty-one, recalled the conversation with President Vladimir Putin: 'I reported to the president from my work place that the submarine was not communicating [and] its location, although at that point it was still to be identified.'

Putin's first reaction was to ask about the state of the nuclear reactors. The crew's fate seemed to be a secondary consideration. He constantly asked whether everything had been done and whether there was anything else that needed doing. Putin also queried whether he needed to break off his family holiday on the Black Sea. Sergeyev reassuringly responded: 'To tell you the truth, I told the president, "Vladimir Vladimirovich, I personally believe that firm command has been organised and the successful deployment of search means, the shorter than expected time taken to find and identify the submarine . . . in my opinion, your presence there is not necessary now." I still believe that my advice was correct.'

President Putin later regretted taking Marshal Sergeyev's counsel, but for the time being remained by the beach. His onerous schedule included appointing the ambassadors to Chile and Jamaica, sending a seventieth birthday card to a famous actress and some jet-skiing. In the West, similar behaviour by a political leader would be unthinkable at a time of such grave crisis. This, however, was Russia, and the old Soviet mentality was still very much in evidence. Putin would learn a few political lessons the hard way as the crisis unfolded.

While Russian rescue ships gathered above the *Kursk* on Sunday morning and all through the afternoon, Admiral Popov told journalists from Itar-Tass, the state news agency, that the naval exercise had been 'a great success'. Broadcast that evening on state TV, the Northern Fleet commander informed the nation that his men had performed with 'utter professionalism'. Everything, he declared confidently, had gone well. Privately, he later admitted he thought at the time that the explosions had killed all or most of the crew.

Back in the *Kursk*'s garrison town, Vidyayevo, stories were already circulating on Sunday morning that the nuclear submarine was in trouble. People had heard that the Northern Fleet's rescue services had been called out very early that morning. Later on Sunday morning, a member of the rescue team returned to Vidyayevo. Buying bread from a shop, the man confessed he was exhausted. 'Why?' someone asked. 'We've been up all night looking for a sub. The *Kursk* is at the bottom of the sea.' A woman fainted on the spot, still holding her grandson. This was how some of the relatives heard their loved ones were in danger. There was no official announcement. In fact, officers in Vidyayevo were *ordered* not to discuss the disaster.

Irina, Captain Gennady Lyachin's wife, was as in the dark as everyone else. On 10 August, Captain Lyachin had left his flat at Zarechnaya 26, telling his wife and son, Gleb, he would be gone for four days. Before he went to sea, Irina usually repeated the same joke: 'Don't flirt with other women and drink only water.' On this occasion, for some reason, she gave it a miss. Originally, Gleb, a submariner cadet, was due to accompany his father on his last mission, but his plans subsequently changed. Gennady had gone to sea on their silver wedding anniversary, marking twenty-five years of marriage to the day. In a typically gallant gesture, a *Mitchman* (warrant officer) later knocked at Irina's door with a beautiful bunch of flowers from her husband, with a message that Gennady would say more when he came back.

Irina Lyachina had met Gennady while they were both teenagers at school in Volgograd, the city formerly known as Stalingrad on the mighty Volga river. A star pupil, Gennady was influenced and impressed by Irina's submariner father. Fascinated by his stories of the 'Silent Service', Gennady decided to become a submariner himself. He made it into the prestigious Leningrad naval academy, marrying Irina after she finished her studies in Moscow. They named their son after Irina's father, Gleb. Respected, dedicated and hard-working, Lyachin was known throughout Vidyayevo. Twenty-two years of service in the Northern Fleet, two decorations and the command of the billion-dollar *Kursk* brought Lyachin a salary of US$200 per month. A local woman who worked at *Kambus*, the officers' canteen at Vidyayevo, said, 'Lyachin stood out. The town is a world apart, where everyone knows one another. Lyachin's reputation was enviable, both as a captain and a civilian. He was the top.'

By Sunday afternoon, rumours were rife in Vidyayevo's close-knit naval community that the *Kursk* was in distress. When you arrive in the 'closed' or secret garrison town, set inside the Arctic Circle, you pass two check-points manned by armed sentries and surrounded by barbed wire. You need a pass to enter or leave the town. Vidyayevo itself consists of grey, shabby apartment blocks, laid out like a giant

Lego set, so beloved by Soviet architects and hated by everyone else. Serving the 20,000 inhabitants are two schools, the naval Officers' Club, a number of shops and several kiosks run by extended families from the Caucasus, in Russia's deep south. Many of the newer shops have been opened by retired or redundant submariners, using their $1,500 pay-offs. They stay in Vidyayevo because they have nowhere else to go.

Anyone wanting a newspaper has to queue at the one kiosk which acts as a link between Vidyayevo and the outside world. A bus, donated by the Russian city of Kursk, helps ferry people around the town. The sub was named after the city to attract sponsorship in post-Soviet days, and fruit, fresh vegetables and recruits regularly flowed into Vidyayevo from the southern Russian city. Vidyayevo itself is set on the treeless and barren Ura Bay, an inlet of the Kola Peninsula leading out to the Barents Sea. It is so cold here in winter that only small bushes can survive in the open. The last snow disappears in June. The Kola Peninsula in this part of Russia's far north is an almost forgotten corner of the country, clinging on to the back of Scandinavia, almost enveloping the White Sea and cutting it off from the Arctic Ocean.

In winter the people of Vidyayevo experience the 'polar night', when it is light only between 12 noon and 2 P.M. For eight months of the year the town is dark, oppressive and covered in snow. The temperature can drop to minus 40°C, with strong bitter winds blowing in from the Barents Sea and the Arctic Ocean. The weather can change markedly several times during the course of a single day. In the 'Land of the Midnight Sun', the short summer months can be very hot, with the sun shining brightly all day and night. Nature around Vidyayevo is pristine, beautiful and clean. You can drink fresh water direct from local lakes, and go night-fishing to catch fish for a breakfast barbecue. Around the time of the equinoxes in March and September, the Northern Lights or *aurora borealis* become visible in the night sky.

Speaking with the families of the *Kursk*'s crew who live in Vidyayevo, it is clear the community spirit is strong. When one apartment has its water cut off, no one has water. Valeria Milyutina, the

young and pretty wife of the *Kursk*'s 28-year-old Captain Third Rank
Andrei Milyutin, remembers that when they arrived in Vidyayevo
with their eight-month-old daughter, they had no cold water for eight
months. The only water available was scalding hot, and they had to
wait for it to cool down before using it. In the summer, there was
often no hot water at all. Andrei and Valeria were relatively lucky.
Milyutin's salary of $130 per month reflected his fairly senior rank as
survivability division commander, based in the *Kursk*'s Central
Command Post in the second compartment. Milyutin's salary was less
than Captain Lyachin's $200 per month, but more than the average
$35–50 per month for the rest of the crew.

The flats in Vidyayevo are generally tiny and tatty. A young officer
couple were lucky if they had a two-room apartment with a bathroom
and kitchen to call their own. The pipes are in a poor condition, the
windows have cracks in them, mould grows on the ceilings, the wall-
paper often peels, the roofs leak, and in winter ice forms on the inside
of the window panes. Walls are so thin you can hear your neighbours
speaking even in low tones. Privacy is non-existent. Single officers
and ratings stay in dormitory-style accommodation, with several to a
room.

Officers and men repair and even make their own heaters, to prevent their families freezing in winter. The radiators are at best tepid,
and the thermometers in the flats sometimes drop to 2°C, even when
the central heating is working. In the decade since the collapse of the
USSR, submariners have periodically taken their wives and children
to live on their docked submarines for several days at a time because
their flats were too cold. At least the submarines were heated. The
flats may have been below-par, but in the words of one officer's wife,
'At least they were our own.' Here in Vidyayevo the officers and their
families avoided the fate of many of their parents, who lived in
cramped communal flats in the city, where over twenty people can
share one bathroom and two ovens.

Life could be hard in Vidyayevo for the *Kursk*'s crew and their families. Senior Lieutenant Alexei Mityayev, the engineer who manually
closed down the *Kursk*'s reactor with Captain-Lieutenant Aryapov,
came from a family of submariners. Both Alexei's father and grandfather

had served on submarines, and he followed the family tradition, despite entreaties from his mother to do something which would give him a better life. Alexei lived in a small flat with three others in Vidyayevo, and three of the four served on the *Kursk*. In the summer of 2000, with Alexei's monthly salary of $50 again hopelessly overdue, he had been living on wild mushrooms (which he picked himself) and mayonnaise. Alexei's parents in St Petersburg offered to send him money but he refused, determined not to be a burden on his family. Like many of the young officers on the *Kursk*, Andrei was serving out of a sense of family tradition, honour and duty. Alexei's view was that 'somebody has to serve the country'.

Alexei's predicament in Vidyayevo was far from exceptional. Lyubov Kichkiruk had lived in Vidyayevo for almost ten years with her husband Vasily and their two children. Vasily, aged thirty-three, was a senior warrant officer with the medical team, based in the *Kursk's* fourth compartment. When they first arrived in Vidyayevo, she remembered, there was a restaurant, but it closed because no one had enough money to go there. Over the years following the collapse of the USSR, living standards seriously deteriorated. Lyubov was head of the *Kursk* wives' committee, and remembers many occasions in the 1990s when the submariners' salaries were months late, although this began to improve under President Putin. She recalled: 'Through the months when salaries were not being paid, we all suffered together. When times were bad we caught crabs and gathered berries and mushrooms to eat instead of shop food. Sometimes we couldn't afford to buy bread and survived by living on the credit we were given at the naval stores. On the day that the money finally arrived, the whole garrison would be out celebrating.'

Officer submariners in Vidyayevo, like many in Russia's armed forces, moonlight as night-watchmen and taxi drivers to make ends meet, in the absence of regular and decent pay. The *Kursk's* 26-year-old doctor, Captain Alexei Stankevich, also based in the sub's fourth compartment, even had to pawn his ID document to pay for food and drink for his wife's visit to the garrison town. Captain-Lieutenant Sergei Loginov, the 27-year-old sonar commander in the *Kursk's* third section, half-jokingly wrote to his partner Natasha: 'I'm learning some culinary secrets. When there is no bread I make my own. It's water, flour, teaspoon of salt and teaspoon of soda. Oats, rice and pasta at this present time are a luxury for me.'

Sergei Loginov summed up the feelings of frustration that many of the submariners felt about their living conditions, and the constant struggle to balance service, survival and a sense of dignity in Vidyayevo:

Hello my darling Natashenka,

I'm writing to you being at sea on my beloved *Kursk*. There is nothing else closer to me here in Vidyayevo. There is also my one-room flat where I can sleep and sometimes eat. It's not for the first time the crew are going out to sea, and their families are living on shore without any money. Everybody makes promises but as soon as the sub leaves they breathe out a sigh of relief. There is no crew, there is no problem.

We swear, we grit our teeth, make fists and live for the sea. Interesting how anyone's soul can take all that and not become an animal with one instinct – to survive and feed oneself; but a human being with dignity, ability to think, to care, to love and to hate?

And how I'm quite fed up with that struggle between dignity and living like an animal.

Another time Loginov wrote to Natasha:

Hello my darling, my love, the only one,

Here we are separated by different towns in our huge and unbelievable Russia. Small Vidyayevo – Oh! When you look at it you want to shiver. The biggest impression I have of it is empty blocks of flats with boarded windows. So Natashenka there are a lot of free apartments – I'm joking!

Once aboard the *Kursk*, the problems of dry land receded. On board they would be fed, they would be warm, they would work hard doing a useful and satisfying job. They could even relax in the sauna, go for a swim in the pool and watch a video if they had any free time. While those at home struggled to make ends meet, the *Kursk*'s crew were insulated from the problems of everyday life. They were proud of the *Kursk*. Aboard the state-of-the-art vessel they were real men, doing a job that gave them back their sense of self-worth and dignity, and instilled in them, in spite of everything, pride in their country.

Conditions were generally so bad in Vidyayevo itself that some of the naval wives refused to live there permanently, staying with their families in St Petersburg, Kursk or Moscow, or living on the family *dachas* for months at a time in the summer. However, for some the posting to Vidyayevo wasn't too bad. At least Murmansk, a city of almost half a million people, was only an hour's bus ride away. Compared to some military postings in the far-flung Russian Federation, like Kamchatka or parts of Siberia, this was regarded as being very close to 'civilisation'.

While Vidyayevo may be a good location for a navy garrison town, it is not designed by nature to support human life. Human beings are unwelcome interlopers in the arctic regions, and trying to survive there is a constant struggle against the odds. Despite the foul conditions in Vidyayevo, or perhaps because of them, there is a tremendous sense of camaraderie and social solidarity in the town. As Captain Roman Kolesnikov told his sons Dmitri and Alex, as they were about to follow in his footsteps into the submarine service: 'You will never earn lots of money. You will lose your health. Nobody will say thank you. But you will make the best friends anyone could in life.' In Vidyayevo there were none of the appalling stories of brutality and beatings suffered by conscripts elsewhere in the Russian armed forces. Many of the teenage conscripts and the young officers' families have truly warm memories of the close friendships they developed in the town during their years of service to a seemingly indifferent and tight-fisted state.

In the city of Kursk, Valentina Staroseltseva was one of several relatives who had forebodings or premonitions of disaster over the weekend of 12–13 August. Her conscript son, 20-year-old seaman Dmitri, had the dubious honour of appearing on the front page of *Komsomolskaya Pravda* after the tragedy. 'I knew something was wrong on Sunday, I felt it,' his mother said. 'I don't know what was going on, but I felt ill.' Nadezhda Alexseyevna, Captain Third Rank Alexander Sadkov's mother, separated by 1,000 miles, had a similar experience. She couldn't explain why, for no apparent reason, she suddenly felt so ill. Svetlana Ivanovna, mother of Alexei Korkin, a bilge specialist in the sixth compartment, was at her family *dacha*. 'On Sunday, towards evening, I began watering our vegetable garden. I bent over the water well, and precisely at that moment, I heard a voice call out loud and clear to me, "Mama." I felt so cold and terrible. When I was leaving our garden, once again I heard a voice loud and clear: "Mama." It was so full of sorrow.' Ludmilla Milyutina, Captain Third Rank Andrei Milyutin's mother, was woken by a strange noise at the door in the middle of the night. When she got up, there was no one there. At 27-year-old Warrant Officer Victor Kuznetsov's home, his mother Olga Romanovna watched in horror as the family's precious icon fell off the wall and smashed into pieces. It had hung there for many years, and Victor's 60-year-old mother took it as a bad omen.

Nor were the crew's relatives the only ones who experienced unsettling premonitions. Several of the crew themselves had seemed uneasy about their immediate futures, including Captain-Lieutenant Dmitri Kolesnikov, who had written several melancholy poems to his wife Olga. Warrant Officer Yashov Samovarov, 23-year-old medical unit chief in the second compartment, wrote a long, puzzling letter to his girlfriend saying he was dying. She was unsure what to make of it.

Before leaving for the Barents Sea, Alexei Korkin wrote to his mother, who heard his voice crying out at the family *dacha* that Sunday. Svetlana Ivanovna received the letter on Friday 11 August, the day before the *Kursk* sank:

I have all kinds of nightmares. Some kind of mystification. It's good we're at our base, not at sea. We would sink, that's for sure. Just like the *Komsomolets* [submarine]. Imagine that! My snapshot would always hang on the wall at the headquarters of our division and our fleet. And the caption under the photo would read: 'Awarded the title of the Hero of Russia for heroism and courage – posthumously' . . . I have this premonition that the world is caving in, that everything is crumbling . . . I have this feeling that something inevitable is going to happen (it would be great if it was my discharge!).

Captain-Lieutenant Sergei Loginov was also acting a little oddly. His partner Natasha recalled that her Seryozha was unusually reluctant to leave Vidyayevo to join the naval exercises, even for just a few days. He was already writing letters to his unborn son, whom he had named Yaroslav. Before leaving on 10 August, Sergei collected together a large pile of pictures of both of them, and took them with him.

## Monday 14 August

On Monday morning the Russian disinformation campaign, designed to cover up the scale of the disaster and the navy's incompetence and beggarly resources, began in earnest. At 10:30 A.M. the news agencies Interfax and RIA Novosti quoted a statement from the press office at the Russian Navy's Moscow HQ that a submarine was lying on the seabed due to 'technical problems'. A 'malfunction' had occurred. The navy categorically denied that there was any damage to the hull, or that the submarine had flooded. Sonar sweeps of the area reported sounds that appeared to be survivors tapping on the hull with metal objects, they said. The navy asserted that the crew had made a 'controlled descent' and that 'liaison with the submarine is established'. The navy also claimed the crew had shut down the twin nuclear reactors on board. Captain Second Rank Igor Dygalo, Russian Navy press spokesman and aide to the navy's commander-in-chief, confirmed there were 'no nuclear weapons' aboard the *Kursk*, that the reactors were off and under control, and that the radiation situation was normal. Admiral Popov, Northern Fleet commander, admitted there were 'technical difficulties' with a submarine, but refused to name it. Radio contact, he said, had been made with the crew, and tubes were supplying them with oxygen and water. The admiral claimed he was confident of a 'positive outcome'. All this, of course, was a complete fabrication. No contact had been made with the submarine, and it would be Wednesday 16 August before any member of the Russian rescue team even saw the extent of the damage to the *Kursk*. When asked later why he had falsely built up relatives' hopes that the crew had survived and were communicating with rescuers, Admiral Popov argued it didn't make any difference what he said. He believed relatives would have flocked to Vidyayevo anyway.

As the day wore on worrying reports started appearing on foreign radio stations like the BBC and US Radio Liberty. Russian TV news reports indicated that the *Kursk* had sunk and the bow was flooded, with independent NTV leading the way. Relatives of those serving on the submarine were glued to their television sets all day and well into the night. Parents and wives packed their bags and made straight for Vidyayevo. Dmitri Kolesnikov's parents heard the news at their family *dacha* in Estonia, and immediately set off for Vidyayevo. Olga Kolesnikova heard at her mother's *dacha* in Boksitogorsk, outside St Petersburg, where she was spending the summer picking fruit and making jam and apple juice. Dmitri and Olga had hoped to retire there one day. Olga joined the exodus to Vidyayevo. In St Petersburg itself, Valeria Milyutina watched the news reports with horror. She took the train first to Murmansk, and then travelled on to Vidyayevo, not knowing whether her husband Andrei was alive or dead.

When Captain Second Rank Sergei Dudko's mother heard the news, she packed her black scarf and set off with heavy heart. Her husband had been a submariner, and she feared the worst. She headed for Northern Fleet headquarters at Severomorsk on the Kola Peninsula, prepared to bury her son where he had been born thirty-one years before. Valery Ivanovich, father of Sasha Khalyepo, a turbinist in the fourth compartment, lived in the autonomous Komi republic, over 1,000 miles to the east. A poor agricultural worker, he hoped one day that his son would rejoin him to work the land, just as he had done for thirty years. Valery Ivanovich, who was owed the comparative fortune of 9,000 roubles ($300) in unpaid back-pay by the local authorities (a familiar story in Russia), had to borrow the fare to Vidyayevo. He had never left his hometown before.

The Russian Navy did not contact a single relative, and was not giving out any information about personnel. None of the families knew exactly what had happened, but they feared it was something terrible. Ludmilla Milyutina thought of her son alone in a dark and cold submarine at the bottom of the Barents Sea. She travelled to Vidyayevo hoping to find her son recovering in hospital from his ordeal. Some relatives were unsure whether their sons, husbands and brothers were actually serving on the *Kursk* or not – the Russian Navy had an annoying habit of cobbling together crews at the last minute, poaching experienced crew members from other submarines in dock. It was a sign of the shortages of experienced crews which plagued the navy, and of the times.

The navy's press office at their Moscow headquarters was still maintaining the 'knocking noises' from the hull indicated that members of the *Kursk*'s crew were trying to communicate. However, the US Navy already knew that this claim was false. Aboard the nuclear sub USS *Memphis*, which was snooping on the manoeuvres, sonar tapes and other acoustic recordings picked up the explosions but no other sounds from the *Kursk*. Within hours of the accident, an account of the torpedo explosions and sinking of the *Kursk* was circulating in US government circles. A detailed intelligence analysis of the tapes, carried out at the US National Maritime Intelligence Center in Maryland, was subsequently leaked to the American media. There were no knocking noises from the crew, or, as later claimed, SOS signals tapped on the hull. Again, this was pure Russian disinformation, which was lapped up by some parts of the media at the time. Popov himself admitted that while he had some reports of knocking noises from the *Kursk*, after acoustic analysis he ruled out any possibility that they came from the crew. It was more likely the short-lived sounds were from dying onboard machinery.

At the UK's Ministry of Defence Permanent Joint Headquarters (PJHQ) at Northwood, north-west London, it was first assumed that the *Kursk* accident was yet another collision involving a US submarine. 'Our immediate reaction was the same as the Russians. We thought the Americans had hit it. It wouldn't have been totally unknown,' one MoD official at Northwood said. Later, as reports of an explosion came in, the view at Northwood shifted in favour of a torpedo malfunction. According to Captain Vladimir Shigin, a staff writer for the Russian language *Marine Journal*, there have been twenty-one collisions involving US and Russian subs near the Russian coast in the last thirty-three years. Although the figures can be disputed, there is no doubt that many collisions were provoked by the rather 'gung-ho' attitude of American sub commanders, who regularly ignored the rule that they should maintain a constant distance from their 'target' of at least five miles. On 11 February 1992 the nuclear sub USS *Baton Rouge* had collided with a Sierra-class submarine it was tracking near the twelve-mile limit off Murmansk. The accident led to protests from the Russian Navy that US subs were operating too close to Russian shores, and an unprecedented Pentagon acceptance that the incident had taken place. Normally, the Pentagon declines to comment on such operations.

The *Baton Rouge* incident had little effect on Pentagon operational tactics, however. A little over a year later, on 20 March 1993, the USS *Grayling* left a big dent in a Delta III Russian submarine while tracking its quarry 105 miles north of Murmansk. The accident occurred in the middle of the Northern Fleet's training range. President Clinton had to offer President Yeltsin a formal apology in the run-up to the Vancouver summit that April, and was furious with the US Navy for muddying the political waters. Clinton declared the incident 'regrettable', and ordered a policy and procedure review. 'I don't want it to ever happen again,' the president stated. The *Kursk* was the sixth nuclear submarine to lie on the seabed after damage or an accident; of these two were American and four were Russian.

The Americans weren't alone in their snooping operations under the Barents Sea. On Christmas Eve 1986, HMS *Splendid*, a Swiftsure-class nuclear attack submarine based at Faslane in Scotland, was tracking a Soviet submarine in the Russians' training range north of Murmansk. The two submarines got too close to one another, with the result that the Russian boat brushed against the *Splendid* and accidentally became caught up in the British sub's towed sonar array. The Russian boat, probably a 172-metre-long Typhoon-class ballistic-missile sub, ended up taking the snagged sonar back to its home base. The huge Typhoons are the largest nuclear submarines ever built, dwarfing the 82-metre Swiftsure boats. The *Splendid*, commissioned back in

1981, is still on active service. The British later went to extraordinary lengths to deny the *Splendid* was anywhere near the *Kursk* at the time of the accident.

On Monday lunchtime, the British Embassy in Moscow passed on an official offer from the British government to help with the *Kursk* rescue efforts. John Spellar MP, Minister for the Armed Forces, was the duty Minister at the Ministry of Defence (MoD) on 14 August, and as such he co-ordinated the British government's response to the *Kursk* crisis. After discussions with Number 10 Downing Street and other government departments, John Spellar made the offer of assistance in a letter to Marshal Igor Sergeyev, Russia's Defence Minister. It was this letter which the British Embassy passed on to the International Relations Department of the Russian Defence Ministry. A copy of the letter was also faxed to the Russian Defence Attaché in the Russian Embassy in Kensington, London. Russia's Ambassador to London, Grigory Karasin, was on leave in Moscow. Spellar offered the Russians the use of the UK's Submarine Rescue Service (UKSRS), particularly the LR5 rescue mini-sub, which was ready for immediate deployment.

Maintained on twelve hours' standby, the manned LR5 submersible was built in 1978, but was extensively modified and refitted in 1983 and again in early 2000. It is one of the most capable and sophisticated rescue mini-subs in the world. LR5 is nine metres long and three metres wide, carries up to sixteen passengers at a time, can operate at a depth of 400 metres, and mate at an angle of up to sixty degrees bow-up. Rumic, the company which operates LR5 on behalf of the MoD, made a direct offer of help to the Russian Embassy in London. The LR5 and its immediate support team is based at Renfrew, Glasgow, and had been prepared to leave for the triannual 'Sorbet Royal' NATO submarine rescue training exercise off Turkey in September. There was no immediate response from the Russians. They merely confirmed that they had received Spellar's offer of help.

The British had reacted with remarkable and commendable speed to the *Kursk*'s plight. Commodore David Russell, then based at PJHQ, Northwood, recalled vividly how quickly events moved that Monday. At 8 A.M. London time, the Royal Navy knew there was a problem with the *Kursk*. By 10 A.M. a recommendation to offer help to the

Russians was sent via civil servants at the Ministry of Defence in Whitehall. By midday, after consulting with other departments, Armed Forces Minister John Spellar had faxed his offer of assistance to Defence Minister Sergeyev in Moscow. In bureaucratic terms, such a swift and united reaction from the Royal Navy, the civil service and the government was extremely rare.

In the United States, Sandy Berger, American National Security Advisor, contacted his Russian opposite number, Sergei Ivanov, the Security Council Secretary. Berger expressed concern for the submariners, and said the US was ready to help in any way it could. Ivanov coolly replied that Russia didn't need any assistance, as they had all the rescue assets they required. As he accompanied Bill Clinton to the Los Angeles Democratic Convention, Berger continued to receive hourly updates on the *Kursk* crisis. Other countries were also showing their concern. Rear-Admiral Einar Skorgen, Norway's Northern Armed Forces Commander, was fully aware of the explosions aboard the *Kursk*. These had been confirmed by NATO's submarines, its P3 Orion sub-trackers in the air, and Norway's intelligence ship the *Marjata*. Skorgen, who knew Popov personally from various naval exchange visits and regarded him as a friend, picked up a 'hotline' direct to the Northern Fleet, set up in 1999 for just such an emergency. Again, the message came back that the Russians had everything under control. Offers of help from Canada, France, Germany, Israel, Italy, the Netherlands, Japan and Sweden were also declined. '*Nyet spasebo*' – 'No thanks', was the clear Russian response.

By Monday evening, the Norwegian and American military publicly announced that their acoustics had picked up two explosions in the Barents Sea. Accounts of the West's offers of help circulated in the media, while it also became apparent that the accident aboard the *Kursk* had occurred on Saturday, not Sunday, as originally suggested by the Russian Navy. As Russian rescue teams were ordered not to talk to the press, Prime Minister Mikhail Kasyanov signed a decree establishing a formal commission of inquiry. The commission was to be headed by Russia's Deputy Prime Minister, Ilya Klebanov, with Navy Commander-in-Chief Admiral Vladimir Kuroyedov as his deputy. Other members of the commission included Vice-Admiral Yury

Sukhachev, Vice-President of the Russian Academy of Science Nicolai Laverov, and Duma Speaker for the Primorye region, Alexei Zhekov. Groups of specialists were represented by the deputy chief of the Nuclear Energy Ministry, the chief designer of the submarine's nuclear power unit, experts from the Rubin Marine Engineering Design Bureau (who designed the *Kursk*), and designers from Nizhni Novgorod and Moscow businesses. Later, nine Duma deputies would also join the commission. Admiral Kuroyedov, faced with demands by the media to explain the disaster, suggested the accident had been caused by a collision with another vessel, probably a NATO submarine. The collision had in turn set off torpedoes aboard the *Kursk*. Meanwhile the Russian Navy still refused to give any details of those serving on the *Kursk*, and during the day reported crew numbers fluctuated between 100, 107 and 116.

## Tuesday 15 August

Tuesday began with the Finnish and Norwegian governments expressing concern at the possible threat of radiation leaking from the *Kursk's* nuclear reactors, a fear expressed the previous day by Norwegian environmental group Bellona. Meanwhile, the Pentagon denied that an American sub had been involved in a collision with the *Kursk*, but heightened suspicions in Russia by refusing to confirm the location of its own submarines in the Barents Sea. White House Press Secretary Joseph Lockhart again reiterated American offers of help, but at the same time the administration indicated there had been no requests for assistance from Moscow. With the *Kursk* rescue operation run by Admiral Popov aboard the *Pyotr Veliky*, more Russian ships headed for the accident site. Russia's only aircraft-carrier, the *Admiral Kuznetsov*, arrived at the scene early in the morning and was joined by the hunter-killer ships *Admiral Chebaneko* and *Admiral Kharlamov*, a coast guard ship and five other rescue boats.

The Northern Fleet organised a press conference in Severomorsk, outside Murmansk. Vice-Admiral Mikhail Motsak, the Northern Fleet's Chief of Staff, known as a blunt-speaking 'Hero of Russia', was replaced at the last minute by the Rubin Design Bureau's Igor Baranov. The St Petersburg-based bureau was responsible for designing the *Kursk*. Baranov, talking about possible damage to the sub, didn't mention the crew once. He did, however, say that in his view foreign rescue subs would find it very difficult to dock with the *Kursk*, as Russian and Western designs were very different. In his view, the crew had only perhaps five or six days' supply of air. The Northern Fleet admitted it had no 'audio' communication with the crew, but said the crew were alive, and were exchanging messages by knocking on the hull. Strong underwater currents were reportedly causing difficulties for the rescue operation.

Later in the day, Ilya Klebanov, Deputy Prime Minister and head of the Commission of Inquiry, said the *Kursk* was at the point of surfacing when the accident happened. He informed the press his commission would look at the possibility of a collision, a torpedo malfunction or the *Kursk* striking a Second World War mine. Klebanov claimed a Force 5 gale had led to the rescue operation being temporarily halted, and suggested a critical situation would be developing on board the submarine because of a lack of oxygen.

Back in the UK, Commander Alan Hoskins and his UK Submarine Rescue Service (UKSRS) team were becoming increasingly restless and frustrated. For the second day running, the team were sitting waiting when they could have already mobilised. With the Russians still saying 'thanks but no thanks' to foreign offers of help, Hoskins and his colleagues were wondering aloud what was stopping them from just going straight to the Barents Sea. After all, the accident had happened in international waters, and they didn't need anyone's permission to deploy to the rescue area. It was clear that political considerations were stopping Hoskins from mobilising the LR5 mini-sub. If the UK's offer of assistance had been immediately accepted on the Monday, the LR5 could have been flown to Murmansk that afternoon, taken a ship out of port the next day and already been in position above the *Kursk* by late Tuesday or early Wednesday. Instead, the LR5 rescue team were left twiddling their thumbs in Renfrew as reports from Russia indicated crew members aboard the *Kursk* were still alive. Commander Hoskins, who had served as a submariner since 1975 on nuclear and conventional subs, was in regular contact with Rumic's Allan Meads and the Royal Navy's Lieutenant Commander Piers Barker. Hoskins was based at Foxhill, Bath, and was part of the Technical Support Cell at the Warship Support Agency's headquarters.

Although the Russians were still not requesting help, the British decided to pull back trucks which were already on the road preparing to deploy the LR5 to NATO's sub-rescue exercise off Turkey. No official decision to abandon the exercise had yet been taken. Nevertheless, the Warship Support Agency's Technical Support Cell started preparations to deploy the LR5 to the Barents Sea, chartering an Antonov heavy-lift cargo plane from Canada. Dan Carmicheal, Vice-President of Operations for Stena, phoned Commander Hoskins to confirm the Norwegian ship *Normand Pioneer II* would be available to transport the LR5 and the UKSRS team out to the rescue area once they arrived by air. British Police, racing by car to Prestwick, delivered vital gauges to the airport ready for deployment with the LR5. The decision to forward-deploy LR5 was formally taken the next morning, still before anything had been heard from the Russians.

In Brussels, a group of Russian admirals caused some confusion and bemusement by turning up at NATO headquarters. The admirals said they had come to discuss co-ordinating the rescue operation with NATO, which caused a few eyebrows to be raised since no one had agreed the *Kursk* rescue was going to be a NATO mission. The appearance of the Russian admirals at best indicated a lack of urgency on the part of the naval High Command, and at worst seemed an excuse for a bunch of top brass to head off on a junket to Brussels at a wholly inappropriate time. Confronted by the media, the Russian admirals seemed somewhat embarrassed to explain just what on earth they were doing wasting their time in Brussels. The trip achieved nothing, and reinforced a sense of total paralysis among Russia's leadership. The lack of direction was underlined by President Putin's self-imposed vow of silence on the Black Sea, which had now lasted for four days following the *Kursk* disaster. While the state-controlled television channels RTR and ORT remained respectfully mute on the president's absence, frustration and anger was growing in the country's independent media. *Moscovsky Komsomolets* newspaper's headline ran 'Damn You, Do Something', while NTV became increasingly critical of the handling of the crisis. The navy told the crew's relatives to watch only the state-controlled channels.

RTR, Channel 2, is wholly owned by the state and had privileged access to the military during the crisis. It was the only television company allowed to film aboard the cruiser *Pyotr Veliky*, which acted as Admiral Popov's HQ for the duration of the rescue operation. The state also owned 51 per cent of ORT, Channel 1, with the remaining shares controlled by the billionaire business tycoon, Boris Berezovsky. Both channels broadly took the Kremlin's line on the *Kursk* crisis. RTR and ORT reached over 90 per cent of the country, with ORT being the more popular of the two. NTV was independently owned by the oligarch Vladimir Gusinsky, who had repeatedly clashed with Putin's government. NTV covered less than three-quarters of the country, reaching a potential 104 million viewers, but competed fiercely with ORT for ratings. Gusinsky, another dollar billionaire, had been briefly imprisoned on conveniently-timed fraud charges the previous June, and was in exile for the second time in his career. Television, much more than the print media, was the main source of information for most Russians on the *Kursk* tragedy.

William Cohen, US Defense Secretary, persisted in offering American help to the Russians. Around 8:30 P.M. Moscow time (11:30 A.M. Eastern Daylight Time) he sent a letter to Defence Minister Igor Sergeyev from the Pentagon: 'My department stands ready to provide any assistance you need: please do not hesitate to ask.' The US had a state-of-the-art Deep Submergence Rescue Vehicle (DSRV) on standby in San Diego, California, specifically designed for submarine rescue missions. The *Avalon* measures 50 feet long, displaces 80,000 lb, can operate at depths of 5,000 feet, and rescue 24 people a trip. Cohen received no immediate reply to his offer, but expected a response the next day at the latest. The Russians didn't reply for two days, and then only asked the US to 'work through NATO channels to co-ordinate' rescue efforts. In effect, the Russians again declined any practical US assistance.

The Northern Fleet's HQ put out information that the crew on the

*Kursk* were still alive, but regular communication with the submarine had stopped. It was now said they would run out of oxygen by midnight on Friday 18 August. At the last press conference on Tuesday night, the press pack accused the navy of not doing enough to save the trapped submariners. Russian Navy press spokesman Captain Igor Dygalo said it was 'not nice' to make that suggestion. They were doing all they could to save the crew. That night the navy established a 'hotline' for the crew's relatives, but still refused to confirm who was on the *Kursk* when it sank. Before midnight, as Tuesday drew to a close, there were twenty-two ships in the rescue area.

## Wednesday 16 August

Wednesday brought the disconcerting news from the Northern Fleet's press office that the navy was still hearing knocking noises from the *Kursk*, despite saying the day before that they had stopped. Captain Dygalo claimed the crew on the *Kursk* had been 'informed' the rescue mission was under way. Quite how the Northern Fleet managed to communicate with the dead is still a mystery. Admiral Kuroyedov, Navy Commander-in-Chief, sitting in his Moscow HQ, proposed raising the *Kursk* by placing two 400-ton pontoons under the sub and then lifting it to the surface. This would be done by pumping air into the pontoons, so that they and the boat would rise from the seabed. There were only a few flaws with Kuroyedov's brilliant plan. The Northern Fleet had six pontoons but they were not prepared and didn't have enough power to lift the *Kursk*; it would take weeks if not months to put into effect; and no one had the faintest idea if it would work. In the middle of the most serious submarine disaster ever to confront Russia, there was a feeling that the navy's High Command was trying to 'wing it'. They simply didn't have any idea what to do, or how to do it. Nor did they have the equipment to try anything, if they had known what to try. The sight of the commander-in-chief trying to devise a submarine rescue system and strategy in the middle of a major accident did not inspire public or international confidence. There was an overwhelming feeling that the Russian Navy was incompetent, reflected in the increasingly angry coverage in the independent Russian print media. The pressure on President Putin to get a grip on the situation was growing.

The Russians were blaming the failure of the rescue mission so far on rough seas, bad weather, a very strong current, and the assertion that the *Kursk* was lying at an angle of sixty degrees. When British and Norwegian rescuers arrived later in the week, they discovered this was a pack of lies. All the talk of sending down diving bells (which were non-existent), repeated contact with the *Kursk* and successful link-ups using mini-subs, were a complete fabrication. Because the Russian mini-subs needed near-perfect conditions to be lowered into the sea by the *Mikhail Rudnitsky*, using two cranes, no Russian mini-sub came anywhere near the *Kursk* until Wednesday, a full five days after the *Kursk* first sank. These old subs were designed to be launched from atop a mother sub and were unsuited to being lowered into the sea using a crane.

The first Russian to see the damaged *Kursk* on the seabed was Captain Third Rank Andrei Sholokhov, commander of the *Priz* mini-sub. He made his first successful descent on Wednesday, working for just over four hours. During the course of the day Captain Sholokhov managed to attach his mini-sub to the *Kursk*'s aft escape hatch eight times, on one occasion mating for about twenty minutes. Sholokhov thought the failure to mate was caused by damage to the escape hatch, which was no longer hermetically sealed. However, on later inspection by Western experts, it became apparent that the reason for the Russians' failure was that the escape hatch had been left in an 'idle' position. Russian subs often left the hatch in this position since it was kept firmly shut by the sea pressure outside. When Sholokhov attempted to mate with the hatch, equalising the pressure, the hatch started to open, breaking contact with the *Priz* in the process. The connecting tube between the *Priz* and the *Kursk* kept filling up with water. Sholokhov could only have succeeded in a successful mating operation with help from the crew inside the *Kursk*, who were already dead.

On board the *Priz* there were personnel from another Oscar II-class submarine who were prepared to enter the ninth compartment if the

*Priz* had successfully mated with the *Kursk*. Surveying the extensive damage to the *Kursk*, Captain Sholokhov and his colleagues were deeply shocked by what they saw. The rubber coating on the outside of the hull was severely damaged, while the front of the *Kursk* simply did not exist. The bow had been blown apart. The fourth compartment looked as if it had been completely steam-rollered by the force of the explosion.

That morning the British LR5 rescue team had been given permission from Whitehall to forward-deploy to Norway. Russia had still not asked for help. By around 11 A.M. in the Barents Sea, the Russians started deploying their second mini-sub, the *Bester*, which could carry up to twenty people at a time. The Russian hospital ship, *Svir*, arrived at the accident site. Igor Dygalo, the press spokesman, again blamed the weather for the repeated failures of the rescue operation, and hinted that Russia might be willing to accept help from NATO. The navy now suggested the knocking noises were 'irregular', and said that it had unsuccessfully tried to supply oxygen to the *Kursk*. At the same time, Captain Sholokhov and the mini-sub *Priz* were finding there wasn't much of the *Kursk* left to supply.

At 2:30 P.M. Captain Dygalo told the press the knocking noises from the *Kursk* had stopped. Russia, he said, was not refusing help from NATO, but it had the 'best technical facilities in the world' to carry out the rescue operation itself. In Sochi, Putin was confronted by journalists and asked what had happened to the *Kursk*. In an unguarded moment, he turned to a Western television crew, smiled inappropriately and said, 'It sank.' Under mounting pressure by the media camped outside his seaside villa, a well-tanned Putin decided to issue a press statement at 3 P.M. Moscow time, which said: 'Situation with *Kursk* very difficult, critical, but fleet has all the necessary equipment for rescue and they will continue to try to rescue.'

Putin accepted assurances from the Defence Ministry and navy that they were doing everything possible to save any survivors aboard the *Kursk*. The military were less than frank about the chances of success given Russia's rescue capabilities, and Putin was politically naïve to take his commanders' word that all was under control. As the hours ticked by, domestic and international pressure piled up on the president to act decisively. The straw which broke the camel's back was a twenty-five-minute telephone call from President Bill Clinton. Clinton again offered US help, and urged Putin to take up the many offers of assistance he had received. Not only Russian domestic opinion but the whole world was concerned about the fate of those aboard the *Kursk*, and felt great compassion for their families. He knew Putin would want to be seen to be doing everything he possibly could to save his submariners' lives, and respond to the genuine offers of help being offered by Russia's friends abroad. The response of the West showed how much things had changed since the end of the Cold War, when NATO and the Warsaw Pact stood as adversaries. After Clinton's call, Putin felt he had no alternative but to accept Western help. To fail to do so would make him look callous, arrogant, and – even worse – a politician in the old Soviet mould. Putin had to show the country, and the international community at large, that his Russia had nothing to hide and was open enough to accept well-meaning offers of help from its partners in the West. The Russian president was eager to dispel any image the West might have of him as a cold, calculating former KGB *apparatchik*.

The Russian military had other ideas, and a different mindset. For the Russian top brass, although NATO was not the direct military threat it had once been, it was still the enemy, and intent on stealing Russia's secrets at every possible opportunity. The Russian Navy may be working more closely with NATO these days, but they didn't trust it one bit. They firmly believed NATO countries would use any Western rescue operation as a chance to steal military secrets. The Northern Fleet, as part of Russia's strategic and tactical nuclear strike force, was historically secretive. The fleet's admirals were instinctively suspicious. After all, the *Kursk* was one of Russia's most modern nuclear submarines, and carried a lot of classified material on board, including secret weapon systems like the Granit cruise missile. The aims and perceptions of the political leadership as now personified by Putin were therefore very different from the aims and perceptions of his admirals. Yet as a former KGB officer, Putin instinctively had sympathy for the navy's desire to protect its secrets. He had always believed that it was the state's duty to maintain secrecy. Belatedly, however, Putin was starting to understand the political significance of the *Kursk* crisis. He could not afford to look ineffectual or indifferent. After all, he had been elected as a decisive 'man of action'. The navy, on the other hand, would still have preferred to try to save their men and fail than bring in the West to help. After Clinton's crucial call, Putin overruled his conservative Defence Minister and ordered his admirals to accept Western assistance.

By 4 P.M. the British team had taken off from Prestwick airport in Scotland. The Antonov was still in the air when the navy's press office announced that Russia would accept help from Britain's LR5 and divers from Norway. Just before 6 P.M. Admiral Kuroyedov said the crew aboard the *Kursk* should have enough oxygen to last until 25 August, the most optimistic prognosis yet. Just under an hour later the British rescue team landed at Trondheim in Norway. Although it would have been quicker to fly straight to Murmansk and take a ship from there, the Russians had refused the British permission to fly directly to the Arctic city. In any event, the British arranged for the *Normand Pioneer II* to take the LR5 direct from Trondheim to the accident site. As the British rescue team, led by Commander Alan Hoskins, arrived in Trondheim, there was still no official co-operation or co-ordination from the Russian side. Hoskins had hoped to be met by some Russians at the airport with drawings of the *Kursk* and an interpreter. There was no one. It was as if the Russians weren't really interested in being helped, a unique experience for the British team. Hoskins feared they might already be too late, as the temperature and oxygen aboard the *Kursk* reached critically low levels. The first twenty-four hours after a submarine accident are always the most crucial, but due to Russian procrastination the British had arrived in Norway a full five days after the initial explosions.

In the garrison town of Vidyayevo, the Russian Navy organised a reception for relatives of the *Kursk*'s crew. Obtaining any official information was a hopeless task. The relatives listened instead to the media for any news of their loved ones. The navy again advised them to listen to the public television channels RTR and ORT, and not the dangerously independent and critical NTV. The so-called relatives' 'hotline' was worse than useless. At around 8:30 P.M. Moscow time the

Russian Foreign Ministry officially asked for help from the UK and
Norway, sending the requests through their embassies in London and
Oslo, copied to the British and Norwegian embassies in Moscow. Later
that evening, as an official bank account was opened in Murmansk to
help the relatives of those aboard the *Kursk*, Russian Vice-Admiral
Ilyin again claimed the navy was hearing SOS knocking noises from
the stricken submarine.

## Thursday 17 August

In the early hours of Thursday morning the British sent three more
Hercules transport planes loaded with equipment to Trondheim. The
Russians had again refused the British permission to fly direct to
Murmansk. John Spellar, UK Armed Forces Minister, confirmed the
LR5 mini-sub crew would consist of two pilots and one operator. The
British rescue mission was also given a code-name, 'Injured Red Lady'.
Nine people from Rumic's LR5 team were to join the *Normand
Pioneer*. On board, the ship's company would comprise over forty
people including twelve crew, nine Rumic personnel, six military
divers, two rescue co-ordinators, two doctors, four other medics and a
group of radiation and nuclear specialists. The trip to the accident site
would take about fifty hours. CNN reported that according to the
Pentagon, there were no signals at all from the *Kursk* following the disaster. The Russian Navy's press office claimed this was US
disinformation.

The ship *Seaway Eagle*, Norway's contribution to the rescue effort,
headed for the Barents Sea after leaving the North Sea the previous
night. There were ninety people on board including twelve divers
(four Norwegians and eight Britons). Their trip would take them
about sixty hours. At 7:50 A.M. the Russian Navy held another press
conference. Here, they stated the damage to the *Kursk* had been catastrophic and instantaneous. The crew had not had time to put on or
deploy any of their rescue equipment, such as their emergency suits or
the accident buoy. All this pointed to an explosion rather than a collision, they concluded.

Defence Minister Sergeyev, however, suggested that morning that the Russians had video evidence of a collision. In the afternoon, he confidently asserted the reason for the disaster was undoubtedly a collision. Admiral Kuroyedov set off from Moscow for Severomorsk to take personal command of the rescue operation.

Foreign offers of help continued to flood in. Sweden offered use of its deep submergence rescue vehicle, which could work at 400 metres. The US checked the readiness of its two DSRVs, *Avalon* and *Mystic*. The Russians suggested they would be of no use, since they could only operate at a maximum angle of forty-five degrees, whereas the *Kursk* was lying at an angle of sixty degrees. The Germans also offered medical and other support. All the offers were rejected. The Russian Navy had gone further than they had wanted to by accepting British and Norwegian help – they certainly didn't want any other rescue teams swarming around the *Kursk*, causing co-ordination problems and snooping around the top-secret sub.

During the day Rear-Admiral Skorgen, Norway's Northern Armed Forces Commander, scrambled an F-16 fighter to investigate six Russian military aircraft heading along the southern coast of Norway, just outside Norwegian airspace. The Russian planes had come from the Kola Peninsula. When he asked Popov the following day what the Russians were up to, he received the startling reply that the Northern Fleet had information that a non-Russian submarine, probably American, was on its way back down the Norwegian coast, and he was searching for it. Later it emerged that the Russians claimed *Pyotr Veliky* had detected the US sub USS *Memphis* on the seabed around the time of the explosions, and had then tracked the boat using one of the cruiser's Kamov anti-submarine helicopters. The *Memphis* is a Los Angeles-class nuclear attack submarine, the backbone of the US underwater fleet, designed to hunt submarines and ships, launch cruise missiles against land targets and gather intelligence. Commissioned in 1977, the *Memphis* was modified in 1994 to act as a 'test' submarine, specialising in intelligence-gathering, and is based at Groton, Connecticut, on America's north-east Atlantic coast.

According to this Russian version, two Ilyushin Il-38 anti-submarine aircraft, piloted by Lieutenant-Colonels Dergunov and

Dovzhenko, deployed hydro-acoustic buoys which recorded the *Memphis* 'limping along' at just 5 knots. The sub was supposedly heading for a Norwegian port for repairs. The clear implication was that the *Memphis* had been damaged in a collision with the *Kursk*. The US nuclear submarine was continuously tracked by Russian ships, planes and satellites until it reached the Norwegian naval base of Haakonsvern, six miles south-west of Bergen. The Russians claimed this trip took seven days, rather than the usual two. During his last reconnaissance flight on 18 August, Lt-Col Dergunov was reportedly unable to detect the *Memphis* due to powerful electromagnetic and hydro-acoustic interference from NATO.

The *Memphis* then allegedly stayed in dock for eight days undergoing 'operating repairs', after which she transferred to an adapted closed dock in Southampton for capital repairs. Russian conspiracy theorists claimed that CIA Director George Tenet secretly arrived in Moscow on 17 August to cover up alleged American involvement in the *Kursk* sinking, and even prevent possible war. Popov's whole show in the Barents Sea, so the conspiracists maintained, was for the benefit of domestic opinion, the West, and its intelligence agencies. The Russian 'search' operation was generally regarded by those in the know as yet another attempt at disinformation, and a rather pathetic effort to deflect blame from the Russian Navy. Desperate to avoid responsibility for the disaster, the Russian Navy's High Command would continue to chase shadows in the Barents Sea.

The Russians went even further to build up the 'collision myth'. Russian intelligence launched a 'black operation' to provide seemingly incontrovertible evidence that the USS *Memphis* had indeed been involved in a collision with the *Kursk*. On Friday 18 August, the daily newspaper *Segodnya* reported that Russian intelligence had intercepted radio transmissions from a foreign submarine, asking permission to call into a Norwegian port for emergency repairs. The story was planted by Russian intelligence itself, but more was yet to come.

The Moscow-based *Versiya* newspaper published a satellite picture of the *Memphis* docked in Haakonsvern on Saturday 19 August, photographed from an altitude of twenty-five miles, allegedly showing damage to the sub's bow. Published on 26 September that year, the accompanying article was written by journalist Dmitri Filimonov. Supposedly sent by an 'anonymous source', the classified photograph had been planted in the media by the SVR, the Russian foreign secret intelligence service, in collusion with GRU military intelligence. Unfortunately, they did not liaise with the domestic security service, the FSB (like the SVR, formerly part of the KGB), which raided the offices of the publishing company responsible for editing the *Versiya* article, demanding to know where they had obtained such sensitive intelligence material. The FSB later seized a computer hard drive from the company and removed data from its server in order to retrieve a back-up image of the satellite picture. Several websites appeared on the Internet pushing the *Memphis* collision theory and querying why the sub had taken a week to travel such a relatively short distance.

In fact, the *Versiya* satellite picture proved nothing. The picture did not clearly show any damage to the *Memphis*. Norwegian admirals who inspected the vessel confirmed it showed no signs of either damage or a collision. The *Memphis* had dropped into port to take off acoustic tapes of the *Kursk* disaster, and to unload its own intelligence personnel to give a debriefing back in the United States. American nuclear subs often call into Norwegian bases to change crews, as they sometimes have problems being welcomed into larger European harbours. On behalf of the US Navy, Vice-Admiral John J. Grossenbacher, Commander Submarine Force, Atlantic, informed this author: 'As the senior operational submarine commander in the US Navy I am aware of all our submarine operations worldwide, at all levels of classification. I know definitively that no US submarine was involved in the *Kursk* tragedy.'

A categorical denial of involvement from a very senior operational commander in the US Navy in such circumstances is unprecedented, and indicates real American confidence that the Russians had no basis for claiming US culpability in the sinking of the *Kursk*. Earlier, at a Pentagon press briefing on 15 August 2000, US Rear-Admiral Craig Quigley had trotted out the more usual navy formula: 'We don't discuss submarine operations, other than to say our submarines operate throughout the waters of the world. But we

don't discuss the specifics of submarine operations or their locales.'
Vice-Admiral Grossenbacher's straight denial of US involvement in
the tragedy showed that *glasnost* had even touched the Pentagon.
Nevertheless, for quite some time the Russian Navy refused to give
up its cherished theory that a collision with a foreign submarine had
sunk the *Kursk*.

In Murmansk, relatives continued to arrive from all over Russia.
Galina Belyaeva, arriving at Murmansk railway station, pushed
through a waiting gaggle of journalists eager to interview the families
of those aboard the *Kursk*. Married to a 43-year-old petty officer on
the stricken sub, Galina spat out her replies to the assembled hacks:
'Of course I hope that he is still alive. He's my husband. And no, I am
not satisfied with the way the navy has handled this at all. I had to
find out my husband may be dying from the television, and I got on
a train to find this place as quickly as I could. The navy said nothing
to me.'

Like the others arriving at the railway station, Galina had been kept
totally in the dark by the navy. She had been told nothing. It was as if
the families of those on the *Kursk* didn't count for anything. Galina
added: 'I don't know why this rescue operation is taking so long if we
and other countries have the equipment to save the men.' Alexander
Selyonov, a retired air force captain waiting for friends at the station,
also felt not enough was being done to save the crew. 'We have the
technology, we could have had those sailors on the surface within
hours,' he asserted. Relatives arriving in Murmansk received no official
welcome and no help to get to Vidyayevo, an hour away by taxi or bus.
Keen to profit from the crisis, local taxis charged an extortionate
200–400 roubles for the trip, up to about $13 or over a week's wages for
a submariner, or half the average monthly pension.

Natalia Rvanina, of Arkhangelsk in north-west Russia, said she
found out more about the fate of her 23-year-old petty officer son,
Nicolai, from journalists than from the authorities. 'I don't expect
them to tell me much. All we can do is wait until the navy admits the
sailors are gone. Obviously, the navy is terribly embarrassed by this and
they don't want people talking about it.' Olga Romanovna, who had
seen her precious icon fall and smash in her living room, feared her son

Warrant Officer Victor Kuznetsov was already dead. His wife and three-year-old son lived in Severomorsk. Olga Romanovna didn't expect to hear anything from the navy unless and until he was shipped home in a coffin. 'Maybe he'll live, maybe he won't,' she said. 'For now I just watch TV – even though they don't tell the truth. Truth is not a part of military life.'

The Russian press stepped up its attack on President Putin for his mishandling of the crisis. *Komsomolskaya Pravda*, a popular tabloid, printed a headline in bold red type:

'The sailors on the *Kursk* fell silent yesterday. Why has the president been silent?'

*Izvestia*, the liberal daily newspaper, also focused on the *Kursk* tragedy: 'Together with the K-141 this has sunk people's faith that the state can protect them from danger. It is the authorities themselves who have hit the bottom.' Meanwhile, showing a lack of urgency which typified the High Command's whole approach to the crisis, Vice-Admiral Pobozhiy wrote to NATO in Brussels asking for a meeting to discuss organisational measures to save the *Kursk*'s crew. The admiral didn't seem to understand it might be a bit late in the day to set up a joint Russia–NATO working party to save the submariners. In any event, as repeatedly made clear to the Russians, this was not a NATO rescue mission. Incredulous journalists were stunned by the admiral's smug bureaucratic complacency and the sheer stupidity of his proposal.

By 9 P.M. on Thursday evening the Russians admitted the *Kursk* was not listing at an angle of sixty degrees at all. They now admitted the tilt was much less, under twenty degrees, or perhaps even as little as twelve degrees. Seasoned commentators came to the conclusion that the Russians had deliberately overstated the *Kursk*'s list to explain their own inability to mate with the boat's stern escape hatch. The same was true of all their stories of storms, bad weather, strong currents and a damaged escape hatch. The Northern Fleet and the navy's High Command had been consistently and repeatedly lying through their collective teeth. At the same time, the navy let it be known that doctors and specialists were saying that the crew's oxygen supplies aboard the *Kursk* would last until 20 August. Many relatives and members of the public still hoped the crew had a chance, albeit a diminishing one.

Late that night, around 11 P.M., the Commission of Inquiry headed by Deputy Prime Minister Ilya Klebanov, meeting in Severomorsk, came to the conclusion that the cause of the catastrophe was a collision with 'an unknown floating object'. The government commission, again showing an odd sense of priorities, had spent eight hours debating the possible causes of the *Kursk* disaster. Klebanov announced the commission's conclusions as 'preliminary', but said that judging by the damage done to the submarine, the object which hit the *Kursk* was of 'very large tonnage'. The Deputy PM confirmed that no vessels of that size had been detected in the vicinity of the accident. The commission continued its deliberations aboard the *Pyotr Veliky* the next day. To all intents and purposes, the Russians looked as if they had given up on the rescue mission and were proceeding with an immediate postmortem. The Russian government and navy needed to find a scapegoat, fast.

Aboard the *Normand Pioneer*, Commander Alan Hoskins, the British rescue team leader, was trying to snatch some sleep. Many of the men had been working non-stop for thirty-six hours. Hoskins was woken to be told he had a phone call from Downing Street. At first he thought someone was pulling his leg. Getting out of bed to take the call, Alan found himself talking to John Prescott, the UK's Deputy Prime Minister. Prescott passed on Tony Blair and Vladimir Putin's personal thanks and appreciation for all the team's efforts. Prescott said, 'I didn't get you out of bed, did I? They shouldn't have woken you up.' He told Hoskins that being a seafaring man, he knew what life at sea was like. Throughout the night the *Normand Pioneer* continued to press on full ahead to the *Kursk* accident site.

## Friday 18 August

The usually pro-Kremlin tabloid *Komsomolskaya Pravda*, having bribed a Northern Fleet officer 18,000 roubles ($600), finally published a full list of those aboard the *Kursk*. *Komsomolskaya Pravda* is controlled by the Interros group, owned by another Russian oligarch, Vladimir Potanin, a former deputy prime minister and founder of the multi-billion-dollar Oneximbank. Power, politics and the press were inseparable in post-Soviet Russia. In one of the biggest scandals of the tragedy, the navy had steadfastly refused to publish a list of serving crew members, citing reasons of 'national security'. The bribe showed that anything in Russia is for sale. Relatives of crew members, thanks to *Komsomolskaya Pravda*, suddenly had confirmation that their loved ones were on the *Kursk*. For some families, the published list came as a shock as they had thought their husbands or sons were serving on another sub. Before heading out to the Barents Sea manoeuvres, the *Kursk* had as usual poached crew members from other submarines. Seaman Nicolai Pavlov, aged twenty, was meant to be serving on the *Voronesh*, an Oscar II sister boat, but was sent on the *Kursk* just for this training exercise. His parents received a letter from him on 15 August saying, 'Hello my dearest father, mother, sister. My health is good. Don't worry about me. Look after yourselves.' At first, Yulya wasn't concerned for her husband, 27-year-old Senior Warrant Officer Vladimir Svechkaryev, because she was confident he wasn't serving on the *Kursk* either. Then Yulya learned he had replaced a colleague on the submarine at the last minute, and realised he was now at the bottom of the Barents Sea. For these families, the navy's obvious indifference was a double blow.

The Commission of Inquiry under Klebanov resumed its deliberations aboard *Pyotr Veliky*. The commission reached a broad set of conclusions. First, at the time of the accident, the *Kursk* was at periscope depth of 16–18 metres when it unexpectedly received 'a powerful, dynamic blow'. Second, as a result of the assumed collision, a hole developed in the bow and the submarine sank swiftly. Experts estimated that this took no more than two minutes. Third, upon hitting the seabed, ammunition detonated in the torpedo room. The commission assumed that three or four torpedoes detonated, equivalent to a two-ton explosion of TNT. Because there were no large surface vessels in the area, the commission presumed that the *Kursk* collided with 'an underwater object'. As the three Russian subs in the exercise area showed no signs of a collision, the commission pointed the finger at 'several' NATO submarines that were monitoring the Barents Sea manoeuvres. After the meeting, Deputy Prime Minister Klebanov announced that 'there still were chances of finding members of the crew in the stern'. Of the twelve versions of the cause of the disaster considered by the commission, the body ruled out nine. The commission considered there were only three possible explanations of why the *Kursk* had sunk: a collision with 'an underwater object' (i.e., another submarine); a torpedo malfunction of some sort; or collision with a Second World War mine. The last was regarded as the least likely. Klebanov specifically denied rumours that a new type of torpedo had exploded on board the *Kursk* during a test launch. The commission was plainly promoting its favourite theory: that a NATO submarine had collided with the *Kursk*, sinking her and setting off torpedoes in the boat's bow. This explanation had the added comfort of letting the Russian Navy off the hook. Their boys had died because of some careless NATO sub, not through the navy's negligence or incompetence.

Klebanov also announced to the press that the commission was considering raising the *Kursk*. While the Norwegians and British rescue teams were sailing flat-out for the accident site, the Russians were already starting to shift their planning from a rescue mission to a salvage operation. In effect, they had given up on bringing any of the submarine crew out alive. The Deputy Prime Minister told the media the *Kursk* would be raised 'exclusively through underwater co-operation'. Lifting the submarine would be an incredibly complicated technical task, he added. A group of design institutes, led by the Rubin Design Bureau, was working on proposals to lift the *Kursk*, which would be submitted to the commission in a fortnight. On 29 August 2000, the Commission of Inquiry would adopt a decision to bring the bodies of the dead submariners to the surface.

In the afternoon, following allegations in the Duma (Lower House of Parliament) of American culpability, Defense Secretary William Cohen categorically stated no US sub was involved in the *Kursk* disaster. At the same time, the Russian Navy refuted the allegation that one of their ships' missiles had gone astray and hit the *Kursk*. Captain Igor Dygalo, a Russian Navy press spokesman, also denied a story doing the rounds that a green and white distress buoy, of a type used by NATO, had been discovered in the Barents Sea. Late afternoon, Deputy PM Klebanov and Navy Commander Admiral Vladimir Kuroyedov flew to meet relatives in Vidyayevo, and had their first face-to-face meeting with the families of the *Kursk*'s crew. Klebanov and Kuroyedov did not have an easy meeting.

Among the relatives who turned out to see Klebanov and Kuroyedov at Vidyayevo Officers' Club that evening were Nadezhda Tylik and her husband Nicolai, and their daughter-in-law, Natalia. Nadezhda's son and Natalia's husband, Sergei, a Senior Lieutenant, was commander of the electrical navigation group in the *Kursk*'s second compartment. Sergei loved the *Kursk*, and had served on the boat for two years. He was twenty-five, and together with Natalia had a beautiful ten-month-old baby, Elizabeth. The couple had known each other for six years. Sergei's father and grandfather had been in the navy, and it was, Natalia said, 'in his blood'. When Natalia asked Sergei why he didn't become a lawyer, so he could earn more than the pitiful $50 per month the navy paid him, he would reply, 'I'm only interested in subs.' Before going to sea, Sergei had told Natalia they were going to test a modified old 'Fat torpedo'. Since the accident, his mother Nadezhda had not been able to sleep. On Tuesday, they had hoped Sergei was still alive, but by now the chance of his still being alive had all but disappeared. Natalia told me what happened at the meeting with Klebanov and Kuroyedov.

The Officers' Club in Vidyayevo was full that night. The gathered relatives were angry and frustrated, none more so than Nadezhda Tylik. Some families weren't present at the meeting, however. The navy had been doling out serious amounts of sedatives to the crew's relatives. Extra doctors and psychiatrists had been drafted in to the garrison town. Valeria, Captain Third Rank Andrei Milyutin's wife, missed the meeting altogether because her dose knocked her out for a whole day. Half of Vidyayevo seemed doped-up to the eyeballs, and some women were in a drugged daze for two or three days. Large or small, young or old, they were all given the same dose. At the meeting itself, Nadezhda was waiting for Klebanov to give an honest explanation of what had been going on, but became incensed when he started repeating the official version of the accident. The relatives thought the official account was a pack of lies. Some women fainted in the audience. Jumping up, Nadezhda shouted: 'Swines! What did I bring up my son for? You are sitting there getting fat but we haven't got anything. My husband was in the navy for twenty-five years. What for? And now my son is buried down there. I will never forgive you. Take off your epaulettes [addressing naval officers] and shoot yourselves now!'

Captured on film by the local Murmansk television station, Deputy Prime Minister Klebanov looked shaken. He would have preferred an egg any day. A naval officer approached Nadezhda to calm her down, but she took no notice. The next instant a female medic approached from behind and injected Nadezhda in the arm, *through her coat*. Nadezhda Tylik immediately collapsed and was carried out of the room. Strangely enough, no one in the room thought much of the injection incident itself. So many of the wives and mothers were on sedatives, they thought it was normal. Most just thought the medics were doing their job, and trying in their way to help a very distressed woman. Of course in the West, the incident was a massive public-relations disaster. The television camera had caught a very angry and upset mother upbraiding the Russian Deputy Prime Minister, and the next minute she was 'silenced' by a forcibly injected sedative. On the front page of the London *Times*, the headline was: 'How the mother of a *Kursk* sailor was silenced.' The newspaper said the 18 August incident was 'a stark reminder of the violent methods employed by the KGB against dissidents, particularly during the Brezhnev era'. While the newspaper was overstating its case somewhat, the impression was left in the West that Russia had not abandoned its former Soviet ways. Here was the proof. Klebanov's 'meet the people' event in Vidyayevo Officers' Club had it all and on camera: lies, incompetence, indifference to suffering and individual repression. At this point, President Putin decided it was better to curtail his summer vacation and return to Moscow.

Commodore David Russell, Deputy Flag Officer (Submarines), DFOSM, was the most senior British Navy officer with the British rescue team. He had been a submariner since 1974, and his years of experience were attested by his silver-grey hair. Russell was also the scene of action commander, with a brief to liaise with the Russians. The previous day he had tried to fly direct to Murmansk, but incredibly the Russians refused him permission to enter Russian airspace, and he was forced to turn back. Frustrated by the lack of co-operation from the Russians, Russell took a helicopter out to the *Normand Pioneer*, arriving in the evening. For the British rescue team, the Russian attitude was inexplicable. They were there, after all, to try to save their men.

Late on Friday, Northern Fleet Commander Popov appeared on RTR television. Looking puffy-faced and with swollen eyes, Popov appeared on the verge of tears. He nervously wrung his naval beret, and said he had tried his best to save his boys. Popov stated the last knocking noise had been heard on Monday 14 August, contradicting the navy's own press office. He looked a broken man. He was. Popov knew that he and the *Kursk* crew were finished together.

## Saturday 19 August

President Vladimir Putin slipped in to Moscow quietly at 4:40 A.M., arriving from Simferopol on the Black Sea. In the United States, experts blamed the sinking of the *Kursk* on a torpedo explosion, supported by seismic reports from Canada, the UK, Germany, Norway and Alaska. The strength of the explosions suggested the first one involved one torpedo, while the second seismic event looked more like several torpedoes exploding at once. At the Warship Support Agency headquarters at Foxhill, Bath, the British announced that they would not enter the *Kursk* if the area below the escape hatch was already flooded. The point here was that the British were only committed to helping with the rescue operation, and saving lives. Traditionally, recovering the dead bodies of servicemen was a very sensitive matter, left to the nation concerned. The British rescue team's first task would be to send a Remotely Operated Vehicle (ROV) video camera to inspect the hatch. The Swedes moved their URF rescue mini-sub to an airport outside Stockholm, just in case the Russians asked for help. Their submersible was compatible with LR5, and could carry thirty-five people at a time. By 7:10 P.M. local time, the *Normand Pioneer*, with over forty people on board, was about twelve miles from the *Kursk* accident site. It was heading for the Russian rescue ship the *Mikhail Rudnitsky*, and was in radio contact with the *Pyotr Veliky*. Having overtaken the Norwegian divers on the *Seaway Eagle*, the *Normand Pioneer* was due to arrive on site at 9 P.M.

Ilya Klebanov, Russia's Deputy Prime Minister, now asserted that there were three foreign reconnaissance submarines gathering intelligence in the area when the *Kursk* sank. He hinted that one was responsible for colliding with the Russian nuclear sub. He said it was 'very possible' that the *Kursk*'s torpedoes had detonated, but only after a collision with a foreign object. Told by the Russians to expect 'stormy weather', the British arrived in the rescue area to find the Barents Sea calm and flat as a pancake. The Russians had lied again.

During the course of the day, a meeting of Russian, Norwegian and British experts was held aboard the *Seaway Eagle*. The meeting lasted between five and six hours. Representing the British were Commodore David Russell, Lieutenant Commander Piers Barker, Captain Simon Lister (interpreter and representative of the British Naval Attaché in Moscow), and David Mayo (project representative). Heading the Russian side was Rear-Admiral Gennady Verich, head of the Russian Navy's Search and Rescue Department, based in Moscow. Verich had overall control of the rescue operation. He gave the impression he was in no hurry. Coming back to brief the Brits aboard the *Normand Pioneer* at 8 P.M. that evening, Commodore Russell said the meeting had proved 'fruitless'. The British rescue team told this writer they were disappointed, angry and disgruntled by the attitude they had encountered. They had been unable to convince the Russians to use the LR5 submersible, and it was clear the Northern Fleet's priority was to send divers down to inspect the *Kursk*'s aft escape hatch. It was apparent from the meeting that the Russians, in a week of operations, had been unable to make a proper inspection of the hatch. Russia's divers no longer had the ability to go down to a depth of 100 metres, and the *Kursk* lay at 108 metres. For professional Western divers, 100 metres was routine. Many commercial divers working from North Sea oil rigs regularly go down to a depth of 320 metres (1,000 feet) or more. The British also faced another problem with the LR5 submersible. The Russians were obviously nervous of the LR5's capabilities. Once the mini-sub went into the water, they would have no control over where it went, or what it saw.

Admiral Skorgen, in charge of the Norwegian rescue operation, and working in co-operation with the British from his command centre in Norway, felt that the Russians were just not coming up with the necessary information. He found the Russian experts he talked to either didn't have the answers required or were afraid to give any information. On the vital question of the aft escape hatch, the Russians offered some handwritten, scribbled notes. Skorgen was starting to lose his patience.

Then it looked as if there might be some progress for the LR5 team. Just before Commodore Russell's briefing, the *Normand Pioneer* received an unexpected helicopter 'protocol' visit from Vice-Admiral Oleg Burtsev, Commander of the Northern Fleet's 1st Submarine Flotilla. Burtsev was a submariner, and speaking through his interpreter, said he knew the *Kursk*'s crew personally. He was a big, emotional man, and was in tears when he spoke about the *Kursk*'s fate. Burtsev discovered that his daughter and Commander Alan Hoskins's daughter had married within a day of each other and celebrated birthdays a day apart. The British LR5 rescue team convinced Burtsev of the submersible's capabilities, and assured him that the mini-sub could take down Russian divers, medical personnel and interpreters.

Whereas the LR5's rubber 'skirt' meant the British mini-sub could mate on difficult surfaces (as little as 6–8 inches thick), the Russian submersibles *Priz* and *Bester* had to dock by linking up exactly with a matching 'o' ring on the outer escape hatch. They were therefore less adept at mating with a distressed sub, and required near-perfect launch conditions to operate at all. Even a one-metre swell would cause problems as a Russian submersible was launched using two separate cranes, with the mini-sub swinging like a pendulum above the water. The British used a purpose-built 'A' frame, part of the *Normand Pioneer*'s structure, which allowed for seamless launches as the mini-sub was winched directly and securely into the sea. Reassured by the rescue team, Burtsev asked what else they needed to launch LR5, and said he would try to get some personnel from a *Kursk* sister sub to help. Despite the negative meeting aboard the *Seaway Eagle*, morale on the *Normand Pioneer* soared, as the team felt that at last they were now 'ready to go'. However, the British never saw or heard from Admiral Burtsev again.

## Sunday 20 August

*Seaway Eagle* and her team of twelve British and Norwegian divers arrived at the accident site at 1 A.M. Later that morning, Deputy Prime Minister Klebanov said that only two of the *Kursk*'s ten compartments were not completely flooded. Vice-Admiral Mikhail Motsak, Chief of Staff of the Northern Fleet, finally admitted that his fleet had no deep-sea, saturation divers. He said that was why the Russians had called in the Norwegians. At 9 A.M., the Norwegians planned to send their first diver down to the *Kursk*, and at 3 P.M. they were analysing video recordings made by an ROV. Later that afternoon, the British and Norwegian divers from *Seaway Eagle* worked on the aft escape hatch, which they found they could unscrew but not lift. The twelve divers worked for the Norwegian company Stolt Offshore. Tony Scott, a British diver, was the first one to reach the escape hatch. He tapped several times on the hatch to see if anybody would reply, but 'there was nothing'. Later he said: 'If we could have saved someone, it would have been brilliant.'

Admiral Skorgen told the author he was furious when he learned that everything the Russians had led him to believe was untrue. The hatch was completely undamaged, as was the mating ring. The submarine wasn't listing at all, it was lying flat on the bottom. The underwater current was nothing like 2–3 knots, in fact it was more like 0.1–0.2. At most, the current reached 0.3 knots. Visibility, previously reported as poor, was good. This meant that everything the Russians had said during the course of the previous week about strong currents hampering the rescue operation was a lie. They just couldn't admit to the world that they didn't have the equipment to save their own men. The Russian Navy's pride, and their desire to keep the West away from the *Kursk*'s military secrets, was more important to them than trying to save lives. They knew from the outset there was little hope of saving anyone, but if they had immediately invited help from the West, in other circumstances there might have been a chance of saving some of the crew. Worst of all, the navy's own shortcomings when it came to faulty hardware (the HTP torpedo), emergency equipment, escape procedures and poor training made the *Kursk* disaster inevitable in the first place. Although the *Kursk* itself was a state-of-the-art sub, the Russians' fatal mistake was to try to economise by using antiquated practice weaponry and cutting back on safety measures, vital maintenance and support services.

Rear-Admiral Einar Skorgen was not going to risk the lives of his men because the Russian military had a psychological inability to tell the truth. He contacted Admiral Popov and told him to give the Norwegians the information they required to do the job, or he would end the operation there and then. Popov immediately agreed. Admiral Skorgen told the north Norwegian daily *Nordlandsposten* the following week: 'I was really angry. I think this was understood as a threat from my side, yes. At times there were so many wrong details and misinformation from Russia that it was close to endangering the divers. We couldn't rely on the information we were getting.'

After Skorgen's ultimatum, two Norwegian divers were flown to the *Oryel*, a sister Oscar II boat in Severomorsk. The divers looked at the aft escape hatch, saw how it worked and took pictures. The Norwegians decided they would need special tools to open the hatch, so set about making them themselves aboard the *Seaway Eagle*. Meanwhile, the British aboard the *Normand Pioneer* were told to stay fifteen to twenty miles away from the accident site. The Russians had six or seven ships in the immediate area, including the aircraft-carrier *Admiral Kuznetsov*. Communication between the *Seaway Eagle* and the *Normand Pioneer* became difficult, but not impossible, when the Russians confiscated the divers' mobile phones aboard Skorgen's ship.

The British LR5 rescue team aboard the *Normand Pioneer* asked the

Russians for a 'trial run' to test their submersible in the rescue zone. The reply came back that they could only go into the water four miles from the accident site, as the Russians were still nervous about letting the LR5 anywhere near the *Kursk*. However, no one told the *Normand Pioneer*'s 'escort', the Russian anti-submarine warship which acted as the British team's shadow. As the Russian warship warned the *Normand Pioneer* it was one and a half miles out of its 'designated zone', its radar and guns started tracking the rescue ship. The British got the message and abandoned the attempted trial run. No one was sure if the Russians would really have opened fire, but neither was anybody keen to put it to the test.

Another long meeting took place on the *Seaway Eagle* that day between the Norwegians, British and Russians. The meeting dragged on for eight hours, and Rear-Admiral Verich was initially as stubborn and immovable as the day before. At one point, the Russians openly suggested the British might use the opportunity to spy on the *Kursk*. 'You could look for weak points,' one Russian told the British team. The divers from the *Seaway Eagle* were not allowed to work forward of the escape hatch, and the Russians were watching them every step of the way. However, once LR5 was in the water, they knew it would be impossible to control its movements. The Russians wanted the Norwegians to wrench the aft escape hatch off with a crane, but they refused to oblige. If the Norwegians had removed the hatch in the way suggested, docking with the LR5 and hence any putative rescue operation would have been made impossible. Again, it looked as if the Russians were more interested in a salvage operation than a rescue mission. The meeting was going nowhere, very slowly. Half-way through the meeting Admiral Verich was summoned to take a call. When he came back, he was all sweetness and reason itself. The atmosphere changed immediately, and the Russians agreed to use the LR5 mini-sub the next morning. They would hold a technical meeting at 7 A.M. aboard the *Normand Pioneer* and launch the LR5 about three hours later. The 'Skorgen effect' seems to have had an impact on Verich, who was ordered by Moscow to be more co-operative. No doubt the navy High Command and the Kremlin were also becoming more aware of the importance of being seen to be accommodating, even though they were extremely reluctant to let the British mini-sub anywhere near the *Kursk*.

As Norwegian divers checked the valves on the stern escape hatch, they were able to move the equalisers. Dye went into the escape tower, indicating the escape chamber was potentially clear. Ignoring the Russians' suggestion to wrench off the aft escape hatch, the Norwegian divers attached a 500 kilogram bag to the outer hatch, called a 'mine bag'. Like a heavy floating balloon, the mine bag was left overnight, with the idea that the gravitational pressure and weight of the bag would open the hatch.

In Moscow, President Putin met Academician Igor Spassky, General Designer and head of the St Petersburg-based Rubin Design Bureau, responsible for designing the *Kursk*. Somewhat late in the day, Putin was at last trying to ensure he was fully briefed.

## Monday 21 August

At 2 A.M. on Monday morning, the *Normand Pioneer* with the LR5 mini-sub aboard, started moving towards the accident site. Between about 5 and 5:30 A.M. the outer escape hatch on the stern of the *Kursk* opened. The 'mine bag' had done the trick. Jon-Are Hvalbye, a forty-year-old Norwegian diver, spoke for the twelve-man diving team. 'It was,' he said, 'an easy task to perform. Technically there were no problems.' At around 7:15 A.M. divers from the *Seaway Eagle* prepared to open the lower escape hatch and look inside the ninth compartment. The chamber between the outer and inner escape hatches was, after all, flooded. No bodies were found in the escape chamber. The lower hatch lid was shut, but the valve was open. Norwegian divers, using the three-pronged tool they had made themselves, opened the inner escape hatch. A puff of gas escaped, and some small air bubbles. They concluded that the ninth compartment was totally flooded. Hvalbye confirmed the whole diving operation to open the hatch had taken between six and seven hours. He said there had been no unforeseen physical complications, despite Russian reports that the hatch was severely damaged. Radiation specialists aboard the *Seaway Eagle* took samples of air, water and the seabed, analysed them and sent samples on to Oslo, Norway. The 'rescue operation' was over. Later analysis of air samples showed there had been a localised fire in the ninth compartment, with the air temperature reaching 300°C.

The Northern Fleet angrily denied that the *Kursk*'s aft escape hatch was undamaged. A Northern Fleet press officer said that any information that the hatch was undamaged was 'absurd'. He claimed it was only the fact that the hatch *was* damaged that had prevented the Russians from linking up with the ninth compartment. The Russian media and the rest of the world saw it differently. On 22 August, Alexander Shaburkin wrote in the newspaper *Vremiya MN*:

> It took Norwegian divers six hours to achieve what had defied
> Russian rescue teams for seven days . . . It's already clear that it
> was too late from the very start. While precious hours were
> wasted in bureaucratic conferences, while the question of
> reporting everything to the top was endlessly debated, while
> attempts were made to conceal the true scale of the disaster,
> while foreign assistance was rejected . . . The navy command
> itself knew how all this would end.

By midday, Deputy Prime Minister Klebanov acknowledged that the operation to raise the *Kursk* would have to be an international project. He accepted that the Russians could not do it on their own. In a belated attempt to control the flow of information, the Russian Navy's press office announced that from henceforth all news on the Barents Sea rescue mission would be provided by the Northern Fleet in Severomorsk.

That morning in the Kremlin, President Putin met his Cabinet. Putin did not make a statement on the *Kursk* but told the assembled press: 'The defence minister has delivered an account of various military-technical aspects of the operation in the Barents Sea. Now we are going to talk about the humanitarian aspects. The families of the sailors will get special help.' As the press were leaving, they heard their president tell his colleagues in a businesslike tone that the agenda included security issues in Central Asia and the tragedy in the Barents

Sea. Putin made it sound as if the *Kursk* was just one of several 'military-technical' issues the Cabinet was concerned with that day. The overwhelming impression was one of bureaucratic indifference. Putin and his ministerial colleagues misjudged the feeling in the country, and still had no real understanding of how deeply people in Russia and abroad had been touched by the *Kursk* disaster. Partly, it was a question of psychology and upbringing. Putin and his Cabinet were creatures of the old Soviet system.

Aboard the *Normand Pioneer*, the early-morning technical meeting was cancelled. At 11 A.M. the British were officially informed that the *Kursk* was flooded. Commodore David Russell was invited aboard the *Pyotr Veliky*, where he met a sombre Klebanov and Admiral Kuroyedov. Meeting for about two and a half hours, Russell found his hosts shocked, thoughtful, polite and grateful. His assessment that the *Kursk* had been sunk by a torpedo explosion was greeted with assenting nods. Russell came away from the meeting thinking that the Deputy Prime Minister and the Navy Commander-in-Chief did not really blame the West for the *Kursk* disaster. Russian pronouncements implicating the West were merely for domestic consumption and to deflect criticism.

Generally kept over ten miles from the site of the accident, occasionally the *Normand Pioneer* had moved within two miles of the location where the *Kursk* had gone down. For the first time, the *Normand Pioneer* was allowed directly over the accident site, where the British team held a memorial service and threw a wreath into the sea. As the British made ready to leave the site, the Russian anti-sub warship which had been their constant shadow executed a high-speed salute. Passing the *Normand Pioneer* at maximum speed, the Russian warship's entire complement lined the deck in salute to the British rescue team. 'We're all hairy-arsed men,' said one member of the team, 'but that high-speed salute brought a lump to the throat.'

The British LR5 team had been on site for 47 hours and 20 minutes, but their highly sophisticated submersible had not even been allowed to get wet. As they left the scene that afternoon, there was a further sour note as one radio journalist aboard a Russian ship reported that the British were leaving as their 'spying mission is now complete'.

Russian paranoia about the West's motives seemed extreme, yet, as will be shown later, they had some real grounds for fearing that the sinking of the *Kursk* could be exploited by several foreign intelligence agencies.

In Vidyayevo, over 200 relatives of the *Kursk*'s crew gathered in the closed garrison town. Three had been hospitalised. The government was finally offering free transport for the relatives and organising special flights to Murmansk. Expert psychiatrists and psychologists from St Petersburg's Medical and Military Academy were arriving in town. When relatives turned up in Vidyayevo, they found a note pinned to the door of the Officers' Club. It told them where they could collect a glass container filled with seawater from the site where the *Kursk* had gone down.

Early evening saw President Putin once again meeting with his Defence Minister, Marshal Sergeyev, in Moscow. They decided to ask Norway for help with recovering bodies from the *Kursk*. The Russian media continued to cite anonymous navy sources who claimed that the accident was the result of a collision with a Western submarine. Vice-Admiral Motsak was one of those openly suggesting the British were responsible for the collision. The allegation was viewed with surprise in London, given improved relations and frequent visits to Russian ports by Royal Navy ships over recent years. The Ministry of Defence denied there were any British submarines in the Barents Sea at the time of the disaster. Later that evening, Sergeyev revealed that he had asked NATO to confirm the whereabouts of its submarines at the time of the *Kursk* sinking. Sergeyev said NATO refused, but indicated there were no NATO boats in the vicinity. However, Sergeyev also said that while Russia's representative was *officially* told there were no subs in the area, *unofficially* he was told that even if there were, NATO wouldn't admit it.

At 9 P.M. the Military Council of the Northern Fleet officially announced that all 118 crew members on board the *Kursk* were dead, and expressed its condolences to their relatives. National television channels began the evening news with solemn music or sounds of the sea and a slow roll-call of the names of all those lost on the *Kursk*. Pictures of distraught relatives were shown, grieving for their loved ones. Vice-Admiral Motsak said: 'Our worst expectations are con-firmed. All sections of the submarine are totally flooded and not a single member of the crew remains alive.' There was no statement from President Putin, and no announcement of a day of mourning. As the country grieved, Russia felt leaderless.

# 3

# Recriminations

Faced with a fresh barrage of criticism from the press, on Tuesday 22 August Vladimir Putin declared the following Wednesday an official day of mourning and finally set off to meet the families of those lost on the *Kursk*. That evening he flew to Severomorsk, where he was met by Deputy Prime Minister Klebanov and members of the government's Commission of Inquiry. Klebanov had just had another bad day. Following a further meeting with the crew's relatives, the Deputy Prime Minister was almost half-strangled by an infuriated family member. Asked when the bodies from the *Kursk* would be recovered, he had nonchalantly replied, 'In a few months . . . maybe a year. I don't know exactly.' According to *Kommersant* newspaper journalist Andrei Kolesnikov, the room erupted. 'A woman . . . shook him. "You swine, get out there and save them." The officers rushed to drag her away. It wasn't easy. She clung to Klebanov and shouted, "You're nothing but scum." '

Speaking on RTR public television on that day, Defence Minister Sergeyev still tried to maintain the official version of events. Asked about the timing of offers of international assistance, Sergeyev replied,

'Foreign help. This is all recorded. On Wednesday the sixteenth of August there was the first offer which was immediately accepted by the navy's Commander-in-Chief.'

The Russian authorities formally appealed to the Norwegian government for help in recovering the 118 bodies of the crew entombed aboard the *Kursk*. Rear-Admiral Einar Skorgen gave his country's initial response during the course of a radio interview. 'With the equipment we have, there is no possibility to do any more than we have done,' he declared, adding that retrieving the bodies was 'a totally different operation'.

Putin and the government were being pilloried by the press. Led by the independent television channel NTV, its stablemate radio Ekho Moskvy, and the newspapers *Komsomolskaya Pravda*, *Novaya Gazeta* and *Vremiya MN*, the media was having a field day criticising Russia's leadership and unpicking contradictions in official accounts of the disaster. *Komsomolskaya Pravda* had led the way the previous week, with a headline in huge red letters: 'Why has the president been silent?' 'People's faith in the state's ability to protect them from misfortune has . . . sunk to the seabed,' wrote *Izvestia*. *Vremiya MN*, echoing many similar headlines, declared: 'The reputation of the Russian leadership lies on the bottom of the Barents Sea.' Nor was the criticism restricted to the Russian press. Western newspapers and TV coverage excoriated the president. The *New York Times* wrote in an editorial on 24 August: 'It is too soon to know if more active leadership on Mr Putin's part could have saved lives, but his performance has been disheartening for those who hoped to see a more democratic Russia shedding the habits of secrecy and indifference to human suffering that marred so many centuries of czarist and Soviet rule.' Three days earlier, the London *Daily Telegraph*'s editorial attacked Putin's leadership, or lack of it: 'His remaining on holiday on the Black Sea until the end of last week looked both callous and irresponsible. His ambition to have the navy fly the flag of a reinvigorated great power around the world, proclaimed by posters reading "Naval might is Russia's glory", appears absurdly vainglorious.'

The *Telegraph* editorial of 21 August also lauded the role of the

Russian media: 'In the style of a Soviet *apparatchik*, Mr Putin sought to stifle the press. That it has rightly rounded on him over the *Kursk* is the one compensating factor in a dismal tale of official hubris, lying and incompetence. One of the key components of a free society has been playing its role with a vengeance.' The role of the Russian media and its relationship with the government was complex. The media had united full-square behind President Yeltsin in his 1996 bid for re-election, running a blatant 'Red scare' campaign against communist challenger Gennady Zyuganov. Previously, the media had been extremely critical of Yeltsin's 1994–96 war in Chechnya, and his opinion-poll ratings had fallen to single figures before the TV and press rallied to his side. Similarly, most of the media had backed Vladimir Putin in his campaign to become president in 2000, indulging in wilful character-assassinations of Putin's main political opponents, former prime minister Yevgeny Primakov and Moscow Mayor Yury Luzhkov. The second Chechen war (1999 onwards) was widely backed by the media, and was crucial in building support for Putin's presidential bid. By the time of the *Kursk* débâcle, the Russian media had started to change its tune. Partly, this was because the oligarchs who were so influential under the rule of President Yeltsin and his 'family' had found themselves suddenly sidelined.

The Media Most conglomerate, owned by Vladimir Gusinsky, was the first to fall out, with his media holdings opposing Putin's presidential bid and backing Primakov. Primakov was also a former foreign minister and head of the SVR, the foreign-intelligence successor to the KGB. Gusinsky's media companies were the most critical of Putin's handling of the *Kursk* disaster, including NTV television, the radio station Ekho Moskvy and the newspapers *Segodnya*, *Novaya Gazeta*, *Obshchaya Gazeta* and *Itogi* magazine. By the time of the *Kursk* disaster, Gusinsky had already been arrested on fraud charges and was in exile abroad. Boris Berezovsky, another oligarch, who owned a controlling share of ORT and TV6 television as well as the newspaper *Kommersant*, also found himself frozen out from the Kremlin and under investigation for fraud. The trio of moguls was completed with Vladimir Potanin, who controlled *Komsomolskaya Pravda* and *Izvestia*.

Although normally pro-government, Potanin could have easily feared his businesses were next in line for criminal investigation. All these oligarchs had made their fortunes in the early days of *perestroika* and post-communism. The way they acquired their companies following privatisation was a bone of contention, especially since the law on private property in those days was a grey area. Any investigation might potentially unravel their business empires, as Gusinsky was finding out. His early purchases of newly privatised media companies were increasingly being called into question.

There was another factor behind the media onslaught against Putin. Most of the Russian media always took it as their duty to support the 'party of power' during elections. They convinced themselves it was necessary for stability, to keep the communists out or to ensure a smooth transfer of power. In any event, supporting the Kremlin's favourite was a way for the media bosses to call in favours later. Once the election was won, however, the media liked to assert its independence. The press, of course, had a vested interest in freedom of speech and freedom of expression, more so than any other part of Russian society. Putin's arrest of Gusinsky in June 2000 had threatened those freedoms. The media felt the president was reneging on the unspoken compact: we will support your re-election, and then you tolerate our freedom of expression the rest of the time. The *Kursk* gave the Russian media the opportunity to 'bite back', to re-assert the independence it had won in 1991, at the time of the attempted hard-line coup against Gorbachev, and subsequently with the collapse of the Soviet Union. Russian editors and journalists decided to remind the president that he had a free press. There were no holds barred, and the criticism was vitriolic. The message that he could not walk all over them or take them for granted was a shot over the president's bows, warning him not to take them on. Putin saw it differently, and was incandescent with rage. In his view, the press was challenging his authority as president, and hence the authority of the state. For a former KGB man, this was just too much. His retribution would come later.

The Russian president's opinion-poll ratings had suffered a setback, reflecting public reaction to his handling of the crisis. The All-Russian

Public Opinion Centre found that his approval rating had dropped 8 per cent in one week, from 73 to 65 per cent. Another poll, conducted by the Romir agency, showed that 28 per cent of Muscovites thought their opinion of Putin had dropped as a result of his mishandling of the disaster. Over three-quarters of those polled believed Russia should have sought international assistance sooner than it did, and one in five blamed the president for the submariners' deaths. Over a third of those asked thought the navy's High Command was responsible for the loss of the *Kursk* and her crew. There was growing anecdotal evidence of a backlash against a president who previously could do no wrong. Mikhail Aleksandrovich, a former army diver on his way to Severomorsk, said of Putin's visit to see the submariners' families: 'The visit won't save anything. His reputation was ruined in the space of two days. So the government is suddenly running around trying to be active, but they should have done that in the beginning. It seems that it is a lot easier to bury a hundred men than open up a state secret.' Staff on the relatives' helpline said they still had not been given a list of the dead crew.

Irina Belozyorova, who lost her husband Captain Third Rank Nicolai Belozyorov and lived in Vidyayevo with her 10-year-old son Alexei, couldn't wait to tell the president what she thought of him. 'I'll just tell him how glad I am that I didn't vote for him. He's not a president. He's just a stooge,' she said with feeling. Although the naval community around Vidyayevo was understandably more bitter than the general public, it was surprising how widespread the feeling of anger and betrayal was throughout Russia. Attending a special memorial mass for the *Kursk*'s crew in Moscow's cathedral of Christ the Saviour, 20-year-old Yevgeny Levlampiyev said of Putin: 'He got to power by exploiting the very strong nostalgia people have for the past, their national sense of humiliation, and the Chechen issue. I never thought he would betray the armed forces.' Levlampiyev had not voted for Putin because he mistrusted his commitment to free speech and democracy. According to another young Muscovite at the church service, 16-year-old Natasha Lemyagova: 'His mistake will cost him dearly. He should have gone to Murmansk on the first day.'

Russia's politicians were also critical of Putin's response to the crisis. Former Soviet Vice-President and Governor of Kursk Alexander Rutskoi, referring to Putin's late arrival at the scene of the accident, said, 'If I was the president I would have arrived on the fastest plane.' Boris Nemtsov, the leader of the Union of Right Forces in the Duma and former reformist deputy prime minister, called for a parliamentary inquiry. Nemtsov, young, articulate and fluent in English, said the inquiry should find out: 'First, the real cause of the catastrophe; and second, did our government and president do everything to save our sailors.' Nemtsov also criticised Putin personally. 'The behaviour of Putin was amoral,' he said. 'As supreme commander-in-chief he has no right to a holiday while his sailors face this drama. Nor is there a reasonable explanation of why he did not accept foreign help before so much time had been wasted.'

Gennady Zyuganov, the 56-year-old former presidential candidate and leader of the communist faction in the Duma, blamed the military and claimed it had not adequately informed the president. Not for the first time, Zyuganov let slip an opportunity to land a political blow against the Kremlin, and showed why he was destined to perpetual opposition. Some commentators suggested the communists had become too cosy with Putin's administration, after doing a deal to gain the Speaker's post in the parliament and carving up important committee places. Zyuganov had always given the impression that he was almost afraid of rocking the boat, and even more afraid of ending up as president. He had failed to beat Yeltsin, despite a healthy early lead, and never looked like beating Putin. History and demography, however, were even more potent reasons why the communist bloc's ageing political support would ensure they remained unelectable in today's modern Russia.

As President Putin arrived in Severomorsk on 22 August he faced a huge challenge to regain the political initiative and shore up his public support. With the press on the warpath, and negative opinion polls staring him in the face, Putin decided to launch a counter-attack. His strategy consisted first of all in travelling to meet the relatives of those lost on the *Kursk*, ten days after the submarine had first struck the bottom of the Barents Sea. He had to be seen offering his condolences to the families who had suffered the loss of their loved ones. Second, he would apologise for the fiasco and offer generous compensation to the bereaved. Third, he would go on the offensive to silence his critics.

Speaking on the same day Putin arrived in Severomorsk, Defence Minister Sergeyev followed the president's lead. Marshal Sergeyev issued a statement offering fresh condolences for the loss of the *Kursk*'s crew: 'We have failed to protect them. Forgive us.' Sergeyev had offered his resignation on Monday, after receiving confirmation that the *Kursk* was flooded, and Admiral of the Fleet Vladimir Kuroyedov and Admiral Vyacheslav Popov, Commander of the Northern Fleet, had offered to resign the next day, but Putin refused to accept the proffered heads.

Following a short meeting with Klebanov and the government-appointed Commission of Inquiry at the headquarters of the Northern Fleet, Putin headed off to meet the crew's relatives in Vidyayevo, arriving around 8 P.M. The media had been kept out of Severomorsk and Vidyayevo, and Putin's visit was covered only by state-controlled RTR television. The president was dressed in a black suit and shirt, buttoned up to the neck, without a tie. One of the first people he met in Vidyayevo was Irina Lyachina, wife of the *Kursk*'s commander, Gennady. The TV camera could not fail to pick up the damp, peeling walls of the officers' accommodation during his meeting with Irina and her daughter. Leaving the flat but still accompanied by Irina, Putin then did a brief walkabout, shaking hands and talking to the large crowd which had gathered. He went on to the submariners' Officers' Club, where around 600 angry and grief-stricken residents of Vidyayevo were waiting for him. Some 350 of the audience had lost their husbands, sons or brothers. Looking sombre, pale and drawn, President Putin was given a hostile grilling for six hours as the tense confrontation continued into the early hours.

Putin had certainly never experienced a meeting like the one he faced in Vidyayevo. Talking to those present, it is apparent that many had turned from loyal presidential supporters to profoundly critical opponents. The anger, hatred even, was palpable. Not all of it was directed at Putin: sitting at his side were the senior navy men Kuroyedov and Popov, and people in the audience repeatedly called for the admirals to resign. The furious relatives bombarded Putin with questions like 'Why have you murdered our lads?' or 'Who are you going to punish for their deaths, and how?' Others asked, 'Do you believe our men are still alive?' One woman in the crowd fainted, while others became hysterical. The questions continued to flow: 'When would the bodies of the submariners be brought home?' 'When will we get them back, dead or alive?' Many simply could not come to terms with the fact that their loved ones were already dead. People shouted their questions, and strained to hear the president's replies. Putin was almost overwhelmed by the onslaught, but maintained a steely calm, listening intently to his hostile inquisitors. Irina Belozyorova, a *Kursk* widow, said, 'I even felt sorry for him. Everyone was shouting questions at once.' Putin tried to console them: 'The grief is immeasurable, there are not enough words for comfort. My heart hurts, but yours hurt even more.' Putin made a mistake by initially trying to patronise his audience: 'Just like you, I'm not an expert.' The audience, full of experienced submariners, balked. Someone asked why international help hadn't been accepted sooner. Putin tried trotting out the official version: 'We accepted Western help as soon as it was offered on Wednesday the sixteenth of August . . .' Before he could finish, however, he was shouted down. Virtually everyone in the audience knew from media reports that foreign help had been offered on Monday 14 August. One woman in the audience shouted, 'They believed in the state, that the state would save them! You don't understand how they believed!' Another person bellowed: 'You could have saved just five! Bastards!'

Swiftly changing tack, Vladimir Putin decided honesty was the best policy, adopting some of his famous bar-room language. During the second Chechen war, this had gone down a storm: 'We'll blast them out, even in the shit-house,' Putin's famous response to the Chechen rebels, had become part of Russian folklore. A submariner's wife berated the president, asking him why Russia had to rely on Norway's deep-sea divers. Putin interjected: 'This country doesn't have a fig.' A little later, warming to his theme, the president told the assembled families: 'I'm willing to take responsibility for my hundred days in power. But when it comes to the last fifteen years, then I'm ready to sit on the bench with you and put the questions to them.' Putin glossed over the fact that he had been prime minister for seven months before becoming president, and before that had been head of the Federal Security Bureau (FSB), successor to the KGB. Although he had only been president for a hundred days, he had been near the centre of power since the mid-1990s.

Putin undoubtedly impressed some with his straight-talking. He also tried to mollify others. So far, the relatives of the victims had only received 1,000 roubles ($37). He now offered the families compensation payments equivalent to ten years' salary. While some of the poorer members of the audience were faintly appreciative, many of those present were sceptical. One ex-submariner commented: 'The officers' wives understood straight away that they were being bought off and that the guilty parties would not be taken to court.' The hostile encounter had been such a bruising experience for the president that only a few seconds of the meeting were shown on RTR state television, minus any soundtrack.

Although feelings on Putin's performance at the meeting were mixed, with some relatives thinking he handled himself well under pressure, others felt he still appeared too cold and self-assured. Vladimir Mityayev, the father of Senior Lieutenant Alexei Mityayev, who perished on the *Kursk*, was at the meeting and gave me his impressions. Mityayev senior had been a submariner like his father before him, and was brought up to respect and trust the authority of the state. He respected Putin as his president, and felt he was a great politician, someone who could be trusted to keep his word. Putin, he said, 'calmed down' the relatives. Mityayev senior's faith in Putin had not even been shaken by the fact that he only heard about the *Kursk* accident on the radio, when his wife picked up that the sub was supposedly 'lying on the seabed'. His absolute belief in his country's leader, despite the evidence of Putin's fallibility, showed just how deeply ingrained the old Soviet attitudes remained in some parts of Russian society. But Mityayev made it clear he had no time for the other politicians and officials, whom he thought were incompetent and 'trying to hide something'.

Vladimir Chaikin had served as a sub-lieutenant on submarines for eleven years. He admitted he had voted for Putin as president, but felt his leader had badly miscalculated: 'He doesn't arrive when his presence is crucial, but he shows up when no one wants to see him.' Olga, widow of Captain-Lieutenant Dmitri Kolesnikov, said: 'Our president made a big mistake. He should have been out at sea supervising the rescue operation. And he should have come straight away to give moral support to us relatives and loved ones. That's what we were all expecting.' Olga Kolesnikova was disappointed and appalled by Putin's performance at the meeting: 'I was waiting for words of condolence and sympathy. What we got was talk about the compensation we'd be paid. It was disgusting, painful.' Some of the families couldn't face going to the meeting. Marina Stankevich, widow of the *Kursk*'s doctor, said: 'I didn't go because I just can't look at that man.' Other relatives were either too upset or too heavily sedated to attend. Lilia Shetsova, of the Moscow Carnegie Centre, later summed it up. 'Putin,' Shetsova said, 'couldn't understand that it was his time, his time to become a leader, and he missed this opportunity.'

Putin received a further setback at the meeting. The original plan was for the president to lay a wreath the next day at the site of the accident, surrounded by the crew's relatives. The event was meant to be the focal point of Wednesday's national day of mourning. The families, however, would have none of it. They didn't want to accept their loved ones were dead, and feared that once Putin's photo-opportunity was out of the way, they and their men would be forgotten. Faced with another public-relations disaster, Putin cancelled the ceremony and returned abruptly to Murmansk and then Moscow. It was the first time anybody could remember the Kremlin abandoning a ceremony because of public pressure. There is no doubt that Putin was shaken by the strength of feeling he encountered in Vidyayevo. It had been the most challenging public encounter of his career, and he had just about survived it. Before the meeting, Vladimir Putin had not really understood the trauma and popular outrage which had gripped Russia following the sinking of the *Kursk*. But he felt it now, and was angry and alarmed that so much of the animus was directed personally at him. Stung, Putin promised the grieving families that he would raise the entire submarine and recover all the crew's bodies for proper burial.

Russia's Orthodox Church tried to come to President Putin's rescue. With Putin under withering attack, Patriarch Alexei, head of the Orthodox church, said in a TV address that he knew how painful the tragedy had been for the president. The Church maintained a cosy relationship with the Kremlin, supporting it over the Chechen conflict and in return seeking government aid in restricting the spread of 'foreign' religions in Russia. The result had been some rather bizarre laws, banning the Salvation Army and the Baptists, for example, and even threatening the existence of other religions in Russia like Roman Catholicism. Only churches registered in Soviet days would be allowed to operate legally in the 'New Russia'. In religious terms, the Russian Orthodox Church was looking backwards to the days when the Soviet Union had given it a state monopoly. The corollary had been limited religious freedom, and a priesthood packed with KGB agents.

Returning to the Kremlin on Wednesday 23 August, President Putin prepared at long last to broadcast to the nation. Appearing on RTR state television that evening on the national day of mourning for the *Kursk*'s crew, President Putin offered a personal apology for the disaster. With the Russian and presidential flags flying at half-mast atop the Kremlin, Putin said: 'I feel a complete sense of responsibility and guilt for this tragedy.' Speaking slowly and carefully, the president showed little emotion. His KGB training often showed through at times like these, and Putin could indeed appear cold and calculating. He said anyone found culpable would be punished, but blame should only be apportioned when 'a full understanding has been gained about what happened and why'. Putin revealed that Defence Minister Sergeyev had offered to resign on Monday, after the Norwegians said the *Kursk* was flooded; and that Admirals Kuroyedov and Popov, commanders of the Russian Navy and Northern Fleet respectively, had offered to resign the following day. He also promised his television audience he would reform the armed forces, but rejected the idea that the navy's honour and the country's pride had sunk with the *Kursk*. 'Our country has survived worse than this,' he said.

Having offered his apology to the nation, Putin pressed on with his three-pronged fight-back strategy which he had devised before visiting the *Kursk* families in Vidyayevo. His target now became the media, and the most remarkable part of his appearance on RTR was his vitriolic attack on the oligarchs who controlled Russia's vast multimedia enterprises. President Putin pointed out that the first to defend the *Kursk*'s submariners and their relatives over the last few days were the same people who 'had long promoted the destruction of the army, the fleet and the state'. He pointed the finger at 'some who had even given a million dollars' to the *Kursk*'s families, apparently referring to a campaign by Boris Berezovsky's *Kommersant* newspaper to raise voluntary donations for the crew's relatives. Warming to his theme, Putin acerbically added a veiled threat: 'They would have done better to sell their villas on the Mediterranean coast of France and in Spain. Only then could they explain why the property was registered under false names and behind legal firms. And we could probably ask the question: where did the money come from?'

The day before Putin's broadcast, the ORT and NTV television channels had carried news reports describing how the Kremlin had tried to limit media coverage of the president's fraught meeting with *Kursk* relatives in Vidyayevo. Boris Berezovsky, who owned ORT television and three major daily newspapers, has a huge villa complex at Antibes on the Côte d'Azur. Berezovsky had just resigned as a member of the Duma to launch a 'constructive opposition' to President Putin. Vladimir Gusinsky, owner of NTV, a range of newspapers, magazines and a radio station, has an expensive villa in Sotogrande, southern Spain. As part of an extensive property portfolio, Berezovsky also has property in London, and Gusinsky property in London, Israel and New York. Vladimir Putin knew exactly what he was talking about. As head of the FSB he had stayed at Gusinsky's Spanish villa as a personal guest of the tycoon. But now Putin was furious at the drubbing he had received at the hands of his erstwhile allies. He was determined to smash them and take control of their media outlets. By referring to the tycoons' allegedly dubious business histories and financial arrangements, which could be applied to virtually all Russia's new business elite (the so-called 'New Russians'), Putin was effectively declaring war on his oligarch critics. This was no bluff. Putin meant to destroy them, and destroy them he would. In the process he would tame Russia's independent media and force them to take a more deferential, pro-Kremlin line. That would also conveniently and felicitously ease his path to re-election in 2004.

On the same day as Putin's broadcast to the nation, Valentina Matviyenko, another of Russia's deputy prime ministers, announced compensation terms for the families of the *Kursk*'s victims. Each family was to receive a lump sum equivalent to ten years of an officer's salary, free housing in any Russian city, free college education for the victims' sixty-five children, and free counselling. This was an unprecedented package for those who had lost their loved ones in military service, both in terms of its generosity and the speed with which it was offered. In fact, in the context of an average wage of around $150 per month, the lump sum of $25,000 was a relative fortune in Russia. With a Moscow or St Petersburg flat thrown in, the *Kursk* families could consider themselves handsomely looked after. In fact the compensation terms were so generous they caused a political backlash in Russia. Veronica Marchencko of the group Mothers' Rights and Valentina Melnikova of the Union of Soldiers' Committees bitterly complained that the relatives of those lost in Chechnya or elsewhere received a pittance from the state. Melnikova thought the government was attempting to 'buy the bereaved families' silence'. And with donations flooding in from across Russia and around the world, the *Kursk* families would eventually receive even more than the agreed state compensation package. Final pay-outs came to around $35,000 per family, not including the cost of brand-new flats or additional sums from charitable sources. Perhaps understandably, this led to a degree of bitterness and jealousy from those who had lost their husbands, brothers or sons in Chechnya or Afghanistan. It also fuelled a degree of cynicism about the government's motives in paying up so quickly and munificently.

Over the next two days following his national address on RTR, President Putin announced pay rises for the military and federal civil servants, and the creation of four new naval rescue centres. The armed forces, police, prison guards, custom officials and tax police were promised a rise of 20 per cent from December. From January 2001, all federal civil servants were also promised an additional 20 per cent. However, these seemingly generous rises would be offset by inflation and tax changes. Inflation was expected to be around 15 per cent in 2001, while military personnel would also have to pay income tax for the first time. Putin's effort to improve the rescue resources of the navy, and boost the pay of the armed forces generally, was only a half-hearted stab at reform. A complete overhaul of the Russian military was urgently required, but Putin showed no sign of being ready or able to tackle such a massive task.

Putin's counter-attack had, however, enabled him to regain the political initiative. He had taken control of the agenda, and shown real leadership. The president had apologised to his people, provided compensation to the *Kursk* families, proposed some reforms and gone on the offensive against his critics. His attack on the oligarchs played well in a country where the leading business figures were often perceived as little better than thieves. The oligarchs were felt to have profited from tainted privatisations and their close connections to the Kremlin and Yeltsin's 'family'. An editor at *Kommersant* newspaper said of Putin: 'He is a cynic, but also a realist. It is too late to undo the system of private property in this country. But he will try to get the oligarchs to pay a little more tax. That's all, but it would be popular with everyone.'

On 24 August the Prosecutor-General's office approved the decision to start criminal proceedings in connection with the sinking of the *Kursk*. The investigation was initially handled by the Chief Military Prosecutor's office. The following day he declared that the investigation would be carried out under Article 263 of the Criminal Code of the Russian Federation (Violation of the Rules for Traffic Safety and the Operation of the Railway, Air or Water Transportation Systems). The Chief Military Prosecutor's press service chief Sergei Ushakov explained that this article had been used since the government's Commission of Inquiry had stated a collision was the most likely reason for the disaster. Charges under the article were normally brought against people who had violated traffic safety, or for negligence. Although prosecutors said the case might later be dealt with under other articles of the criminal code, the investigation was treating the *Kursk's* crew as suspects. If found guilty, any living person could expect a sentence of four to ten years in jail. The search for scapegoats had begun in earnest.

# 4

# The Spying Game

Despite the end of the Cold War the intelligence agencies of Russia and the West have not abandoned their love of the spying game. Although the rivalry is not so intense these days, everyone still tries to steal everyone else's secrets. In the first three months of 2002, two defence workers at the British-based multinational BAE Systems were arrested for allegedly trying to sell secrets to the Russians. One involved technology designed to cloak combat aircraft from enemy radar, another documents about the Harrier aircraft and the Apache attack helicopter. Two months after taking power in 2001, President George W. Bush expelled fifty Russian diplomats accused of spying from Washington. The mass expulsions were seen as the US response to the arrest earlier that year of Robert Hanssen, a senior FBI counter-intelligence agent who had been selling secrets to the Russians for twenty-two years. Moscow quickly retaliated by expelling four US diplomats for 'activities incompatible with their status', a diplomatic euphemism for spying. A 56-year-old family man, Hanssen accused the FBI of 'criminal negligence' in making it so easy for him to spy for the former Soviet Union and Russia, receiving illicit payments of about

$600,000 in the process. He had passed the Russians 6,000 pages of documents and twenty-seven computer disks, while also helpfully telling them the Americans had dug a surveillance tunnel under their Washington Embassy. The year before, the Russians had been caught out when police arrested a senior Japanese official accused of passing secrets to a military attaché who was a member of the GRU. Nor, of course, were these human intelligence ('Humint') operations a one-way street.

Platon Obukhov, a 30-year-old Russian diplomat and author of espionage thrillers, was sentenced to eleven years in prison in July 2000 for spying for Britain's secret intelligence service, MI6. Arrested in 1996 while broadcasting classified information of a 'political and strategic defence character' to MI6's headquarters in London, Obukhov had been caught red-handed by the FSB, the Russian Federal Security Service. His controller was allegedly Norman MacSween, a Secret Intelligence Service (SIS) officer working under-cover as counsellor in the Moscow Embassy. Obukhov was reportedly recruited in Estonia by Pablo Miller, another SIS agent working as a First Secretary in the British Embassy in Tallinn. According to the FSB, MI6 had been interested in information on Russian spies in Britain and other NATO countries; details on the personnel and struc-ture of Russian counter-intelligence; the political situation in the run-up to the presidential election; and how the arm of Russian intel-ligence dealing with electronic surveillance (FAPSI) operated. Although a junior diplomat who had previously been based in Norway, Obukhov's father was a former Soviet deputy foreign minister, and well connected. At his trial, at which he wore a dunce's hat, odd socks and laceless shoes, Obukhov's parents criticised MI6 for recruiting a 'sick person', claiming their son had been mentally unwell since childhood, and suffered from schizophrenia. Since his arrest Obukhov has spent most of his time in secure psychiatric units. Britain has never denied that Obukhov was one of their agents. His arrest sparked the biggest spy row between Britain and Russia since the collapse of the Soviet Union, with each country expelling four diplomats for spying. Such 'tit for tat' expulsions were common during the Cold War.

Meanwhile, the Americans were also busy trying to steal Russian naval secrets. In December 2000 Edmond Pope, a former American naval intelligence officer, was sentenced to twenty years for espionage by a Moscow court. Pope, aged fifty-four, was the first US citizen to be convicted of spying in Russia for forty years. He was sent to Moscow's notorious Lefortovo jail after being convicted of illegally obtaining classified blueprints of the Shkval high-speed rocket torpedo used by the Russian Navy. Pope denied the charges, saying the information was already in the public domain and had been published abroad. The Shkval or 'Squall' rocket torpedo was so secret that some still doubted its existence. Press reports in Russia and elsewhere had speculated that a Shkval torpedo had exploded while being prepared for a test-launch aboard the *Kursk*. Deployed for the first time in 1977, the Shkval torpedo was the most powerful weapon developed by the USSR in the dying days of the Cold War. In 1995, Jane's Intelligence Review said the torpedo had 'no Western equivalent'. Powered by a rocket motor, the torpedo can travel underwater at 230 miles per hour, approximately five times faster than the torpedoes currently used by NATO's navies. Frictional drag slows any bodies moving underwater. The Shkval rocket torpedo gets around the adverse physics by using redirected thrust ejected from its nose and skin, and moving through the water in a semi-vacuum bubble or 'supercavity'. According to *Scientific American*, the new technology 'could mean a quantum leap in naval warfare that is analogous in some ways to the move from prop planes to jets or even to rockets and missiles'.

The Shkval travels so fast that no US defence or countermeasures can stop it. It is particularly designed to attack large ships like aircraft-carriers. The rocket torpedo also enables Russian submarines with inferior sonar to knock out American subs before the slower US wire-guided torpedoes can hit their target. The Shkval's high speed means it can punch a hole in most ships without the need for an explosive warhead. Jack Spencer, defence analyst at the US Heritage Foundation, confirmed the Shkval's prowess: 'We have no equivalent. Its velocity would make evasive action exceedingly difficult, and it is likely that we have no defence against it.' The 6,000-pound weapon has a range of about 7,500 yards, and is guided by autopilot rather than a homing head as on most torpedoes. The original Shkval was designed to carry a tactical nuclear warhead, detonated by a timer clock. The Russians have since developed a homing version, which runs at high speed, then slows as it searches for its target. First tested by the Pacific Fleet in the spring of 1998, a conventionally armed version of the Shkval was being marketed in early 1999 – featuring at the Abu Dhabi IDEX '99 arms exhibition, for example. It is also advertised in *Military Parade*, the magazine of the Russian military–industrial complex. Its detailed design plans remain secret.

According to US intelligence reports, China purchased some forty Shkval rocket torpedoes from Russia in 1998. Richard Fisher of the US Jamestown Foundation believes China is acquiring a fleet of blue-water submarines armed with the Shkval. China is aiming to build a navy capable of operating far from the Asian continent, armed with a combination of silent subs, supersonic nuclear-tipped Stealth missiles and the Shkval. China has also purchased four Russian Kilo-class conventional submarines. Fisher states: 'The Kilo 636 is said to be nearly as quiet as the early version of the US Los Angeles-class nuclear submarine.' The Chinese are also seeking to build a new type of nuclear sub, the Type 093, using Russian technology. The Type 093 weighs more than 5,000 tons, is over a football field in length, and is armed with eight 21-inch torpedo tubes large enough to fire the Shkval torpedo. Between four and six new Type 093s are due to enter service by 2012.

The combination of the Shkval rocket torpedo and the upgrading of the Chinese submarine fleet are causing extreme anxiety in Washington. The Chinese acquisition of the Shkval, allied with the purchase of the four Russian-built Kilos, could threaten US naval supremacy in the Far Eastern Pacific. Without US Seventh Fleet dominance of the Formosa Strait between China and Taiwan, Taiwan itself could be vulnerable to Chinese invasion by a reinvigorated People's Liberation Army. Beijing has never given up its claim to the lost province, and since the restoration of Chinese sovereignty over Hong Kong, its 'One China' policy is more clearly focused on recovering Taiwan.

Because of the strategic threat posed by the Shkval, US intelligence would give its eye teeth to get hold of the weapon's blueprints, or even better a whole Shkval rocket torpedo. Edmund Pope had been an officer with US Navy military intelligence, with a specific remit to collect information about maritime weaponry. Retiring in the mid-1990s, he had founded CERF Technologies International, a company assessing and buying foreign naval equipment. Pope protested his innocence when he was arrested in April 2000. 'I have already spent eight months in prison in Russia. I am not a spy.' A frequent visitor to Moscow, Pope claimed he did not understand why he had been accused and condemned. For the FSB, Pope's protestations carried little weight. In their view, he was still working for US military intelligence, and he would have to be pretty dim-witted to think obtaining blueprints of the ultra-secret Shkval torpedo would be looked upon with equanimity by the obsessively secret Russian military–industrial complex, much less the FSB. Pope's wife and lawyers claimed he suffered from a rare form of bone cancer, and asked for clemency. US Secretary of State Madeleine Albright raised the case with Russian Foreign Minister Igor Ivanov, and President Bill Clinton personally asked Putin to release Pope on the grounds of ill-health. The Russian prosecutors were sceptical about the severity of Pope's illness, however, and Putin said that he would not intervene in the trial. But after a decent interval Vladimir Putin pardoned Pope, and the Americans got their man home.

The *Kursk* submarine had itself undertaken an intelligence-gathering mission reminiscent of the Cold War in the summer of 1999. Leaving its base at Bolshaya Lopatka on the Litsa fjord in the Kola Peninsula, the *Kursk* had travelled through the Barents Sea towards the GIUK (Greenland–Iceland–UK) Gap. Following the route of many Soviet nuclear ballistic 'boomer' subs before it, the *Kursk* passed the GIUK Gap near the Faroe Islands and headed into the wide North Atlantic Ocean. The *Kursk*'s crew knew they were in danger of being picked up by several SOSUS (sound surveillance system) acoustic listening stations. A SOSUS line or 'acoustic fence' covered the whole GIUK Gap, made up of thousands of sensitive hydrophones strung out along the bottom of the ocean. Travelling south, the Russian sub then passed the British colony of Gibraltar and entered the Mediterranean. Commanded by Captain Gennady Lyachin, the *Kursk*'s task was to find and follow 'the enemy', identifying as many NATO ships and submarines as possible, checking their routes and operational activities. In effect, the *Kursk* was spying on NATO operations in the Mediterranean much as the submarines USS *Memphis* and *Toledo* were monitoring the Russian Barents Sea exercises in August 2000. The mission would also allow the *Kursk* to test its life-support and other systems, in close to battle-like conditions.

The *Kursk*'s appearance in the Mediterranean caused quite a stir. Ten years before, such Russian missions to the Med were routine, but since the collapse of communism they had become extremely rare. As ever, the main reason had been the catastrophic reduction in funding and resources for the Russian Navy. Politically, President Boris Yeltsin was too dependent on Western financial support to tweak NATO's nose. The crisis in the Balkans, especially Kosovo, had altered the political atmosphere, with Moscow keen to be seen giving their historical allies the Serbs at least some moral support, following NATO's eleven-week air campaign against Serbia. Although Belgrade and President Milošević had been pummelled into submission by NATO, diplomatic arm-twisting from Moscow had helped end the conflict.

To be sure of securing influence in post-conflict Kosovo, on 13 June 1999 the Russians had even raced ahead of NATO with 200 paratroops to seize control of Kosovo's Pristina airport. The Russian forces were the first foreign troops to enter Kosovo, much to NATO's surprise and chagrin. The airport seizure enraged the Atlantic Alliance's Supreme Allied Commander Europe (SACEUR), General Wesley Clark. General Clark's demand to seize the airport from the Russians, by force if necessary, was firmly rebuffed by the British commander on the ground, Lieutenant-General Sir Mike Jackson. General Jackson told his nominally superior officer, 'I'm not going to start the Third World War for you.' It is generally accepted that some purple Anglo-Saxon words were then aired in a full and frank exchange of views. Gaunt, severe and extremely direct, General Jackson was known as Darth Vader or the Prince of Darkness by his men, and commanded the K-For troop deployment in Kosovo. General Clark, like Bill Clinton a native of Little Rock, Arkansas, and also an Oxford Rhodes scholar, was subsequently replaced as SACEUR three months early. Clark's premature removal was widely seen as a reprimand for his handling of the Kosovo conflict.

Against this background, the appearance of one of Russia's most capable and modern multi-purpose nuclear submarines in the Mediterranean set nerves on edge in NATO.

According to the Russians, the US spent tens of millions of dollars trying to track the *Kursk* in the Med, with mixed success. The US Sixth Fleet, based at Naples, became extremely active in the search for the *Kursk*. By Russian accounts, the US Sixth Fleet restricted the operation of its large ships and aircraft-carriers to stay out of the Russian sub's possible area of activity. Captain Lyachin was certainly proud of the *Kursk*'s performance, later saying that the boat had received a lot of attention from NATO's subs, ships and planes, but 'we almost always spotted them first'. NATO found it difficult to establish prolonged surveillance and contact with the *Kursk*. In these circumstances, in addition to using subs and surface vessels, NATO would hunt the *Kursk* with American P3 Orion aircraft.

The four-engined Orion workhorses had been in operation for forty years, and could find any submarine by picking up the noise of its propellers, or through detecting heat, an electro-magnetic field, or the smell of diesel. Each Russian submarine's propellers made a distinctive noise, and each one had been recorded and chronicled so that any sub in the Russian fleet could be readily identified by NATO. The Orions would also drop sonar buoys into the sea to track and trap an 'enemy' submarine. If a Russian sub on the surface realised it had been spotted, a shout would ring out aboard the boat: 'Radar on aircraft above working. Signal strength three points.' The captain would order, 'All down, immediate dive!', and the crew topside would then drop six metres down the central well from the bridge, sliding down the rails using their hands only. Crew members had 1.2 seconds to get from topside to the Central Command Post inside the sub. Any longer in battle conditions and the Orion could sink the boat. In peacetime, any dalliance would allow the Orion to summon anti-sub warships to track and corner the submarine.

Lyachin felt the *Kursk* achieved all its military objectives on its 1999 mission, annoying the Pentagon in the process. On arriving back in Russia, Lyachin was personally received by then Prime Minister Vladimir Putin in the Kremlin, who asked him some questions and congratulated him on his mission. As a result of the operation, Lyachin's name was put forward to receive the golden star of the Hero of Russia, which he was awarded posthumously. The rest of the crew were posthumously awarded the order of Muzhestva. As Nicolai Cherkashin wrote in his book *Unesyonnye Bezdnoi* ('Drawn into the Bottomless Pit'), the Kremlin thought the 1999 mission was a great success because it let everyone know the Russian Fleet 'was still alive despite ten years of disintegration'. The idea was to let NATO and the world know that Russia was still a military and diplomatic force to be reckoned with. Despite the loss of its USSR superpower status, Moscow was asserting its claim to be taken seriously as a 'Great Power'. The Russians were desperately concerned they were being increasingly ignored and sidelined by leading Western countries, especially the United States. Russia felt it had no real influence over major decisions taken by the international community affecting the Balkans, the Middle East, Iraq and the future of NATO. All these areas were of vital strategic importance to Moscow, but its views were dismissively discounted. Under President Yeltsin the Russian Federation was progressively treated like an impoverished and embarrassing eccentric aunt, whom the rest of the family tried to quietly ignore at social gatherings. The *Kursk* mission was an attempt at national self-assertion, and at the same time it was a gesture to restore a sense of lost Russian pride.

The *Kursk*'s Mediterranean mission was meant to mark the beginning of the Russian Navy's resurgence. This reinvigoration was one of Putin's core aims, along with rebuilding the other armed forces, strengthening the security apparatus (especially the FSB and the SVR) and centralising power in the hands of the president. In July 2000, Russia was planning to send an aircraft-carrier group into the Mediterranean by the end of the year. Led by Russia's sole surviving carrier the *Admiral Kuznetsov*, the battle group would comprise a fleet of warships which packed more of a punch than the former Soviet Mediterranean naval squadron. On 30 July, Navy Commander-in-Chief Admiral Kuroyedov told the press: 'We plan to return to the

Mediterranean. I can assure you that the group of vessels flying the St Andrew flag will have greater power than the power of the Soviet Mediterranean squadron in its time.' The same day, President Putin visited Baltiisk, headquarters of Russia's Baltic Fleet, to celebrate Navy Day. Putin told the assembled sailors: 'When the navy becomes weak, it is always worse for our country. When it stood on its own feet, Russia also rose up and was able to call itself a great state.' President Putin believed in re-creating a 'Great Russia', and was committed to the 'Russia First' policy espoused by President Boris Yeltsin, following the end of the Yeltsin administration's honeymoon with the West. The Russia First strategy reflected a shift away from Western political and economic values and models in favour of a more balanced view encompassing Russia's traditional, historic and strategic interests.

To this end, in June 2000, Putin approved a new fifteen-page for-eign-policy doctrine entitled 'The Foreign Policy Concept of the Russian Federation'. The document gives a concise insight into Putin's foreign-policy thinking. As its main objectives, the paper refers to achieving 'firm and prestigious positions in the world community, most fully consistent with the interests of the Russian Federation as a great power, as one of the influential centres of the modern world'. Russia, the document asserts, already exerts 'significant influence on the formation of a new world order'. Russia would pursue a balanced foreign policy as one of the largest Eurasian powers. It sought to reduce and limit conventional armed forces, and interact with influential western European states like Britain, Germany, Italy and France in defence of its national interests in European and world affairs. On Afghanistan, Russia pledged to co-operate with other states to achieve a fair and lasting political settlement while 'interdicting the exporta-tion of terrorism and extremism from that country'. Finally the paper warned:

> There is a growing trend towards the establishment of a unipo-
> lar structure of the world with the economic and power
> domination of the United States . . . The strategy of unilateral
> actions can destabilise the international situation, provoke
> tensions and the arms race, aggravate interstate contradictions,

national and religious strife . . . Russia shall seek to achieve a multipolar system of international relations that reflects the diversity of the modern world with its great variety of interests.

The Russian complaints of US unilateralism in the foreign-policy field pre-dated the new administration of President George W. Bush, and similar grumbles from many of America's European allies.

Vladimir Putin stressed the need to rebuild and reform the country's armed forces in order to protect Russia's domestic and international interests. The same week he visited the Baltic Fleet, the president addressed a group of senior military officers: 'Today the factor of military strength is of great importance, most of all in preserving the stability of the country and guaranteeing its peaceful and progressive development.' During the 1999 Kosovo conflict, Moscow considered sending Russian ships into the Med to support their paratroops occupying Pristina airport. Captain Richard Sharpe, editor of *Jane's Fighting Ships*, said: 'If the *Kuznetsov* had deployed off Montenegro during the Balkan conflict, it could have caused severe embarrassment to NATO. The presence of large-scale flying operations not in co-operation with NATO had the potential to seriously disrupt alliance movements.' The *Admiral Kuznetsov* can carry around forty aircraft including Su-27 fighters. When it was last deployed in the Mediterranean in 1996, the carrier's presence had a similarly unsettling effect on NATO to the *Kursk*'s Mediterranean excursion three years later. The proposed deployment of the *Admiral Kuznetsov*'s battle group to the Mediterranean was indefinitely postponed following the *Kursk* sinking. Billboards in Moscow at the time of the disaster carried posters for the navy: 'A Mighty Navy for the Glory of Russia.' After the *Kursk* went down, they looked cruelly sardonic.

The US Navy has been one of the most active players in the spying game, as Sherry Sontag and Christopher Drew have recorded in their excellent book *Blind Man's Bluff: The Untold Story of Cold War Submarine Espionage*. Although the number of US nuclear-powered attack submarines has almost halved since 1989, the number of intelligence, surveillance and reconnaissance missions they undertake has nearly doubled. The US began using submarines to spy on the USSR as far back as 1948, when it sent two subs, the USS *Sea Dog* and *Black Fin*, to record radio communications and measure the speed of propellers aboard Soviet ships. This information could be used later to identify individual Soviet destroyers and merchant vessels. In 1949, the experimental sub USS *Cochino* lost six of its crew when a battery exploded while it was on a spying mission in the Barents Sea. The US sent boats under the Arctic on an annual basis, and its intelligence missions became increasingly brazen.

Between 1971 and 1972 the submarine USS *Halibut*, specially refitted for special operations, laid a tap on a Soviet telephone cable under the Sea of Okhotsk, off Kamchatka in the USSR's Far East. The cable linked the nuclear missile submarine base at Petropavlosk on Kamchatka's east coast with Pacific Fleet headquarters in Vladivostock on the Chinese border, which in turn was linked to Moscow's naval HQ. By attaching a recording pod on to the cable, the Americans were able to tap into this flow of military communications, giving the US military an invaluable insight into the workings and operational abilities of the Soviet Navy. In 1979, the Americans launched a similar operation in the Barents Sea. The sub USS *Parche* headed for an area off the northern coast of the Kola Peninsula, and succeeded in tapping a communications cable which linked the major bases of the Northern Fleet with their headquarters outside Murmansk. Both the secret Barents and Okhotsk missions violated the USSR's three-mile limit recognised by the USA, let alone the Soviet Union's twelve-mile territorial limit.

The USSR discovered the Sea of Okhotsk tap in 1981, tipped off by John A. Walker Jnr and his US-based spy ring. Walker was a retired US Navy submariner and a communications specialist, and enlisted his son, brother and another communications expert to spy for the Soviet Union. They came relatively cheap. Over eighteen months the Walker spy ring cost the USSR $1 million. The ring was rounded up in 1985 when John Walker was betrayed by his wife, who feared her daughter would be the next KGB recruit. When the Soviets recovered the recording pods from the Sea of Okhotsk, there could be no doubt who had placed them there – inside one of the pods, a component was marked 'Property of the United States Government'. Washington did not have the cheek to ask for its return.

Cold War operations like these sometimes came at a considerable cost, however. By the end of 1975, for example, the US Navy had registered at least nine collisions with hostile submarines during the previous ten years. Over the same period, there had also been more than 110 possible detections of US surveillance subs actively operating against the Soviet Union. Latest Russian figures suggest there have been up to twenty-one collisions involving US and Russian subs near the Soviet or Russian coast over the last thirty-three years. The collisions involving the USS *Baton Rouge* and USS *Grayling* off the Kola Peninsula in 1992 and 1993 were part of a familiar pattern. While Soviet subs also operated off the United States' east and west coasts for similar reasons, the US Navy deliberately encouraged bravado and risk-taking among its secret submarine elite. Successfully gathering intelligence and closely shadowing the Soviet 'boomers' seemed to be the way ambitious US sub commanders caught their superiors' attention and won promotion. For the US Navy, the priority was to get the upper hand over their Soviet rivals and dominate the oceans. Safety at sea seemed to take a back seat. The result was a long list of accidents dating back to the 1960s.

The case of the USS *Augusta* is an interesting example. Allegations of a collision in 1986 between the Los Angeles-class American sub and the Russian Yankee-class strategic nuclear sub K-219 have been strongly denied by the Pentagon. Aired in Peter Huchthausen's book *Hostile Waters*, the suggestion is that the collision was caused by the reckless proximity of the shadowing US sub, which was tracking K-219 in the Atlantic, north of Bermuda. The collision resulted in an explosion aboard K-219, and a critical situation in one of the boat's nuclear reactors. The boat sank with the loss of four Russian submariners. The Yankee-class boat had two nuclear reactors and carried sixteen nuclear missiles, which sank with the submarine to the bottom of the Atlantic Ocean. The crew believed that they had prevented a huge nuclear catastrophe, at some personal cost, by manually shutting down the two onboard reactors. The authors of *Blind Man's Bluff* say that US Naval Intelligence officials and the *Augusta*'s crew deny colliding with the

1. The *Kursk* moored on the Kola Peninsula.

2. Captain Gennady Lyachin in October 1999, after his sub's successful mission to the Mediterranean. The *Kursk*'s presence in the Med caused quite a stir with NATO and the US Sixth Fleet.

3. The 'closed' or secret garrison town of Vidyayevo, where most of the crew lived.

4. Captain Third Rank Andrei Milyutin and his bride Valeria, on their wedding day.

5. Captain-Lieutenant Dmitri Kolesnikov and his wife Olga posing in front of the *Kursk* at Severomorsk naval base. The couple were married less than four months before the disaster.

6. The last known photo of the *Kursk* before 12 August 2000. On the right is Andrei Milyutin; on the left, Captain Third Rank Ilya Shchavinsky (fifth compartment).

7. The torpedo compartment aboard an Oscar-class nuclear submarine, similar to the *Kursk*. It was here that the initial explosion occurred.

8. The *Mikhail Rudnitsky* rescue ship lowers an obsolete Russian submersible during the operation in the Barents Sea on the morning of Friday, 18 August 2000, six days after the disaster.

9. The state-of-the-art British LR5 manned rescue submersible aboard the *Normand Pioneer*. Frustratingly for the British team, the LR5 was never allowed in the water by the Russians.

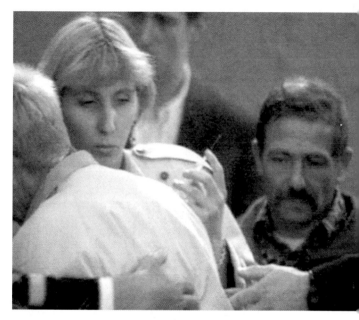

10. Nadezhda Tylik, the mother of *Kursk* submariner Senior Lieutenant Sergei Tylik, is injected with a sedative at a public meeting on 18 August 2000. The apparent forcible silencing of a victim's relative caused outrage in the West.

11. Vice-Admiral Oleg Burtsev leaves the *Normand Pioneer* after meeting the British rescue team on 19 August 2000. The British never heard from him again.

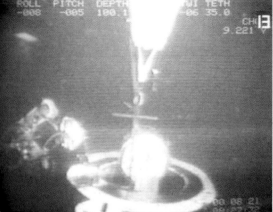

2. Norwegian and British divers from the eaway Eagle open the *Kursk*'s aft escape atch on 21 August, using a 500-kilogram nine bag'.

3. The *Normand Pioneer*'s 'shadow', the Russian 650 anti-submarine warship, executes a high-speed lute to the British rescue team with the ship's entire complement on deck, 21 August.

14. Russian Defence Minister Marshal Igor Sergeyev, pictured at a Cabinet meeting in Moscow, 22 August 2000.

15. Meanwhile President Vladimir Putin meets relatives of *Kursk* victims on a walkabout in Vidyayevo, watched by Captain Gennady Lyachin's widow, Irina (centre).

16. Two days later, some of the relatives are taken out into the Barents Sea, near where the *Kursk* sank, to pay their respects.

7. Putin announces he will recover the bodies of the crew, 19 September 2000. With him (left to right) are Deputy PM Ilya Klebanov, Admiral Vladimir Kuroyedov, and Security Council Secretary Sergei Ivanov.

8. A Russian boy stands by memorial to the *Kursk*'s crew in Vidyayevo on the first anniversary of the disaster.

19. The Northern Fleet's Vice-Admiral Mikhail Motsak and Dr Igor Spassky, head of the Rubin Design Bureau, embrace after the successful operation to recover the *Kursk*, 9 October 2001.

20. Russian Prosecutor-General Vladimir Ustinov (right) addresses a press conference in Roslyakovo on 23 October 2001, with Commander of the Northern Fleet Admiral Vyacheslav Popov at his side.

21. On the same day the *Kursk* re-emerges from the depths after fourteen months as the conning tower becomes visible in dock at Roslyakovo.

22. Graves of *Kursk* crew members at Serafimov cemetery, in St Petersburg's northern suburbs, December 2001.

Yankee-class K-219, and insist they hit a Russian Delta I-class sub instead. However, there is no proof that a Delta-class sub was involved in this incident.

According to the US account, K-219 sank because of a problem with one of its missile tubes, and not because of any collision with the *Augusta*. In 1988, the Soviet hydrographic research ship *Keldesh* reportedly went back to the accident site in the Atlantic Ocean. Sending down a pair of remote cameras, the Russians found the wreck of K-219 sitting at a depth of about 18,000 feet. The boat was split in two aft of the conning tower. Mysteriously, the remote cameras apparently discovered the missile silo hatches open, and that the sixteen Russian nuclear missiles and their warheads had disappeared. The Pentagon still maintains no US sub was responsible for sinking K-219, and the evidence on this remains inconclusive.

With such a long history of collisions between Soviet and NATO submarines, it is no wonder that the Russians first assumed the *Kursk* had hit an American or British boat.

It was the logical thing to assume, and some people in the UK's Ministry of Defence initially thought the Americans might have been responsible for the accident. Russia's perversity was to continue pressing the collision theory when this was patently not the cause of the *Kursk* tragedy. Russia's naval High Command had already come to the conclusion that the continued brinkmanship shown by submarine captains would eventually lead to a major disaster, and questioned whether such risks were justified in the post-Cold War era. Rear-Admiral Valery Aleksin voiced these concerns in 1993: 'We walk on a razor edge. Some day this hunt will end in a disaster. I am sure, too, that if such a practice doesn't stop, the disaster is inevitable.'

The Americans, however, felt the Russians were losing their appetite for playing the submarine spying game because they could no longer cut the mustard. Admiral James Watkins, former US Chief of Naval Operations and Secretary of Energy, had another view of the secret sub operations: 'The fact that you get caught periodically is historical. So what. You know everyone's in the game.' In 1972, the United States and the USSR had signed the bilateral Incidents at Sea Agreement, which sought to put an end to games of 'chicken' and clashes between American and Soviet surface vessels. As the US Navy had insisted, the agreement did not apply to submarines operating below the sea's surface. Washington still has no intention of giving up its technical superiority and edge in the submarine spying game. While 'The Bear Still Swims', as the US Navy says, the Americans will keep watching the Russians.

The Russians' seaborne spying operations tended to be low-budget, even in the days of the Soviet Union. The USSR's favourite method of spying at sea was to strategically locate specially converted 'trawlers' to eavesdrop just outside US naval bases or in the vicinity of naval exercises. A Soviet trawler had cheekily picked up an American practice torpedo from the Pacific in 1979, fired by the missile sub USS *Sam Houston*. The trawler was 'persuaded' to abandon the torpedo over the side after it was surrounded by two aircraft-carrier battle groups, and following diplomatic pressure from the US State Department. The US, on the other hand, seemed to have limitless funds to spend on its underwater espionage operations. The most contentious, and certainly the most expensive US undersea mission revealed to date, was 'Project Jennifer'.

Recounted faithfully in Edwyn Gray's *Few Survived: A Comprehensive Survey of Submarine Accidents and Disasters* and again in *Blind Man's Bluff*, Project Jennifer is revealed as a costly grand folly, promoted by the CIA against the advice of almost everyone else. The idea was to raise an ageing Soviet diesel submarine from where it had sunk in the summer of 1968, almost three miles down in the mid-Pacific. The drama had begun when the Americans began tracking the NATO-designated Golf II-class submarine as it left its base in Vladivostock on 24 February 1968. The Soviet boat belonged to a class of conventional diesel submarines built after the first Zulu-class boats, which were converted to carry nuclear missiles, and the new nuclear-powered missile boats. The Soviet Golf displaced 2,350 tons and had a crew of eighty-six officers and men. The submarine was carrying three ballistic nuclear missiles. Closely monitoring the Golf's progress, the US Navy tracked the Soviet sub to a position 1,000 miles north-west of Hawaii in the Pacific. A surveillance officer then picked up the sound of a faint explosion. The engines stopped and the

Golf struck the seabed, 16,580 feet down. The explosion may have come about because of a build-up of hydrogen, as the 450-ton sulphuric acid battery was changed. The 1950s era Golf sub was already becoming obsolete, and was far inferior to the latest US submarines, but still, the CIA became excited about the prospect of getting hold of the Soviet boat's nuclear warheads, its 'crypto-codes', decoding machines, burst transmitters and receivers. The CIA hoped this would enable the navy to decode all the communications it had intercepted over recent years.

In 1969 the CIA offered the reclusive billionaire Howard Hughes, and his company Global Marine, $350 million to recover the Soviet sub. Two top-secret salvage ships were specially constructed at a huge cost to the American taxpayer. The ship designed to raise the Golf, the *Glomar Explorer*, was the length of three football pitches and built by Hughes's Summa Corporation. The CIA code-named their secret operation 'Project Jennifer'. Some suggested the whole idea was dreamed up as a way of paying off President Nixon's political debt to Howard Hughes. Specialists in the US Navy opposed Project Jennifer, thought it couldn't work, and believed the whole idea was a massive waste of resources. The CIA thought they knew better than the marine experts.

Six years after finding the Soviet Golf in the Pacific, the CIA had recovered about 10 per cent of the submarine, bringing a 38-foot piece of it to the surface. The CIA planted stories in the US media that they had recovered the forward third of the 300-foot sub. In fact, the small part of the boat they did recover was insignificant. As they tried to raise the sub from the depths, it fell apart and down to the seabed, as the navy's experts had predicted it would. The CIA didn't get their codebooks, decoding machines, transmitters, receivers or nuclear missiles. The whole operation was a costly $500 million fiasco, a testament to the blind arrogance and incompetence of the CIA. The CIA did, however, recover six bodies from the wrecked sub, and held a videotaped burial service, in case the USSR ever demanded information about the recovery operation. Clyde Burleson's contention in his book *Project Jennifer* that the CIA's recovery mission was a magnificent achievement beggars belief. It is a view shared by very few outside the CIA's headquarters in Langley, Virginia. Project Jennifer did, however, show the Russians just how far intelligence agencies in the United States would go to steal their naval secrets, a lesson they had learned well by the time the *Kursk* sank.

The United States was definitely interested in knowing more about the *Kursk*, and the weapons systems it was carrying. Before the onset of the Barents Sea exercises in August 2000, the Pentagon might have assumed the *Kursk* could be carrying Shkval rocket torpedoes. The US would have welcomed any opportunity to witness a Shkval in action, and a rumour circulated that a Chinese naval officer was on board the submarine to observe a test-firing of the top-secret weapon. As it turned out, the *Kursk* was only test-firing an old practice torpedo, but there were unquestionably other weapons aboard the boat which interested the US Navy. Chief among these were the Granit cruise missiles.

Manufactured in the late 1970s and early 1980s by the Reutovo branch of the Mashinostroyeniye company, under the direction of Soviet Academician Vladimir Chelomeyev, the SS-N-19 Granit can be fired from both ships and submarines. The submarine version is launched when the sub is underwater from tubes which on the *Kursk* were situated at an angle of forty degrees between compartments two and five. The Granit is a top-secret long-range supersonic cruise missile, reaching a velocity of mach 1.5 and with a warhead equivalent to 618 kilograms of TNT. The Granit can carry a nuclear warhead, but the nuclear version has not been in service in Russian submarines since the signing of the START arms reduction treaty. Designed to be used against surface ships, the Granit was seen as a particularly effective weapon against large aircraft-carrier battle groups. The Soviet military concept in the early 1980s was to create an 'asymmetrical' response to superior US aircraft-carrier battle groups, by establishing a fleet of nuclear submarines armed with long-range supersonic anti-ship cruise missiles. The Oscar II-class *Kursk* carried three times as many anti-ship cruise missiles as the earlier Charlie and Echo II-class Soviet submarines – normally, twenty-four, although at the time of its sinking the *Kursk* had only twenty-two aboard.

According to Gerbert Yefremov, General Director of the

Mashinostroyeniye company, the Granit's strongest point is its unique guidance system. The system is based on 'artificially intelligent' electronics which operate on the 'one ship, one missile' principle. The missile's onboard computer holds tactical data on ship formations, modern classes of ships, countering radio-jamming signals, and tactics to avoid enemy countermeasures. The computer can identify the type of threat, such as a convoy, aircraft-carrier group or landing assault force, and attack the main target. After the Granit missiles are launched in a volley, they can decide among themselves which missile will hit which target, and calculate their own attack pattern. After the main target is eliminated, the remaining Granits attack other ships in the formation, ensuring that only one missile is unleashed against each target.

Western intelligence agencies have gathered quite a bit of information about the Granit missile, but have never seen one up close. Unlike most Russian weapons, including the Shkval rocket torpedo, Granits are not displayed at international arms fairs. Edward Hooton, editor of *Jane's Naval Weapons Systems*, said of the Granit: 'We know a lot about how the Granit works, but not everything. There is no doubt that some people in Britain and America would love to get their hands on one.' Hooton added: 'The Russians are dead against the West inspecting one. The last thing they need is for us to find out what the Granit's weaknesses are. For instance, just by inspecting the type of fuel and its fuel capacity we would be able to establish its exact range.' At $840,000 each, the Granit missiles are an expensive piece of ordnance to lose. With twenty-two undamaged Granits sitting on the bottom of the Barents Sea, they remained a multi-million-dollar prize to whoever recovered them. The Russians were determined to stop the United States or another NATO country getting hold of a Granit, or getting near enough to inspect one.

The Russians took the threat of espionage around the sunken *Kursk* so seriously that they had warships guarding the wrecked submarine around the clock. For a year after the sinking, to ensure that it had enough vessels to guard the *Kursk* accident site, the Russian Navy cancelled all large exercises and indefinitely postponed its proposed mission to the Mediterranean. But the Russians went to further, extraordinary lengths to protect the *Kursk*'s secrets. On 15 November 2000, the Norwegian NORSAR seismological observatory reported that it had recently recorded a number of 'relatively weak' seismic signals near where the *Kursk* sank in the Barents Sea. NORSAR stated that between September and November that year it recorded more than forty small controlled explosions. The magnitude of the explosions measured between 1 and 3 on the Richter scale. NORSAR's assessment was that 'a possible explanation might be that the Russian military wants to keep foreign submarines away from this area'. The Russians had been using depth charges to discourage foreign submarines or intelligence-gathering operations in the vicinity of the *Kursk*.

Were the Russians paranoid the Americans would launch another 'Project Jennifer' in their backyard, and did they have other reasonable grounds for fearing Western defence and intelligence agencies would try to snoop around the *Kursk*? The answer to both questions is yes. Western intelligence agencies would feel they were failing in their duty if they didn't try to glean intelligence from the *Kursk*'s sinking. As US Admiral Watkins, former Chief of Naval Operations said, 'Everyone's in the game.' The Americans were not alone. The British too had a proud tradition of spying on the Soviet Navy. Don Camsell, a former member of Britain's Special Boat Service (SBS), the Royal Navy's equivalent of the army's Special Air Service (SAS), proudly recalls his days spying on the Russians for crown and country. His book, *Black Water: My Secret Life in the Special Boat Service*, makes interesting reading for those wanting to understand the Russians' apparent paranoia. A chapter of the book, 'Spying on a Russian's Bottom', recounts the occasion in 1978 when Camsell swam beneath a Kirov-class heavy cruiser (like the *Pyotr Veliky* in the Barents Sea) to spy on the ship's hull. The Kirov cruiser was on a goodwill visit to Gibraltar at the time, and Camsell jauntily suggests that it was routine to launch underwater spying operations when Soviet ships called into British ports on exchange visits. The navy divers, working with British intelligence, were particularly interested in onboard sensors, weapons and propulsion systems.

Special-forces divers in either the United States or Britain would be very capable of undertaking an intelligence-gathering mission in the Barents Sea. The UK's Special Boat Service used to be known as the Special Boat Squadron, but was renamed in the early 1990s. The SBS motto is 'Not by strength, by guile'. The SBS's origins lie in the Second World War, when specialised units were created for reconnoitring and raiding enemy coastlines. Since the Second World War, the SBS have fought in Oman and Borneo, and were involved in the 1982 recapture of South Georgia in the Falklands War. During the 1991 Gulf War, the SBS staged diversionary raids along the Kuwaiti coast, drawing Iraqi forces away from the main point of attack. Usually working in four-man teams like the SAS, recruits are all volunteer Royal Marines (RM) with at least two years' service. At any one time there are around 200 members of the SBS, whose headquarters are in Poole, Dorset. Entry is extremely competitive, with a tough three-week selection course followed by fifteen weeks' gruelling training for the chosen few. The training course covers demolition and advanced weapons skills, the use of closed-circuit aqualungs, seamanship, navigation, reconnaissance work and the use of small amphibious craft. The SBS work with the Klepper Mark-13 collapsible canoe and the larger Gemini equipped with a 40-horsepower outboard motor. Advanced weapons handling includes training with the silenced version of the Heckler & Koch MP5 submachine gun. SBS trainees must also pass a four-week parachute course before joining an operational unit. SBS teams may be assigned to the Royal Marine Commando Brigade for operational purposes, and members of the SBS wear standard Royal Marine uniforms, with the commandos' green beret and a globe and laurel badge. SBS personnel also wear RM parachutist wings on the right shoulder, and a Swimmer Canoeist badge on the right forearm (the latter is not worn by SBS officers). The SBS handle all special operations from the high-tide mark to twelve miles inland, and the SAS all others.

It was common knowledge that the *Normand Pioneer*, sailing to the aid of the stricken *Kursk* in the Barents Sea with the LR5 rescue mini-sub on deck, had British military divers onboard. What was less well known was the fact that the six naval divers were members of the UK's special forces. In fact, they were members of the Special Boat Service, highly trained in sabotage, intelligence-gathering, reconnaissance, demolition and equipped with the SBS's standard Gemini craft. The Royal Navy tried to keep the special-forces divers' presence low-profile.

If the Russians had known about the presence of these divers they would have been even more suspicious and wary than they already were. The Russian Navy knew what units like the Special Boat Service were capable of, and had been on the receiving end of their operations many times before. For the SBS, diving to 108 metres and spying on the *Kursk* would be a piece of cake. They would also be able to remove any code books or other sensitive material lying about on the sunken sub, if they were able to gain access. In the Russians' mind, they could also form part of a co-ordinated operation to remove a Granit cruise missile or other secret weaponry. After all, this had been part of the plan with Project Jennifer. Special-forces divers could also conduct a detailed inspection of the *Kursk* and take photographs of the boat and its hidden secrets. The Russians were very careful to ensure that Norwegian and British civilian divers from the *Seaway Eagle* only worked on the area around the *Kursk's* aft escape hatch. Combined with the capabilities of LR5, the Russians feared they would have no control over what the British might photograph, or perhaps remove altogether. It was the fear of a special-forces operation, using specialised underwater craft, which led the Russians to pound the area around the *Kursk* with forty depth charges. In any event, *Normand Pioneer* and LR5 were only allowed near the *Kursk* accident site on the very last day of the rescue mission, to lay a wreath. Even if the British had wanted to launch an intelligence-gathering mission, the Russians saw to it that they had no opportunity to do so. The *Normand Pioneer* was kept too far away from the *Kursk* site to be an effective operational base for any special forces based onboard.

The UK special-forces divers did have a legitimate role aboard the *Normand Pioneer*, and although they do not officially comment on special-forces operations, the British authorities will deny there was ever any intention to launch a special-ops intelligence-gathering mission against the *Kursk*. Divers were required to support the launch and recovery of the LR5 mini-sub. The divers would support the LR5 as it came to the surface, operating in a Gemini, connecting it to its 'lift-line'. They would also be on hand if there was an emergency, and operate the decompression chamber if necessary. It was entirely logical that these divers should be military, and would be trained to work with LR5 during NATO's submarine rescue training exercises. This is not the type of work which can easily be 'contracted out' to commercial civilian divers. It was more efficient and faster to have professional navy divers on permanent standby, who knew the ropes and what was required of them.

Nor, for the record, is there any evidence that a special-ops mission against the wrecked *Kursk* was planned, executed, cancelled or intended in the first place. However, the presence of SBS divers was not likely to have assuaged Russian fears of possible Western espionage, hence the need for the Royal Navy to keep their participation quiet.

Britain has offered £80 million to improve nuclear safety in the former Soviet Union, with the European Union also keen to clear up the world's nuclear graveyard in Russia's far north. However, Russia has so far stalled on allowing Western remedial teams into the Murmansk area, concerned that the West will use the operation to spy on its Northern Fleet's sensitive naval bases. The decline of the Northern Fleet mirrored the decline of the Soviet and Russian navies. Between 1989 and 1994, the number of nuclear submarines in the navy had almost halved from its peak of 196, and by 2000 the number of subs in the Northern Fleet had fallen to just 39. Only three of the Northern Fleet's submarines are on patrol at any one time, due to the cost of fuel and the difficulty of maintaining a seaworthy fleet. This decline has come to pose an environmental threat to Russia's neighbours, the Arctic wilderness and to the rest of the entire world. Russia's loose control and disposal of its military nuclear waste, redundant reactors and obsolete weapons strikes fear into even the least environmentally aware. Some 100 Russian submarines, 300 nuclear reactors (about one-fifth of the world's total) and thousands of spent fuel rods are simply left to rot in fjords and on open ground. Scores of inoperable Russian nuclear submarines lie like beached whales around the Kola

Peninsula. Admiral Oleg Yerofeev, Commander-in-Chief of the
Northern Fleet at the time, said in April 1995:

> The problems of storing spent nuclear fuel, radioactive waste,
> inactive submarines and the lack of servicing for the sub-
> marines in active service are a problem not only for the
> Northern Fleet, but also for the Russian state. Therefore, it
> would be natural not only for the Fleet to take necessary
> action, but also for the Ministry for Situations of Emergency,
> Emercom, also to act. If measures are not taken to address the
> situation today, over a period of time the situation could
> become critical and lead to an ecological disaster.

The Norwegian-based environmental group Bellona has repeatedly
clashed with the Russian authorities over the issue of nuclear dumping
and the ecological threat it poses. The Russians reacted by arresting
and trying one of Bellona's supporters, former naval officer Captain
Alexander Nikitin, for spying. Nikitin's interest in the state of Russia's
nuclear submarines and radiation pollution on the Kola Peninsula
was treated as a case of pure espionage by the FSB. Nikitin was arrested
in 1996, tried for high treason and imprisoned for twenty-two months.
He was only released after his case had come to court thirteen times,
despite international condemnation of his arrest. Nikitin could at
least count himself luckier than his whistle-blowing counterpart in the
Far East, Grigory Pasko, an investigative journalist who worked for the
Pacific Fleet's newspaper.

Former naval captain Pasko was stripped of his rank, convicted for
high treason and imprisoned in Vladivostock on 25 December 2001,
after writing reports on the Russian Navy's poor environmental record
in the Far East. According to the Russian authorities, Pasko was a spy.
Arrested on 20 November 1997, Pasko was acquitted by the Pacific
Fleet Court for treason and espionage, but sentenced to three years for
misusing his position and released on general amnesty. Both sides
appealed the verdict and Pasko was sent for retrial at the Pacific Fleet
Court after the previous verdict was quashed by the Military Supreme
Court. The prosecution wanted him to serve twelve years in a labour

camp. The retrial started on 11 July 2001 and ended on 25 December, with Pasko being sentenced to four years' hard labour for treason. Pasko spent his first few weeks in a cell without window panes, as Vladivostock experienced its worst snowstorms for over forty years. His cell was as cold inside as out, with temperatures falling to minus 15°C.

The Russian authorities maintain that the absence of prison window panes 'lets in fresh air' to overcrowded cells, and prevents broken glass being used as a weapon. With violence and diseases like tuberculosis endemic in the Russian prison system, and a hard labour regime little changed from the gulag days described by Alexander Solzhenitsyn, Pasko would normally be lucky to survive four years' incarceration. The international and domestic concern at Pasko's arrest may yet be his salvation. The European Parliament passed a resolution condemning his arrest, and Amnesty International adopted him as a prisoner of conscience, saying his prosecution seemed 'motivated by political reprisal for exposing the practice of dumping nuclear waste'. President Jacques Chirac also raised the case with President Putin when the Russian leader visited Paris in early 2002. Putin confidently asserted that even Pasko's lawyers accepted he had passed a document marked 'secret' to Japan, but was plainly rattled by the subsequent grilling at the hands of the Paris press pack. As a result, Pasko got his window panes and the luxury of a four-man cell to himself.

Pasko's conviction revolved around a meeting of the Pacific Fleet Council on 11 September 1997, at which he took notes. The court concluded that Pasko *intended* to hand these notes to the Japanese journalist, Tadashi Okano, who worked on the *Asashi* newspaper. The notes allegedly contained an analysis of naval manoeuvres carried out between August and September 1997. The boss of the local FSB in the Russian Pacific Fleet reputedly toasted Pasko's conviction, and the role his secret servicemen had played in bringing the case. FSB Major Alexander Egorin was officially commended for his 'distinguished work' on sending Pasko to jail. While the now Kremlin-controlled ORT television station produced a programme on 7 February 2002 presenting Pasko as a Japanese spy, a sympathetic programme by the independent television station TV6 on Pasko's plight was axed when the station was shut down on a financial pretext by those close to the government.

To a certain extent FSB and Russian Navy paranoia over Nikitin and Pasko is understandable, if not laudable. Nikitin co-authored the Bellona environmental group's report on the Northern Fleet, which is extremely comprehensive. The report details not only the navy's nuclear dumping strategy (or lack of it), but also the type, location and characteristics of the Northern Fleet's strategic and tactical nuclear submarines and their bases. Bellona's report also includes detailed maps, and photographs of many submarines tied up at jetties in the various closed or 'secret' bases. The FSB and the Northern Fleet's commanders were doubtless horrified to see all this information so clearly in the public domain, and were suspicious of where and how Bellona had got hold of this supposedly secret material. Among defence and intelligence agencies this reaction is not unique. Both the UK and USA remain secretive about the operational details of their nuclear submarine forces, and the two countries still refuse to confirm that their subs operate in the Barents Sea, which they patently do. Britain and America's coyness about their operations does not extend to locking up environmentalists who write damning reports, but both still restrict details and access to their strategic submarine bases. If in doubt, ask Faslane's anti-nuclear demonstrators in Scotland how welcoming they find the UK's Ministry of Defence.

The worst example of this type of sensitivity in the West was the sinking of Greenpeace's *Rainbow Warrior* in Auckland harbour in New Zealand, on the night of 10 July 1985. The French secret service operation must rank as the most crass and heavy-handed attempt to preserve nuclear secrecy in history. The *Rainbow Warrior* was trying to monitor France's nuclear tests on the Mururoa Atoll in the Pacific, but the French resolved to deal with this intrusion by holing and sinking the ship with the loss of one Greenpeace member's life. Fernando Pereira, a Portuguese photographer, was drowned trying to save his cameras. New Zealand Prime Minister David Lange called the *Rainbow Warrior* bombing nothing more than 'a sordid act of international state-backed terrorism'.

Back in Russia, the security agencies showed signs of wanting to re-establish Soviet-era controls over academics, human rights and environmental pressure groups. The arrests of Nikitin and Pasko were just the start of an attempt by the Russian security services to regain past influence and re-assert their lost authority. The election of Vladimir Putin as President in March 2000 accelerated this process. Putin had been in the KGB for sixteen years, and had been head of the FSB security service under Yeltsin. As president, Putin consciously sought to boost the role and status of the security services to a level unseen since the days of the pre-Gorbachev Soviet Union. Sergei Ivanov, a KGB colleague from St Petersburg, was promoted to be head of the Security Council, and then Defence Minister. Victor Ivanov, another KGB colleague, was brought in to run the Kremlin's personnel department. Nicolai Patrushev, another former KGB crony, became head of the FSB and was put in charge of the war against Chechnya in January 2001. Sergei Grigoryants, a leading human rights activist and head of the Glasnost Foundation, said: 'It's unprecedented that the army and the interior ministry troops are put under the secret police. That's a new direction for Russia.' Of the thirteen new regional governors elected in the thirteen months following Putin's own election, four were army or navy officers. Of the seven presidential representatives appointed by Putin to run the new Federal Districts or 'super-regions', five were army or ex-KGB. Twenty of Putin's senior appointments went to former colleagues from the president's native St Petersburg, many with security backgrounds.

Putin was essentially rebuilding the security apparatus dismantled after the 1991 abortive coup against Mikhail Gorbachev, which had been instigated by the KGB's then head, General Vladimir Kryuchkov. Boris Yeltsin had systematically divided and emasculated the KGB's sixteen directorates, creating five separate security agencies. The KGB had eight heads in less than a decade. Putin, on the other hand, wanted to rehabilitate the former KGB and the security services as the very embodiment of selfless and incorruptible service to the Motherland. As a young man, he always believed the secret service to be an honourable and respectable career, worthy of public admiration. He wanted to re-create the KGB's old image as defender of the state's interests, and a service committed to the public good in a corrupt world. The new-style security services would also bolster the authority and status of the president, accreting power to the centre.

Others saw Putin's security policy as a threat to individual liberty, democracy and the freedom of the press. In February 2001, Yabloko liberal party leader Grigory Yavlinsky said Putin was 'building a police state'. Former liberal Prime Minister Yegor Gaidar said around the same time that the jury was still out on whether President Putin was committed to democracy. Gaidar noted 'a very serious increase in the role of the secret service' and 'selective pressure' on the free media. 'All this,' he added, 'shows that the Russian leadership at least is not very decided on the issue of democracy being necessary.' In December 2000, Putin spent the evening with senior secret service officers celebrating the eighty-third anniversary of the Cheka's foundation in 1917. The Cheka were the Bolsheviks' secret police, the precursor to the infamous KGB, who were responsible for arresting and killing millions during Stalin's purges. During Stalin's *Yezhovshchina* or Great Terror between 1936 and 1938, the KGB arrested 7 million people of whom an estimated 3 million died, either through execution or because of the appalling conditions in Soviet labour camps. Among the victims were ten close associates of Lenin, three marshals, six Politburo members and over half the generals in the Red Army. Quite something to celebrate. Speaking of the KGB's Moscow headquarters, the notorious Lubyanka (which also doubled as prison, torture and execution block), an apparently inebriated Nicolai Patrushev, chief of the FSB, declared: 'The history of the Lubyanka in the last century is our history. We should retain and increase everything in that history which worked for the benefit of Russia.' The Lubyanka remains the headquarters of the FSB, successor to the KGB.

In the spirit of the good old days under the KGB, the FSB installed a 'telephone trust-line' at the Russian Foreign Ministry so that staff could denounce colleagues to the security service, anonymity guaranteed. As Sergei Lebedev, the head of the SVR foreign intelligence service, told a Moscow newspaper in December 2001: 'Being an agent means being reliable. It means dedication to the homeland, to comrades, it means being noble.' Putin couldn't have put it better himself.

If it also meant informing on your disloyal colleagues and putting them away, so much the better.

In June 1991 a leaked directive from Russia's Academy of Sciences advised the country's scientists to report all contacts with foreigners to their institute's authorities. The directive was meant to prevent the leakage of classified information to the West, but human rights groups saw it as an attempt to re-impose Soviet-era restrictions. The decree stated that foreigners should not have access to 'information concerning national security', and should provide the Academy with details of international co-operation contracts, research grants from abroad and foreign scientific trips, as well as supplying copies of articles submitted for international publication. An Academy official said: 'There is nothing new or sensational in the fact that the Academy has an instruction aimed at preventing damage to Russia and warning researchers and institutions against divulging confidential information.' The Russian Academy presented the directive as a routine measure to protect sensitive know-how in a market economy system.

However, the arrest and trial of another academic, Igor Sutyagin, seemed indicative of a growing pattern. Sutyagin, a 35-year-old security affairs specialist, collates and analyses information from newspapers and periodicals for the Moscow-based US–Canada Institute. The US–Canada Institute is a highly prestigious and influential foreign-policy think-tank, regarded as liberal and pro-Western in outlook. Igor Sutyagin was put on trial for espionage in Kaluga, south-west of Moscow, in February 2001, almost a year after Putin was elected president. He was accused of giving state secrets to the United States. Sutyagin insisted he had no access to classified information and had only analysed sources already in the public domain. Valery Borshev, head of the human rights section of the Duma parliamentary legislation committee, said, 'The effect of putting Sutyagin on trial is to create a climate of fear. Yet again, the hunt is on for enemies of the state.' A former KGB general now working as a banker said of the situation: 'There's a new fear. It's a new situation. There's a sense of the KGB's return. For ten years those guys were sitting around silent. Now they see their chance.' Disillusioned and demoralised by a loss of status and power, many of the KGB's officers had left to join security firms or work in business, often providing 'protection'. Those who remained in the FSB were poorly paid and often disgruntled. They had either stayed in the security service because they believed absolutely in the old KGB ideals, or because they weren't bright or young enough to find jobs elsewhere in the 'New Russia'. Some were unemployable hardliners who had bided their time. They knew they had nowhere else to go. For these men, Putin's election in 2000 after ten years in the wilderness meant that it was pay-back time.

In autumn 2001, there was a seemingly significant victory for Russian human rights campaigners when the Moscow Supreme Court struck out parts of a Defence Ministry decree which had been widely used to prosecute researchers for espionage. A group of human rights advocates had challenged the 1996 decree, which defined military secrets and a list of classified data. Ironically, the Defence Ministry decree is classified, so that academics and journalists do not know which data is covered. The decree could also be used retrospectively to classify a document on security grounds without specifying further details. In effect, the Defence Ministry could declare a researcher, scientist or journalist had breached national security without giving a reason. Various state agencies could also have different levels of classification, so that information which was made open and freely available by one was secret and protected by another. According to the human rights groups, the list of classified information should be determined by federal law, as laid down in the constitution. Captain Alexander Nikitin, himself arrested for espionage, said: 'We want state secrets to be preserved, not agency secrets, as is the case now.' Nikitin added: 'A new term has appeared: analytic espionage. As a result of their work, scholars, environmentalists and journalists can create a document that can be made secret.'

The Supreme Court ruling was, however, only a partial victory. While ruling against elements of the Defence Ministry decree, the Supreme Court would not give details. Because of the nature of the issue, the court hearing had been closed to the public. Transparency in the law governing espionage was still some way off. Nicolai Gastello, spokesperson for the Supreme Court, would only say that 'some clauses' of the decree had been struck out. Since the court was expecting an appeal from the Defence Ministry, he refused to comment further. The murky world of Russia's espionage cases remained as opaque as ever. Journalists, academics, human rights and environmental campaigners are still unsure of where the boundaries lie between legitimate exposure and national security.

The terrorist atrocities in New York and Washington on 11 September 2001 led to unprecedented co-operation between Russian intelligence services and their Western counterparts. In their eighth bilateral summit in two years, Prime Minister Tony Blair and President Putin established a joint working group on terrorism, comprising senior officials from the UK Foreign Office, Ministry of Defence, MI6 and their Russian opposite numbers. Having virtually run the Afghan intelligence service from 1979 to the early 1990s, the Russians were able to identify over fifty al-Qaeda and Taliban terrorist bases in Afghanistan. One senior British source said that post-September 11 'the co-operation on terrorism has been very close, particularly on intelligence. Our intelligence people sit down with theirs and go through some very detailed stuff. There is a sense of mutual trust. The intelligence people are really struck by the way the Russians have engaged with them.' Tony Blair told the Russian Interfax news agency: 'In the last century, Russia and Britain vied for influence in Afghanistan as part of the "Great Game". Now we share a common interest in the development of Afghanistan as a viable state ready to take its place in the community of nations.' Britain and the USSR had played a twentieth-century version of the 'Great Game' as recently as the 1980s, when members of the SAS were sent to Afghanistan to help train the anti-Soviet *mujahideen*, which at that time included a certain Osama bin Laden. The *mujahideen* also received backing from the CIA and Pakistani intelligence, the ISI.

More recently, in April 2002, the Russian security service showed the value of the new intelligence co-operation when they tipped off British military intelligence about an arms shipment to the IRA. According to Russia's security services, the IRA had purchased at least twenty AN-94 rifles, which can fire 1,800 bullets a minute and pierce body armour. The guns can be used as machine guns or as deadly high-velocity sniper rifles. The guns had apparently been sold to the IRA in autumn 2001 by a renegade group of Russian special forces officers in Moscow. The story was reported in the UK's *Sunday Telegraph* on 21 April 2002, after the newspaper was contacted by British military intelligence officers. The shipment of arms was worrying for the British government, especially since it seemed to imperil the Good Friday ceasefire agreement and the Northern Ireland peace process. It also showed how shockingly easy it was for terrorists to buy technologically advanced weaponry from the former Soviet Union.

The United States also found the Russians extremely accommodating post-September 11, even to the extent of not objecting to US forces using bases in the former Soviet 'backyard' republics of Central Asia, particularly Uzbekistan, Tajikistan, Kyrgyzstan and Kazakhstan. The West's war against terrorism chimed nicely with Russia's long-standing claim that it had been fighting a lonely battle against terrorists in the breakaway republic of Chechnya, in the Caucasus. At last Russia felt that it was receiving a sympathetic hearing from the West on Chechnya, rather than the endless complaints of human rights abuses in the region and demands for a political settlement with Chechen leaders. For years, Russia had unsuccessfully tried to link its wars in Chechnya with the UK's struggle against terrorism in Northern Ireland, without any perceptible effect. Moscow hoped for other benefits from its new intelligence co-operation and moral support in the global war against terrorism, including support for Russia's entry into the World Trade Organisation, a closer relationship with NATO and the rescheduling of the country's debts.

There were some setbacks on the road to a new world order after September 11, however. NATO's enlargement continued apace, without giving Russia its hoped-for veto over future military engagements. The USA unilaterally announced its withdrawal from the 1972 Anti-Ballistic Missile Treaty and persisted with its National Missile Defence shield, despite Russia's misgivings. US belligerence towards Iraq, Iran and North Korea threatened Russia's vital strategic and trade interests in those regions. Despite the co-operation over terrorism, there was no indication that Russia and the West's intelligence agencies would stop spying on one another, or even that they truly trusted each other. Not far below the surface, the old suspicions and rivalries persisted. In April 2002, for example, the FSB announced that it had thwarted a plot by two CIA agents to recruit an expert in a secret Russian Defence Ministry arms plant. A spokesman told the Interfax news agency that the FSB had 'irrefutable proof of the CIA's spying activities against Russia'. The Russians claimed the CIA agents were working under diplomatic cover in Moscow and another former Soviet republic, and had tried to obtain secrets about new Russian military projects and its security co-operation with former USSR countries. According to the Russians, the CIA were foiled when the intended 'target' turned double-agent for the FSB.

Sergei Lebedev, Russia's foreign intelligence chief, summed up the underlying ambiguities. September 11 was, in his view, a 'real turning point'. Giving a rare interview, his remarks were published in the mass circulation *Trud* newspaper on 20 December 2001. 'Exchanges of information between the countries of the world community now take place on a different, improved level,' he told the newspaper, but added:

Suppose the operation in Afghanistan is completed and Bin Laden is found and all of a sudden everyone goes back to their 'own' camps. Will we again believe that each side has its own terrorists, its own cockroaches to be rid of? In the next few years, we will see whether mankind has become smarter after this drama or whether memory endures only a few years.

It is to be greatly hoped that the events of September 11 will finally see an end to the rivalries engendered by the Cold War. The real fear is that in the intelligence world, it is already back to business as usual. What all the recent history of espionage has shown, both at sea and on land, is that the struggle between intelligence agencies in the West and Russia continues unabated. Both Russia and the West are actively spying on one another, and there is no evidence that the scale of intelligence operations on either side has seriously diminished since the fall of the Berlin Wall. The mutual distrust this creates underpinned Russia's reluctance to accept Western help during the *Kursk* tragedy. As the *Kursk* lay on the bottom of the Barents Sea, it was apparent that whatever the rhetoric at the political level, Cold War suspicions remained as strong as ever in Russian military and intelligence circles. Protecting the *Kursk*'s military secrets from the West's prying eyes seemed more of a priority than saving any survivors aboard the *Kursk*.

As a product of the Soviet Union's intelligence community, Vladimir Putin sympathises with the importance of protecting state and military secrets. Instinctively, he agreed with his admirals that they should handle the situation without involving the West. Putin not only sympathises with protecting the 'secret state'; through his policies he has sought to strengthen it. The ex-KGB chief believes in enhancing the role of the secret services in Russian society and re-imposing Soviet-era disciplines. His background, mindset and domestic security policies show why Putin so readily took his admirals' advice to keep the *Kursk* rescue an all-Russian affair. Like his admirals, he didn't want to let the West get their hands on the *Kursk*'s secrets. The level of espionage operations carried out against Russia since the implosion of the USSR shows Putin was right to be concerned. He was mistaken, however, to take the Russian Navy's assurances that they had everything under control at face value. Even worse, Russia's political and military leaders can be accused of believing that when it came to protecting Russia's secrets, the *Kursk* and its crew were simply expendable.

# 5

# Raising the *Kursk*

On 19 September 2000, Vladimir Putin took the formal decision to recover the submariners' bodies from the sunken *Kursk*. Two weeks before, the Russian president admitted the crew had probably died quickly after the *Kursk* sank, and that they had never sent any signals from the distressed sub after it went down. A $5,800,000 contract for the recovery operation was signed with the Norwegian branch of the American firm, Halliburton. The expedition set off from the Norwegian port of Bergen, arriving at the *Kursk* accident site in the Barents Sea on Friday 20 October. With stormy weather closing in, there wouldn't be much time to recover the bodies aboard the *Kursk*. The operation to salvage the submarine itself was postponed until the following summer, when the weather would be better, and the sea calmer. The man in charge of the recovery operation was the obdurate Rear-Admiral Gennady Verich, head of the navy's Search and Rescue Department, which had proved so obstructive to Britain's LR5 mini-sub rescue team.

Halliburton supplied the expedition with the Norwegian floating platform *Regalia*, two Kolokol-type diving bells and a decompression chamber. There were six foreign 'saturation' divers and twelve Russian divers. The foreign team included Norwegian, British, South African and Dutch nationals, and had been training in Norway weeks before starting the recovery operation. Since the *Kursk* sinking, the Russian divers had received Western deep-sea training. They would have to cope with intense cold and darkness as they worked 100 metres below the surface of the icy Barents Sea. The Russian divers were led by Captain First Rank Vasily Vasilevich Velichenko, commander of the 328th expeditionary detachment of the Department of Searching, Emergency and Rescue Works. The 328th rescue team had been in existence for seven years, and half the team were officers, the other half warrant officers. Captain Velichenko had personally selected the men to work on the *Kursk* recovery operation. On 8 September 2000 the Russian divers flew from St Petersburg's Levashovo military airport to Murmansk, where they prepared to depart for the Barents Sea. The divers would work in groups of three, with two Russian divers accompanied by one foreign diver. Working in four-hour shifts around the clock, only Russian divers would be allowed to enter the *Kursk*, while their foreign colleagues assisted from inside the *Regalia*'s decompression chamber lowered to the bottom of the Barents Sea.

That October the *Regalia* joined several Russian ships above the wreck. Besides the frigates *Admiral Kharlamov* and *Admiral Chabenko* (now used as Admiral Kuroyedov's flagship), there was the *Altai* rescue ship, the hydrographic survey ship *Semion Dezhnev* and the heavy cruiser *Pyotr Veliky*. Northern Fleet commander Admiral Vyacheslav Popov joined Kuroyedov aboard the *Admiral Chabenko*. Accompanying Kuroyedov were two *Kursk* widows, who brought flowers to cast into the water and home-baked pies for the divers. At 1 A.M. on 21 October, four Russian and two foreign divers descended to the *Kursk*. Hampered by bad weather and storms, over the next few days the divers made holes in the *Kursk*'s outer hull, so they could access the eighth and ninth compartments in the boat's stern. Radiation checks by remote-controlled cameras lowered inside the submarine showed an absence of radioactive isotopes. The sub's nuclear reactors had not leaked.

After five days of gruelling work, early on Wednesday 25 October the international diving team cut a hole over 1.5 metres wide through the sub's 40 cm hull. Six more holes would have to be made in the hull to allow access to all the sealed compartments. Water was pumped into the boat under high pressure to remove silt and debris which could make the recovery operation more difficult and hazardous. Sharp and jagged metal was covered with protective material to prevent the divers' suits from being punctured. Due to the ever-present danger of divers ripping open their pressure suits or puncturing their air hoses on mangled debris and equipment, Admiral Kuroyedov warned that he might have to cancel the recovery effort completely. He promised to end the operation immediately if divers were endangered. Relatives of the *Kursk*'s crew had begged officials not to risk further lives in recovering bodies from the submarine. The relatives' feelings on the whole recovery enterprise were mixed. Some thought the submariners should lie where they died, undisturbed in their final resting place. Seventy-eight relatives had written to President Putin demanding that the men's bodies should only be recovered together with the whole submarine. In the meantime, they called for the recovery operation to stop altogether.

At 3 P.M. on Wednesday 25 October, Russian diver Warrant Officer Sergei Shymgin entered the eighth compartment in the flooded sunken hulk of the *Kursk*. Shymgin, wearing full diving gear, passed with difficulty through about five metres of the eighth compartment to the partly opened connecting hatch, linking the eighth and ninth sections. In pitch darkness, looking for bodies by touch, Shymgin found everything seemingly burned and melted by a terrible fire. He could not fully open the narrow hatch and, peering dimly inside, nor could he make out any bodies. With visibility near zero, Shymgin found his way back out of the sub. It was a nightmarish experience, made worse by not knowing what would be found in the dark recesses of the stricken boat. Returning to the *Kursk* later that day, Shymgin and his colleagues eventually recovered four submariners' bodies, gently and carefully placing them in a metal basket one at a time, which was then hauled to the *Regalia* on the surface. Three Russian and one Norwegian diver worked together on the grisly task. Psychologists had warned the divers not to look the dead men in the face. Once aboard the *Regalia*, the bodies were taken to shore for examination at Severomorsk naval hospital.

Among the dead were Captain-Lieutenant Dmitri Kolesnikov, so badly burned from the waist up that his upper half was skeletal. But Kolesnikov's note to his superiors and his beloved Olga, still protected by his charred arm and clutched to his heart, threw the whole of Russia into a frenzy of self-doubt and recrimination. Up to that point the country and the international media had assumed the whole crew had died instantly, perishing when the *Kursk* had been shattered by two cataclysmic explosions. Ilya Klebanov, Deputy Prime Minister and head of the government's Commission of Inquiry, had told the public that almost all the crew would have died before the *Kursk* struck the seabed. Kolesnikov's note proved that some of the crew had survived for several hours after the explosions, perhaps for several days. It added credence to the early reports of messages from the crew, signalling 'SOS, water' for up to three days. Now the Russian people and the media were again questioning whether some of the crew could have been saved, particularly if Russia had accepted offers of international help sooner. For the Russian government, President Putin and the navy's High Command, Kolesnikov's note pointed an accusing finger from beyond the grave. Almost three months after the *Kursk* sank on 12 August, the government and navy were once more being accused of incompetence, indifference and ineptitude.

The divers initially worked on the upper third of the *Kursk* submarine, with storms again preventing other attempts to recover more crewmen's bodies. Cutting more holes in the *Kursk's* outer hull, Russian divers were able to re-enter the submarine on Saturday 28 October. Over the next two days another eight bodies were recovered, bringing the total to twelve. Among those found were Kolesnikov's best friend Captain-Lieutenant Rashid Aryapov, Captain-Lieutenant Sergei Sadilenko, commander of the eighth compartment, Senior Lieutenant Alexander Brazhkin, Senior Warrant Officer Andrei Borisov and seaman Alexei Korkin. Work continued until 7 November, but became increasingly difficult and dangerous. The divers found that the first and second compartments were completely destroyed. TV cameras showed the third compartment was such a wreck it was impossible to send the divers in. The compartment was located beneath the conning tower, equivalent in height to a five-storey building. The fourth wasn't in a much better state. Over two days, 5–6 November, the divers could move forward only two metres. Any further exploration of the fourth compartment proved impossible. It was thought that some of the submariners' bodies would have been discovered on the lower decks in the fifth compartment. But in full diving gear it was not possible to access the lower decks, which had to be reached via narrow hatches, 60 centimetres wide. Drilling holes in the fifth compartment, one of the sub's strong points, would weaken the whole structure of the boat and put at risk the lifting operation planned for 2001. The whole sub might fall apart when moved.

After a meeting aboard the *Regalia* on Tuesday morning, 7 November, representatives from the Rubin Design Bureau and Halliburton agreed to abandon the search for any more bodies. Conditions had simply become too dangerous for the divers, and there was little more they could do in any case. They had, however, managed to locate some log books, which they removed from the sub. The divers completed an examination of the hull and the surrounding seabed, including the heavily damaged bow section. The information collected would prove useful to the future lifting operation. After a final farewell and memorial ceremony, the *Regalia* left the accident site at around 2 P.M. in the afternoon. The *Pyotr Veliky* and the hydrographic survey ship *Gorizont* were left behind to guard the *Kursk* from prying eyes, and to monitor radiation levels.

Before the *Regalia* left the Barents Sea, rumours were circulating that a second note had been found in Dmitri Kolesnikov's pocket. According to the journalist Yelena Guseva, who worked for the Russian newspaper *Zhizn*, the note contained information about the disaster and was addressed to the navy's High Command. It was dated Tuesday 15 August, four days after the *Kursk* sank. Guseva claimed she had discovered the existence of the note while posing as a waitress at a restaurant in Severomorsk, the Northern Fleet's administrative headquarters. According to Guseva's account, a military expert at Severomorsk's naval laboratory told her about the second note, which was clearly dated 15 August. Unlike the first note, dated 12 August, the second one was far more difficult to read, especially since the lines overlapped. Vice-Admiral Mikhail Motsak, the Northern Fleet's Chief of Staff, allegedly told the experts to keep quiet about the second note. Motsak revealed the existence of Kolesnikov's first note on national television, hours after it was discovered. Although REN TV in Moscow aired the *Zhizn* story on 30 October, there has been no independent confirmation that such a second note ever existed. The publicity surrounding Guseva's article nevertheless added to the general perception that some of the *Kursk*'s crew had been abandoned by the state and condemned to a slow death.

The bodies of the twelve submariners recovered from the *Kursk* were returned to their home towns and cities for burial. Captain-Lieutenant Dmitri Kolesnikov's body was laid to rest in his native St Petersburg on 2 November 2000. His closed coffin first lay for a time in a grandiose hall in his old Admiralteiski Naval College, the resplendent former imperial headquarters of the czarist navy. The hall was filled with mourners bearing flowers and holding candles. Columns were draped in red and black ribbons, and young naval cadets from the college wore red and black armbands. Outside, two dozen sailors stood to rigid attention as the coffin left the former Admiralty building. From central St Petersburg, next to the Neva River, Kolesnikov's coffin was taken to a special 'heroes' section of the huge Serafimov military cemetery in the northern suburbs. Serafimov is a dignified, serene place, full of lost heroes and servicemen dating back to the Second World War and before. A framed copy of part of Kolesnikov's last letter was placed beside his coffin by one of his relatives, with two words from the note, 'Don't despair', added as a title. A postmortem examination earlier in the week had established that he had died from carbon monoxide poisoning.

Attending Dmitri's funeral were his parents Roman and Irina, his submariner brother Alex and his widow Olga. Also there were St Petersburg Governor Vladimir Yakovlev, and Northern Fleet Commander Vyacheslav Popov. Popov told the mourners: 'His fate will become an example of serving the Motherland for everyone. I will teach the officers, sailors, midshipmen of the Northern Fleet according to his example.' A volley of shots was fired over Kolesnikov's last resting place by sailors wearing black dress uniforms.

Thirty-two graves were prepared to receive crew members whose families decided they should be buried in St Petersburg. No one who has been to Serafimov can fail to be moved by the sight of the graves of those young and not-so-young submariners, who faithfully served and died on the *Kursk*.

For some families, the loss of their loved ones and their recovery from the *Kursk* was almost too much to bear. Alexei Korkin's mother, Svetlana Ivanovna, had heard her son calling to her in her *dacha*'s vegetable garden after the *Kursk* went down. Alexei, a bilge specialist in the sixth compartment, was one of the first submariners found on the wreck, and was buried with full military honours. 'It is terrible for me to imagine what our boys lived through in that ninth compartment when they were waiting for help,' Svetlana Ivanovna said. 'After all, they believed and hoped that help would come. How long did that last? The question will torture me until my dying day.' Alexei's mother, who had identified her son's body, added: 'What did Alexei live through that his hair turned grey at the age of nineteen?'

Other relatives were inconsolable. Sixty-year-old Olga Romanovna, Victor Kuznetsov's mother, did not survive her bereavement. Warrant Officer Kuznetsov, aged twenty-seven, had been a senior assistant turbine operator in the eighth compartment. Olga had been horrified to see the family icon fall off their wall and smash into pieces on 15 August, but hoped her son would survive despite the bad omen. Three hours before she was due to identify her son's body, which had been recovered from the *Kursk* in October, Olga Romanovna died, apparently grief-stricken. Mother and son were buried on the same day in their home city of Kursk, in south-west Russia. Before the coffins were taken to two different cemeteries, they lay together near their home, watched over by Alexei's father.

Dozens of local men signed up to serve on the submarine named after their city, and sadly seven of the crew who lived in Kursk or the immediate area would be coming home in coffins. Some families, given the choice of having new flats anywhere in Russia, would decide to come to live and have their men buried in the city. Sixteen submariners' widows said they wanted to move from the garrison town of Vidyayevo to Kursk, where some had spent their annual holidays. The people of Kursk had been very loyal and supportive to the submarine which bore its name and the submariners' families over the years. Relatives from Vidyayevo remembered with affection and gratitude the apples, sugar, flour, chicken and sweets freely donated to the crew's families. There was also the Kursk city bus, donated to the Vidyayevo garrison for the use of the *Kursk* submariners and their kin. In the hard days following the collapse of the USSR, the free supplies from the city of Kursk were a godsend.

To his credit, President Putin kept his promise to raise the 18,000-ton *Kursk* and retrieve the bodies of those lost. It was, and remains, an expensive promise to fulfil. The salvage operation alone would cost $65 million, and this did not include the earlier costs of the operation to retrieve the twelve submariners in October 2000, or the later costs to recover the bow of the submarine. The whole recovery and salvage operation was estimated to cost about $130 million. The sum allocated to the salvage operation alone was equivalent to almost twice the navy's budget for operating all its submarines for a year. There were those in the service who quietly criticised the recovery operation as a costly, politically-led face-saver for the Russian president. Others felt that the operation was not only financial folly, but environmentally dangerous as well. If the reactors leaked during the course of the *Kursk* lifting operation, the result could be an underwater Chernobyl, with devastating consequences for the Arctic ecosystem and the rich fishing grounds of the Barents Sea. The Norwegians were understandably nervous. Including the *Kursk*, there were six nuclear submarines quietly rotting at the bottom of the ocean by the summer of 2001, two American and four Russian, buried at depths of up to 5,000 metres. As yet, no one had successfully raised one to the surface.

Given the catastrophic public-relations meltdown of the previous year, Putin and his government decided to handle the *Kursk* recovery operation in a completely different manner. They were going to be totally transparent and frank. For the Russian hierarchy, the level of openness displayed was wholly unprecedented. The Russians held an online press conference on the lifting operation in Moscow on 28 June 2001. Representatives included Vice-Admiral Mikhail Barskov, Deputy Commander-in-Chief of the Russian Navy, head of the naval press service Igor Dygalo, and representatives of the recovery consortium. The group answered questions from the assembled journalists, as well as questions from Internet users around the world. On 8 August 2001, the Russian government launched a website in London providing comprehensive information on the _Kursk_ lifting operation. Run by the National News Service Strana Ru in association with the Interfax news agency and ORT television, the site[*] was an unparalleled venture to give official day-to-day information on the progress of the lifting operation. The site also provided a great deal of background information on the _Kursk_ tragedy, commentary, expert opinions and video footage of the wreck. The impetus for the website came from President Putin himself and his closest advisers. Putin and the Kremlin ensured that from now on they would set the news agenda, not follow it, as they had done during the darkest days of the _Kursk_ crisis.

To reinforce the point, Sergei Yastrzhembsky, one of Putin's closest aides and a master Kremlin spin-doctor, was put in charge of co-ordinating information about the _Kursk_ lifting operation. He told the press conference during the website launch that 'our presence here, the fact that we are here today to promote the new website and answer your questions, I think is evidence of the Russian government's commitment to find the truth about the _Kursk_. So far we don't have all the answers about what happened last August. Our investigation is looking at all possibilities.' He promised to share the findings with 'not only the Russian people and Russian society, but with the rest of the world'. Honesty, transparency and clarity. The scene in London was in stark contrast to the mendacity, obfuscation and incoherence displayed by the Russian government and naval High Command the year before. Yastrzhembsky acknowledged that lessons had been learned. Putin's spin-doctor also proudly announced that the Russian authorities had accredited around 1,000 journalists to cover the salvage operation, and that the government was opening a special

[*]_www.kursk141.org_ / _www.kursk.strana.ru_

International Press Centre in Murmansk to accommodate them all. This was serious media management.

For some, the new openness was difficult to stomach. The old Soviet-era ways died hard, especially for the older generation. Gennady Sorokin, press secretary to Igor Spassky, head of the Rubin Design Bureau which designed the *Kursk* and most modern Russian submarines, found it especially hard to change the old Soviet mindset. Contacted by journalists and researchers for information on the progress of the investigation into the *Kursk* disaster, he was inclined to brush aside questions as Western-inspired attempts to undermine the Russian defence sector and influence the outcome of the government's official inquiry into the sinking. Luckily, his boss Igor Spassky was more forthcoming and media-friendly, lacking the paranoia so often found among the older generation in Russia's military–industrial complex. Sorokin's view that the best information is no information – somewhat bizarre for a press officer – typified the sort of instinctively secretive attitude which had so hobbled the reaction to the *Kursk* sinking in the first place. Many in the Russian Navy's High Command had the same response as Sorokin. By their very nature they had been trained to say little and give away less.

Two rival Dutch bidders for the salvage contract to raise the *Kursk* agreed to form a joint venture in May 2001. Mammoet, a former unit of the Nedlloyd shipping group and mainly used to moving heavy equipment overland, was chosen as the lead operator. The other partner was Smit International, a Rotterdam-based marine services company, and the more experienced of the two. Both Dutch companies had been part of the original bidding consortium including Halliburton Subsea, a Norwegian division of the US Halliburton company. The Halliburton consortium had been dropped after it declared it was not willing to compromise safety by trying to raise the *Kursk* by the end of 2001. The consortium's experts had believed it was just too risky to attempt to raise the submarine in such a short time. Nevertheless, the Russian government believed that it was essential to meet the 2001 deadline if the *Kursk* families were to have any chance of burying their dead. Mammoet guaranteed it would do the job on schedule. The contract to carry out the salvage work and raise the boat was signed on 18

May. It had been drawn up in about ten days, which Deputy Prime Minister Klebanov claimed was a 'world record' for contracts of such scope. On the Russian side, Mammoet's partners would be the Russian Navy and the St Petersburg-based Rubin Design Bureau.

A team of Russian, British, Norwegian and Dutch divers arrived at the *Kursk* accident site on the evening of 15 July 2001 to begin the first phase of the salvage operation. They were joined by the diving mother-ship DSND *Mayo*, operated by Mammoet but based in Aberdeenshire, Scotland. Other ships at the site were the anti-submarine warship *Severomorsk*, the *Iceberg* missile warship, and the *Romuald Muklevich* and GS-87 hydrographic vessels. The headquarters of the so-called 'Special Mission Expedition' were aboard the *Severomorsk*, and commanded by Vice-Admiral Motsak. An unmanned submersible was lowered the same day to examine the seabed around the *Kursk* and monitor radioactivity. This enabled the salvage team to draw up a detailed chart of conditions in a fifty-metre radius of the wrecked submarine. While the two hydrographic ships monitored levels of radiation and the weather, the *Severomorsk* and the *Iceberg* were assigned to guard the sunken *Kursk*. The Russians still feared Western attempts to gain access to classified material and weaponry aboard the nuclear sub.

Divers from Halliburton and the Russian Navy, who had already been in training for this part of the operation, began clearing deposits around the submarine and cutting holes in the hull. Sand and silt which had built up within the submarine was flushed out of the boat. Working in temperatures around zero, within a few days the divers would start work with robotic cutting instruments to slice off the *Kursk*'s severely damaged front section. There were fears that sawing open the front section of the boat, which included the torpedo magazine, would be extremely hazardous. The torpedoes, which had survived eleven months underwater without exploding, could be accidentally detonated, blowing apart the fifth reactor compartment and resulting in a massive leakage of radiation. The Norwegian environmental group Bellona accused Russian officials of rushing the work. Bellona's Igor Kadrik estimated there were seven tons of TNT explosives still scattered around the submarine's bow. 'The equipment they are using has never been tried in this kind of operation and some of it has never been tested underwater,' Kadrik said. 'This is what we define as rushed.' Some environmentalists thought the $130 million budgeted for the *Kursk* salvage and recovery operation would have been better spent on clearing up the Northern Fleet's nuclear contamination of the Arctic, including its 113 rusting nuclear subs laid up on the Kola Peninsula. Norway's Nuclear Protection Board was also nervous. A spokesman said: 'There is a risk of the lifting operation itself going wrong, that they could, for example, lose the submarine. That could result in the reactor being more damaged.' The Barents Sea is one of the world's cleanest oceans, and the Norwegians wanted to keep it that way. The Russians did not underestimate the dangers. 'Everything is possible, considering that we are dealing with a submarine loaded with torpedoes,' naval chief Admiral Kuroyedov disconcertingly admitted.

Meanwhile, a huge 24,000-ton barge, the 122-metre *Giant 4*, was being modified in Rotterdam to carry twenty-six thick lifting cables. Each winching cable was strong enough to lift 900 tonnes. Over the course of the summer, divers would cut twenty-six 70 cm-wide holes in the *Kursk*'s inner and outer hulls, using powerful underwater jets. During the lifting operation, the winching cables would be lowered from *Giant 4* and attached through the holes, using large steel clamps to keep them in place. The 'grippers' would be inserted into their respective holes and used to secure the lifting equipment to the wreck. The cables would be connected to hydraulic jacks anchored to the *Giant*, and used to raise the *Kursk* about 100 metres, just below the barge. The raised *Kursk* would then be towed for three days to Roslyakovo, a small port just outside Murmansk. Once at Roslyakovo, two specially built pontoons would ease the submarine into dry dock. This stage of the salvage operation was scheduled to take place on or about 15 September. Russian officials were concerned to finish the operation before the reactors could corrode, leading to a possible radiation leak. They rejected environmentalists' fears that they might be proceeding too hastily. 'The first and main reason to raise the *Kursk* is to get the nuclear reactors off the seabed,' Vice-Admiral Motsak said. 'Secondly, we have to raise it to fulfil our human obligation to all those who died on board and to give them a respectable burial.' Almost a hundred journalists were taken to the accident site above the wreck to witness the start of the 'active phase' of the salvage operation. Again, the Russian Navy was showing it had learned lessons from its disastrous handling of the tragedy the previous year.

On Monday 17 September, the massive *Giant 4* barge left Kirkenes in Norway's far north. *Giant 4* was heading for the accident site, eighty-five miles north-east of Murmansk. The week before, remote-controlled cable saws had successfully cut right through the hull, detaching an eighteen-metre section of the bow. What was left of the bow was to be left behind on the seabed until the following year, when a further recovery operation would attempt to retrieve it. With the salvage operation already running ten days behind schedule, there were doubts whether the work could be completed by the end of September, when deteriorating weather might make further progress impossible. Vladimir Kuznetsov, of the Russian branch of the Green Cross, expressed the widespread concern that the recovery timetable was dictated by political expediency. 'The official information gives the impression that the work is being conducted too quickly, too chaotically, and is of a purely political nature,' he said. Retired Vice-Admiral Yury Senatsky, former head of the Soviet Navy's salvage operations, felt the whole operation was really about fulfilling President Putin's promise to raise the *Kursk* and bury its dead. 'Nobody will tell the president that his promises are worthless,' Senatsky said. 'Many of the admirals agree with me. Putin says the main thing is to bring up the bodies. But the main thing now is to find out the reasons for the sinking, because we have another nine submarines like the *Kursk*.'

The Russian Navy vigorously denied accusations that it was deliberately leaving the *Kursk*'s bow section on the seabed because it had something to hide. Captain Igor Dygalo, press spokesman and aide to the navy's commander-in-chief, refuted an allegation in August from a group of retired St Petersburg submariners that the *Kursk* had been struck by a surface vessel. Dygalo said it was necessary to sever the bow 'in order not to upset the lift operation and the centring of the submarine'. Igor Spassky of the Rubin Design Bureau estimated that the bow section of the *Kursk* had split into more than fifteen fragments after the two explosions. Captain Dygalo was especially concerned that the compartment 'might fall off during the lifting operation or might cause dangerous fluctuations in the hull'. He said that the compartment was being severed to ensure complete safety, adding: 'Towing a sub with a destroyed compartment is impossible and dangerous. Once the compartment has been severed, naval experts will examine it with the aim of obtaining further information about the original cause of the tragedy.' The bow fragments would be examined in detail by experts once they were brought to the surface. Dygalo made the point that the bow had just not been holed; it had been blown to pieces by the force of the two explosions which sank the *Kursk*. Vice-Admiral Mikhail Barskov said that the bow was in such poor condition it couldn't be lifted as a whole. 'It doesn't exist,' he said. Nevertheless, the salvage consortium managed to retrieve seven bow fragments when the main part of the submarine was lifted free of the seabed.

Some persisted in seeing conspiratorial reasons for not raising the bow section, including the Northern Fleet's *bête noir*, Bellona's Captain Alexander Nikitin, whom the FSB security service had repeatedly attempted to imprison for treason. Nikitin claimed in late September that the *Kursk*'s bow was being left on the seabed to hide the true cause of the sinking. He accused the Russian authorities of a deliberate cover-up. Dygalo, speaking for the navy, reacted indignantly. 'Not a single country in the world has demonstrated such maximum information transparency as in the situation around the *Kursk* salvage operation,' he asserted. Dygalo dismissed Nikitin's allegation as 'groundless and unsubstantiated' and praised the salvage mission's 'media transparency'. The navy's High Command was more interested than anyone in finding out what caused the catastrophe, he said. Even so, Dygalo did not hide the fact that the Russians were still preoccupied with security: 'A combat ship is being brought to the surface. Questions concerning the preservation of a military secret are only natural, but they have nothing to do with concealing the causes of the *Kursk* disaster.'

In a parallel development, chief military prosecutor Mikhail Kislitsyn promised to discover the cause of the explosions. Interfax reported that Kislitsyn would join sixteen task groups charged with examining the *Kursk* once it was brought into dry dock, following monitoring for toxicity and radiation. Also taking part in the investigation would be Vladimir Ustinov, the Russian Federation's prosecutor-general. Kislitsyn revealed that the Russians had not given up on the collision theory. 'At present, we are working on three main versions of the disaster: an accident in the first compartment, i.e., the explosion of a torpedo; a collision with some extraneous object; or hitting a mine of World War Two vintage,' he said. In effect, the Russians were clinging on to the three versions of the accident that the government's Commission of Inquiry had identified over a year before. In the rest of the world, the vast majority of experts and commentators put the explosion down to a torpedo malfunction. The Russian authorities still hoped, somehow, to put the blame on someone and something else.

At midnight on Sunday, 7 October 2001, the lifting operation finally got under way, a full fourteen months after the *Kursk* sank with all hands. Preparation for the lift had taken eighty-eight days, twenty-four days longer than planned. Bad weather and complications had delayed the lifting. The work had been particularly badly hit back in August, when divers discovered that they would have to cut holes in the hull by hand, rather than using robots, because the void between the inner and outer hulls was filled with pipes, wiring, air-pressure canisters and supports. Vice-Admiral Motsak, overseeing the final lifting operation, honoured an old naval tradition by spitting three times over his left shoulder for luck. Jan van Seumeren, Mammoet's president, just said calmly, 'Let's get started.'

At 3:55 A.M. Moscow time, the lifting gear gradually raised the *Kursk* four metres above the seabed. Igor Spassky of the Rubin Design Bureau couldn't hold back the tears. He had expected major difficulties, but was astonished when everything went in a 'surprisingly smooth way'. Spassky told Russian television: 'When we lifted the submarine, I felt as if a huge burden fell off my shoulders.' Rear-Admiral Gennady Verich, head of the navy's Search and Rescue Department, was also feeling fraught with emotion. 'For me, it was a night that dissolved all doubts, a night of hope in memory of those who had given their lives for the Fleet and the Motherland.' For one awful moment, it appeared that the bow section was buried deep in silt and still attached to the rest of the submarine. But the first compartment was successfully separated from the rest of the sub, and the lift continued unimpeded. A net was placed across the open end of the submarine to prevent the contents tumbling into the sea.

The *Kursk* continued to creep up from its resting place on the seabed, rising at a rate of ten metres per hour. At 11 A.M. reports came in that the weather was about to worsen seriously. Instead of waiting for the sub to be raised enough to be fixed under the *Giant* barge, the tugs *Atrek* and *Smit* began towing the *Kursk* while the boat still continued its slow ascent from a depth of forty metres. It took fifteen hours to lift the submarine into place. By about 8 P.M., the *Kursk* had travelled ten miles from the accident site and had settled into its special 'cradle' which held it in place under the *Giant*. The *Kursk* was suspended inside the barge, together with its two nuclear reactors, twenty-two Granit cruise missiles and the earthly remains of 106 submariners. The conning tower and the boat's stern fitted snugly into niches cut into the *Giant*. The barge crawled along at a pace of two and a half miles per hour in the direction of Roslyakovo, 120 miles away. Because Roslyakovo was so near to Murmansk, and its population of 400,000 people, there was understandable concern about the possibility of radiation leaks from the *Kursk's* two reactors. Dismantling the reactors could pose a particular threat, and classes were held at schools in Murmansk to teach children what to do in the event of a nuclear accident. Chernobyl was ever-present in people's minds. As the *Kursk* left its bow section behind at 108 metres below the surface of the Barents Sea, divers placed a marble tombstone beside it on the seabed. Eight Russian ships passed over the accident site, with crews at attention and ships' sirens sounding, laying wreaths for the lost submariners in a final salute.

According to the Russian Navy, the site where the bow lay remained closed for reasons of 'security, not secrecy'. Admiral Popov told Interfax that the parameters of the official accident site would be reduced to one-tenth of their previous proportion. Navigation and fishing would be prohibited in the accident zone to 'ensure maximum safety, so that fishing in that area would cause no excesses'. The Russian Navy were still fearful that the bow fragments could be targeted by Western intelligence agencies.

The lifting operation was a bold and magnificent technical achievement. During months of planning, Valentin Pashin, director of Russia's Krylov research institute, had made innumerable calculations and carried out hundreds of experiments and model simulations. Drawing the embedded submarine from the pull of seasilt suction went better than many of the scientists and engineers could have hoped. Raising and securing the *Kursk* to the salvage barge had gone largely without a hitch, despite the threat of bad weather and the rocking action of the waves. Igor Spassky admitted they had been 'very lucky with the weather'. Conditions in the Barents Sea had been unusually calm for so late in the year. The Russian Navy, the international divers and the salvage team could feel immensely proud of a difficult job done well. Many had doubted it was possible, many more wondered whether it was wise. That the lift went smoothly, despite all the things that could have gone wrong, was a triumph of modern marine engineering. The presence of nuclear reactors had made the operation doubly dangerous. Vice-Admiral Motsak probably understated the mood when he said: 'Once we reach the shore, we will have a good drink, according to Russian custom.' A good number of vodka bottles were emptied when everyone reached land.

Mark Girdlestone, a 42-year-old former Royal Navy 'saturation diver', could be proud of what he had achieved. He was one of a team of twelve deep-sea divers who spent up to a month at a time working on the *Kursk*'s hull. His job had involved attaching twenty-two-ton lifting gear into the holes bored into the *Kursk*'s inner and outer hulls, working punishing seven-hour shifts. Girdlestone operated at seabed pressures ten times greater than those the human body was used to on land. Every day he would be lowered to the seabed in a pressurised diving bell with two Russian divers. At the end of the shift, the diving bell was winched back on board the Norwegian-owned *Mayo* diving support ship, and clamped to a decompression chamber. At risk of developing 'the bends' or decompression sickness, Mark had to spend his time between shifts in the permanently pressurised chamber aboard the *Mayo*. Food, drink, clothes and other needs were supplied via an airlock, which could also be used to pass notes back and forth. Confined with two Russians in a decompression chamber the size of a bathroom, the British diver spent a lot of time sending e-mails home. He also sent e-mails to the BBC's Real Time website, describing his experiences.

Girdlestone normally worked as a deep-sea diver on oil rigs, platforms and pipelines in the North Sea. Previously he had helped recover the Royal Navy's first submarine, HMS *Holland*, which had sunk back in 1913. Before beginning four days of decompression at the end of the salvage operation, Mark Girdlestone wrote: 'A lot of the divers and crew are ex-armed forces and felt an affinity for the Russian sailors lost on the *Kursk* and those we have been working with.' When the *Kursk* was finally raised, Girdlestone said he felt 'pleased, relieved and proud of a job well done. I also felt we have helped the relatives of the lost Russian sailors.' Diver Jim Irvine, from St Andrews in Scotland, shared the sentiments. 'It feels great to be part of a team that has brought these Russian sailors home,' he said. 'We have achieved something for the Russian people as well as the Russian government.' Many of the British divers, employed by Aberdeenshire company DSND, became close friends with their Russian colleagues.

When the *Mayo* arrived back in her home port of Aberdeen on 22 October, she was met by an official civic ceremony led by the city's Lord Mayor, Margaret Smith. The *Mayo* had left Aberdeen in July, spending over three months in the Barents Sea. Onboard the *Mayo* was search and rescue chief Rear-Admiral Gennady Verich, the diving team and crew. Honouring the team, the Lord Mayor praised the mission's 'unqualified success', sent her condolences to the *Kursk*'s families, and said the lifting operation would make it possible to pay homage to the memory of the lost crew. Sean Pople, DSND onshore manager, said that despite the technical difficulties of the operation, 'the crew never forgot that the *Kursk* was a grave, where many men had perished'. Three memorial services were held on the *Mayo* while she was at sea, in remembrance of the crew. '*Mayo* was the testing ground for the most advanced diving technologies,' Admiral Verich told those assembled in Aberdeen. 'There were doubts, and we are pleased that such a difficult project was eventually so successful. In many respects, we owe it to the exceptional professionalism of the participants in the work.'

On 10 October, the 44,000-ton combined colossus of the *Kursk* and the *Giant 4* barge, cradling the submarine just beneath the surface, finally reached Roslyakovo in the Kola Bay. Russian naval ships sounded their sirens in salute and sombre crowds lined the shore in silence as the *Giant* came into view. Around 5 P.M. local time the *Giant* was attached to floating anchors 500 metres from the shoreline. Deputy Prime Minister Klebanov tried to reassure the public there was no risk of a radiation leak. 'We are absolutely confident nothing will happen to the reactors,' Klebanov said. 'If there had been a one-in-a-million chance that something would happen, we would never have carried out the operation in Roslyakovo.' Not many locals believed him. Despite twenty-four-hour monitoring of radiation levels aboard the *Kursk*, local schools intensified their nuclear accident training classes. Roslyakovo officials prepared evacuation plans and stockpiled medical supplies. To allay local concerns, a screen with continual radiation readouts was placed in the centre of the port town. The unexploded Granit missiles still aboard the *Kursk* were also considered a major risk. 'Unloading missiles is dangerous even in normal conditions,' observed Admiral Popov. Popov added that the navy was taking 'extra safety precautions'. If it was not possible to lift the missiles out of their individual silos, the navy would cut each silo out of the *Kursk*'s hull. Popov's remarks made the locals more nervous than ever.

Roslyakovo's inhabitants remained remarkably calm given the circumstances. Local people displayed typical Russian stoicism, partly borne out of a lifetime of accepting decisions handed down by the authorities. In the West, the public reaction would have doubtless been somewhat different. When the British nuclear submarine HMS *Tireless* called into Gibraltar in May 2000 needing a minor repair to a cooling pipe near the boat's nuclear reactor, all hell broke loose, causing an international incident and a crisis in Anglo-Spanish relations. Local Gibraltarians objected strongly to the damaged submarine being brought to the Rock at all. Greenpeace activists from Spain, Germany,

Austria and Italy arrived in the British colony in rubber dinghies and attempted to board the Royal Navy submarine. Eight Greenpeace members were arrested after unfurling a banner on the sub reading 'For a Nuclear-Free Sea'. Environmentalists claimed that even a small radioactive leak could contaminate a radius of up to 100 kilometres. Spanish Premier José María Aznar formally asked the British to remove the *Tireless* after widespread protests in Spain. The London *Sunday Times* wrote of the possibility of a 'Chernobyl-style meltdown', and residents of Gibraltar threatened the British Ministry of Defence with legal action. After convincing locals and the Spanish government that it was safe to carry out repairs, HMS *Tireless* finally left Gibraltar in May 2001, almost a year after it had arrived. In Roslyakovo, despite the possibly unstable presence of two nuclear reactors, twenty-two cruise missiles and an unknown quantity of unexploded torpedoes, there was not a single public protest. Everyone from the naval High Command down knew it was a highly risky exercise, but just kept their fingers crossed.

A seventy-metre-wide dock awaited the *Kursk* in Roslyakovo, the Russian Navy's largest dry dock. Navy shipyard engineers prepared to ease the first of two massive pontoons under the combined *Giant* and *Kursk*. Shallow water meant the *Giant* needed the support of the pontoons to ease into dock. The pontoons were filled with water to lower them beneath the *Giant*, then filled up with air to expel the water, raising the whole structure six to seven metres. Once inside the dock, the pontoons would be filled with water again, so that the *Kursk* could be manoeuvred on to a support as the structures holding it finally moved away. After radiation monitoring, the water would be drained from the dock, and the work of inspecting the exposed *Kursk* and removing bodies could begin. Technical difficulties meant that moving the *Kursk* into its dock became an extremely slow process. Navy experts needed to improve the locking devices that would secure the *Giant/Kursk* to the buoyancy pontoons, and other checks were needed on the pontoons' pumps and draining devices. The unknown state of the *Kursk* made precise design calculations difficult. Dutch contractors Mammoet–Smit International requested a delay on the docking operation as they made further checks on the *Kursk*'s joints and mechanisms. Captain Vladimir Navrotsky, spokesman for the Northern Fleet, explained that the timing of the job had been changed 'because of the unique character and complexity of the docking and safety precautions'.

As work proceeded around the clock, checks on the submarine's hull continued, and a remote-controlled submersible was used to verify the boat's nuclear reactors were not leaking. On Sunday 14 October, giving his final briefing at the international media centre in Murmansk, Admiral Popov told reporters time 'was of no importance' in moving the *Kursk* to its Roslyakovo dock. Installing the pontoons was a tricky operation which required important engineering decisions to be taken. Unlike the rest of the salvage operation, the docking was not dependent on weather conditions. There was no need to rush this last stage, and everything would be done thoroughly, Popov added. An official later confirmed that safety considerations were now the priority. The media was promised access to the wrecked submarine after the boat was safely in dock and had been drained of water. Twelve hundred reporters from twenty-seven nations had covered the *Kursk* lift operation over the previous hundred days. The professional handling of the media was in stark contrast to the fiasco over a year before.

Work to submerge the first of two pontoons under the *Giant* only began on 17 October, and took twenty-four hours to complete. It took the *Giant* until 21 October to dock successfully. By Monday 22nd work had begun to remove the clamps or 'grippers' which held the *Kursk* to the *Giant 4* barge. In the afternoon, released from all twenty-six grippers, the *Kursk* was resting underwater supported by blocks on the floor of the massive dock. Just before noon on the morning of Tuesday 23rd, *Giant 4*, supported by the pontoons *Mar* and *Gon*, left the Roslyakovo dock and headed for home. For the Mammoet and Smit International consortium, the salvage operation was over. As the *Giant* headed into Kola Bay, the crew lowered wreaths into the water in memory of the lost submariners.

It was now time for the huge dock and the *Kursk* itself to be drained, exposing the submarine's severed hull. The draining operation was expected to take three or four days. The submarine could not be drained immediately, because of the fear that water turbulence would disturb important evidence. A sudden decrease in the water level could alter the position of bodies or material aboard the boat. According to Admiral Kuroyedov, Navy Commander-in-Chief, the investigators wanted to see 'everything left as it was'. Russian Northern Fleet spokesman Vladimir Navrotsky said officials only expected to find thirty or forty bodies onboard, since the others had probably been vaporised by the massive explosions aboard the nuclear sub. Responsibility was now shifting from the salvage consortium and the Russian Navy to the prosecutor-general's office. Igor Dygalo, the navy's indefatigable press spokesman, told Interfax that from now on, all information to the media would come via the prosecutor's office.

Gradually, as the dock drained during the course of 23 October, more and more of the *Kursk*'s outer hull became exposed to the naked eye. At first, only the conning tower, with its shattered glass windows on the bridge and Russia's emblematic double-headed eagle, could be seen above the water-line. Then, as more of the submarine came into view later in the afternoon, Prosecutor-General Vladimir Ustinov led senior navy officials and forty investigators on to the *Kursk*'s deck. Before stepping on to the submarine, Ustinov and his colleagues observed a moment's silence in honour of the dead. First on board the *Kursk* was Gleb Lyachin, son of Captain Gennady Lyachin, late commander of the submarine. Then followed Ustinov, Admiral Kuroyedov, Admiral Popov and the large team of investigators, including explosive, radiation, legal and fire experts, forensic medical specialists, biologists and criminologists. Lyachin's son and the others managed to walk down the deck as far as the fourth compartment. Further forward, the hull had simply been blown apart.

By Thursday 25th the *Kursk* had emerged fully from the receding water. In the early hours a two-centimetre hole was drilled in the submarine's fifth compartments to measure radiation levels emitting from the reactors. Engineers installed gutters channelled to collectors to prevent any irradiated water reaching Kola Bay. A first team of investigators, including six military prosecutors, chemical, biological, radiation and other specialists, then prepared to enter the submarine's hull. They would have to wear protective suits and gas masks to protect themselves against the toxic fumes which had built up within the submarine over the past fourteen months. With tons of unexploded weaponry and twin nuclear reactors onboard the team faced an extremely hazardous mission. During the first day, the investigators recovered four bodies from the *Kursk*'s ninth compartment, where the twenty-three survivors of the first blast had retreated. Prosecutor-General Ustinov told Russian television that what he had seen defied description. 'The clearest example of the massive destruction . . . can be seen in the first three compartments where there is a pile of twisted metal,' Ustinov said. 'It is a very, very remarkable sight.' Work was now going on around the clock to retrieve the bodies. Fears that the remains would be unrecognisable after fourteen months in the frigid water seemed unfounded. Those recovered could be identified visually, and had been remarkably well preserved in their watery tomb. Experts dismissed claims that the Granit missiles might accidentally be fired, citing the lack of necessary electric power in the submarine.

Film released by the prosecutor-general on 28 October showed the extent of the damage to the *Kursk*. The footage showed that much of the submarine had become a mass of mangled metal. 'I would like to stress that what was going on in the compartments was hell, a hell which you can only try to imagine,' Ustinov declared. Russian experts estimated the temperature in the fire's epicentre reached 8,000°C, and the whole sub was flooded within eight hours. Fires had raged in all sections apart from the reactor compartment. The investigators searching for bodies had been carefully selected and psychologically screened, but even so a number found it impossible to carry on. 'We investigators are, generally speaking, hard people used to various aspects of life, including death, corpses and the like. But the tragedy of the submarine is a difficult case,' said Ustinov. It had taken a year to select and train the investigators and 'not everyone stood the test'. The prosecutor-general went on: 'Most psychologically firm people passed muster – top experts, still young but highly professional.' Northern Fleet spokesman Captain Vladimir Navrotsky said that those entering the *Kursk* faced an onerous task: 'We have picked the strongest men for the job, but it's hard to say whether they will be able to endure the mess inside,' he said. They would be walking into a nightmare. In spite of their training and psychological preparation, some of the experts found the scenes aboard the *Kursk* so horrific they had to be replaced.

By Friday 2 November, fifty-five submariners' bodies had been recovered and forty-five identified. Thirty-nine of those found had been returned to their relatives. A thousand mourners attended a funeral ceremony in St Petersburg on Saturday 17 November for eleven *Kursk* submariners. The submariners joined Dmitri Kolesnikov and Alexander Brazhkin, buried at Serafimov cemetery twelve months before. The eleven submariners came from Russia, the Caspian, the Crimea and elsewhere in the Ukraine, but their families had asked for them to be buried at Serafimov alongside their colleagues. Sergei, Captain Third Rank Vasily Isayenko's fifteen-year-old son, attended his father's funeral wearing his naval cadet's uniform. Also present in the deep snow were the parents of Senior Lieutenant Alexei Mityayev, who had lived on wild mushrooms before going to sea on the *Kursk* for the last time in August 2000. Vladimir and Marina, who lived in St Petersburg, had a chance to bid a proper farewell to their son. His mother touched Alexei's forehead, and whispered goodbye. Vladimir said that when he identified his son's body 'my wife and I both felt that the weight which had hung on our souls for a year fell right off'.

There appeared to be some confusion among the Russian authorities about the prospects of getting to the bottom of the *Kursk* disaster. In early October, President Putin was quoted pledging that everything possible would be done 'to reveal and show to the public the true causes of this tragedy'. At the same time, Russian Prosecutor-General Vladimir Ustinov was also promising to reveal all. 'There must be no "blank spots" in this tragic story. The relatives and the dear ones of the seamen who died, as well as all Russians, have the right to know the truth, no matter how bitter it might be,' he said in an interview with *Rossiskaya Gazeta*. He assured the newspaper that the investigators would try to find answers to all the questions surrounding the disaster. However, that would only be possible after a 'detailed examination of all material evidence obtained from the submarine'. A week later, Ustinov told the press that there will be 'no motives, including political ones, for concealing what caused the death of the heroic seamen'.

He had already obtained all the relevant documents from the Northern Fleet and from Russia's naval command relating to the tragedy. Only state secrets would be withheld, and the investigators' conclusions would be made public. Criminal cases would be instituted against guilty parties. 'If the guilt of officials is revealed during the investigation – officials who nonetheless exerted every effort after the disaster to speed up lifting the submarine – no exceptions will be made for them either, whatever ranks they may have,' Ustinov added. Among witnesses already questioned were senior commanders in the Northern Fleet and the Russian Navy, as well as top personnel from the Rubin Marine Engineering Design Bureau.

Deputy PM Ilya Klebanov was meanwhile trying to play down expectations of what the investigation would divulge. It was his belief, he said on 23 October, that 'nothing new will be found in the raised submarine' that could assist 'in understanding the causes of the *Kursk* catastrophe'. Ustinov now agreed. 'Without examining the bow of the boat, it is impossible to clarify the cause of the disaster.' He said that he had told Klebanov all along that the investigators could not come to a final conclusion until the bow section had been recovered. Klebanov sowed further confusion by changing his mind yet again ten days later. 'I cannot say with one hundred per cent certainty, but it is likely that we might obtain data making it possible to find out what caused the *Kursk* disaster,' he said on that occasion. The truth is that the Russians didn't have a clue whether they would find out why the submarine had sunk. One minute they hedged their bets by saying they would have to wait until the bow was raised, another they were quite bullish about discovering the reasons for the disaster. They didn't really know what they would find aboard the *Kursk*. It was possible, they knew, that they might have to wait until they raised the remaining bow fragments. The earliest that could happen would be the spring or summer of 2002. There was still some doubt about whether the Russian government would want to spend another $65 million on retrieving what was left of the bow.

The prosecutor-general told a press conference on Wednesday 24 October that the Russians were still sticking to their three main theories for the accident, first propounded fourteen months before.

'The analyses, which we will conduct on the submarine, will give the answer with seventy to eighty per cent certainty as to why the explosions took place,' Ustinov now said. 'The final answer will be given after the remaining compartment is raised from the seabed. Some parts of the torpedo compartment have been raised just recently, but the whole section is scheduled to be raised by the spring,' he added. In reality, the operation would take much longer, with work scheduled to begin in the summer. Indicating the broad scope of the inquiry, Ustinov also promised a full investigation into how the fateful Barents Sea naval exercises had been conducted and prepared for. Various rumours circulated about how the navy had made many mistakes before and during the course of the exercises preceding the *Kursk's* loss. All this would be fully explored. Investigators hoped to discover the submarine's log books, journals, notes and the boat's recorders, which are usually switched on during military exercises.

Opinion polls showed the Russian public overwhelmingly supported the lift and salvage operation. For President Putin and his administration, the polls were a huge endorsement of the government's policy to raise the *Kursk*. It also showed that his strategy to regain the political initiative following the initial public relations disaster was a great success. President Putin's reputation had been substantially rehabilitated in the public's eyes. At a projected cost of $130 million, Putin probably thought it was cheap at the price.

In some ways the haul of information from the *Kursk* was disappointing. The boat's logs were found in the fifth compartment in early November, and left to dry out. Admiral Popov told journalists on 11 November that the logs would be of no help in determining the cause of the disaster. He said the notes were 'purely technical and are of no use as far as the cause of the catastrophe is concerned'. Earlier, a farewell message in a bottle had been found aboard the *Kursk*. It was Senior Warrant Officer Oleg Borisov's personal message to his wife and son, and was sealed in an empty mineral water bottle. The message contained no clues about the accident. In the New Year, on 3 January 2002, investigators removed secret documents and encrypting equipment from the *Kursk*. Although the Russians were relieved to retrieve the material, it again told the investigators nothing. Three automatic data recorders or 'black boxes' had earlier been discovered in the submarine's central section, and were sent to the St Petersburg-based Prometei research centre for analysis. Two other empty black boxes were also recovered. Around eighty hours of recordings were uncovered in total. So far seventy-nine submariners had been recovered from the *Kursk*, six of whom remained unidentified. All that had been found of Captain Gennady Lyachin was his captain's suit and his ID card. The work to retrieve the submariners' bodies was set to last for months.

The twenty-two Granit missiles onboard the *Kursk* were a real cause for concern. They had been lying on the seabed for over a year. However, as the silos appeared undamaged, the Northern Fleet hoped the weapons could be removed without any undue risk. If the Granits blew up, they would obliterate the Roslyakovo shipyard and perhaps a good part of the port town with it. The Russians turned out to be wrong – some of the missile silos *had* been damaged by the explosions. Initially the unloading went smoothly, and five of the missiles were removed apparently intact. The situation abruptly changed on 5 November, as personnel working in the *Kursk* were hurriedly evacuated after 150 kilograms of TNT were discovered. The explosive came from torpedo warheads which had been blown from the first compartment into the boat's second and third sections. Investigators also found that the massive explosions had blown machinery and equipment from the second section through to the fourth compartment. From that day on, the investigators and other personnel worked only in daylight.

By 19 November, 400 tonnes of ammunition, nineteen fragments in all, had been removed from inside the submarine. A further 44 kilograms of explosives were removed by the end of the month (bringing the total found to 444 kilos), plus a total of 550 tonnes of mangled steel and thirteen service pistols. Investigators continued their slow search, fearing yet more explosives could be hidden beneath the twisted metal in the second, third and fourth compartments. The threat of explosions aboard the *Kursk*'s wreck was real: during early August, while the divers were working on the lifting operation, there had been three small explosions inside the *Kursk*, and when Russian

divers entered the fourth compartment on 4 August, some munitions
had exploded. Luckily no one was hurt. Two other minor explosions
occurred when foreign divers were inside the wreck, but the most they
suffered was painful eardrums.

Silos containing six missiles near the bow were badly deformed by
the explosions that rocked the *Kursk*, and some on the starboard side
had filled with water. Sixteen missiles were recovered from the submarine without complications. The Russians decided to leave the
other six missiles onboard and move them together with the submarine to a designated secret naval scrapyard. The entire submarine and
the damaged missile silos were taken to the Nerpa shipyard, situated at
the mouth of the Olenya Guba bay in the Murmansk region. There
the missiles and the *Kursk* herself, the former pride of the Northern
Fleet, would be scrapped as part of the United States Congress's Co-
operative Threat Reduction Programme. The $3.1 billion project was
established in 1997 with the aim of scrapping missiles, their submarine
and silo launch systems, and chemical weapons. The American taxpayer was thus contributing to the *Kursk*'s ignominious demise.
Sevmash, an enormous industrial engineering complex in
Severodvinsk, twenty-two miles from Arkhangelsk in north-west
Russia, was also involved in the disposal operation. With a 30,000-
strong workforce, Sevmash is Russia's largest submarine manufacturer.
Since the end of the Cold War, orders for new submarines had
slumped spectacularly, and Sevmash had tried to switch to civilian
production, shipbuilding, heavy-duty oil and gas equipment, and the
manufacture and disposal of military equipment. It still has the capacity to manufacture nuclear and diesel-electric submarines up to 25,000
tons, as well as surface ships and other vessels. The Russian government can rarely afford to build them.

The *Kursk*'s forward section was now sealed, and the whole submarine was prepared for transportation by floating dock to the Nerpa
scrapyard, where the break-up was planned to last around three
months. It had been decided that the cruise missiles would not be
returned to service. They were to be dismantled and broken up for
spares. The salvaged Granits were sent to a Northern Fleet armaments
depot, where their warheads and boosters were removed. Some

components of the missile firing system and other parts would be sent for further analysis by special weapons designers. After the submarine's nuclear fuel had been removed, the nuclear reactors would be cut from the hull and deposited in Sayda Bay, one of the Northern Fleet's bases on the Kola Peninsula. The missile silos themselves would be disposed of at a naval test site. Part of the sub's conning tower, including the emblem of the two-headed eagle, was destined for a memorial in honour of the crew in the southern city of Kursk.

Saturday, 23 March 2002 saw the funeral service of Captain Gennady Lyachin and six other crew members in St Petersburg. Hundreds of mourners came to pay their last respects. After attending so many funerals for other *Kursk* submariners, Gennady's widow Irina, and his son, Gleb, could bid a final farewell to their own loved one. Admiral Kuroyedov told the mourners that the *Kursk*'s crew had forestalled a nuclear catastrophe. 'Today we say goodbye to the heroes of our fleet,' he said. 'At the cost of their own lives, the commander and his team saved hundreds of thousands of other people's lives in northern Russia and in the Scandinavian countries by preventing a possible explosion of the nuclear reactor.' The navy was convinced the crew had manually shut down the reactors, preventing a nuclear meltdown. Broadcast on national television, the St Petersburg funeral service was the last burial ceremony for the *Kursk* submariners held in Russia. Russian warships lowered their flags to half-mast as a sign of respect, and a guard of honour fired a gun salute during the service.

Gennady and the other submariners had only been identified the week before, as the investigators wound up their gruesome task. Just 3 of the 118 crew members remained unidentified, far fewer than anybody had expected. Fears that many of the crew had been 'vaporised' were unfounded. Most of the crew had died by drowning, and many had also been badly burned.

A week before Gennady Lyachin was buried, the Northern Fleet announced it had established a special team to retrieve the *Kursk*'s bow. The operation to recover the bow from the bottom of the Barents Sea was scheduled for summer 2002. As the bow was so badly damaged, the plan was to cut it up where it lay and raise it in pieces weighing between five and twelve tonnes. Igor Spassky, head of the Rubin Design Bureau, was responsible for presenting the plan to raise what was left of the *Kursk*, which this time would involve only Russian divers. With the dry-dock examination of the *Kursk* completed in April 2002, the nuclear submarine embarked on its last journey to the Nerpa scrapyard at Snezhnogorsk on Friday 26 April. As the *Kursk* made ready to leave, Murmansk deputies in the regional legislature bitterly complained that the state had not paid for the work carried out at Roslyakovo shipyard. The government owed Roslyakovo 150 million roubles or $5 million for the use of the dry dock, and the deputies wanted the bill paid.

Its break-up for scrap was a humiliating end for the *Kursk*, which had only been launched back in May 1994, but it was symptomatic of the failure of the modern Russian state. The *Kursk* had been built as a symbol of Russian pride. It had been a state-of-the-art submarine, but it had been maintained on a shoestring, and had only been in dry dock once in five years. What had started with so much hope and ambition had become a farce. The *Kursk* had meant to embody Russia's Great Power pretensions. Roman Kolesnikov, Captain-Lieutenant Dmitri Kolesnikov's father, was scathing in his criticism of the Russian Navy. 'The fleet's repairs base has collapsed,' he said. 'The repair workers don't get paid and go on strike. Then the boat's commanders do the repairs themselves. They sit there all day and night doing the repairs. The boats are leaking.' Now the Russian government couldn't even afford to pay the bill for scrapping the submarine. From superpower to impoverished Third World country, in less than a generation. That was the story of the *Kursk*, and its sorry end at the Nerpa scrapyard. The *Kursk*'s fate really did represent Russia's lost pride.

# 6

# Retribution

As the investigators continued their work aboard the shattered wreck, the Russian Navy's day of reckoning came ever closer. For sixteen months the navy's High Command and the government's Commission of Inquiry had tried to maintain the fiction that the *Kursk* had been sunk after a collision with a foreign submarine. This self-delusion in the face of the facts could not be maintained indefinitely. As the prosecutor-general prepared an interim report for President Putin, a raft of senior Russian Navy officers faced the sack for incompetence and deceit. Deputy Prime Minister Ilya Klebanov felt his own position in government becoming increasingly insecure. The purge, when it came, was shocking in its scope. Nothing like it had been seen in Russia since Mikhail Gorbachev used the landing of Matthias Rust's light plane in Red Square in 1987 to purge military hardliners. Prosecutor-General Vladimir Ustinov presented his report to Putin in the Kremlin on 1 December 2001. Also present at the meeting were Defence Minister Sergei Ivanov, Navy Commander-in-Chief Admiral Kuroyedov and the Chief of the General Staff of Russia's armed forces, Anatoly Kvashnin. The prosecutor-general's report was lacerating. Ustinov told Putin his investigations had discovered serious derelictions of duty both in the day-to-day work and combat training at all levels of command in the Northern Fleet. There were 'major breaches' during preparations for the August 2000 naval exercises in the Barents Sea. Much had gone wrong at sea, in chart rooms and in planning sessions.

According to Ustinov, although they had not discovered a direct link to the disaster, it was plain that 'traditional negligence' had caused the sinking. The president told his colleagues he was appalled by the navy's lack of preparation for the Barents Sea exercises. Putin was genuinely furious with the navy for landing him in the middle of a major crisis, but Ustinov's report also presented him with a useful political gift. The Russian president was in effect handed a list of scapegoats who could take the blame for the *Kursk*'s loss, conveniently getting him and the rest of the government off the hook. Although the High Command and the Northern Fleet had conspired to keep the president blissfully ignorant in the early days of the tragedy, it was not their fault that the Russian Navy had been chronically underfunded for over a decade. Even better from Putin's point of view, a purge would allow him to get rid of some dead wood and send a powerful message to the rest of the navy and other armed forces. His purge would show the services not only who was boss, but that old anti-reformist and obstructionist ways would not be tolerated by the Kremlin. Putin wanted reform, and he didn't want any more opposition from the Soviet old guard. Some of the military top brass were opposed to cuts in Russia's armed forces, particularly the nuclear strategic deterrent, and were fundamentally suspicious of Putin's policy of cosying up to the West. But Putin was determined there should be a new, slimmed-down professional military, and those who didn't like it could get out before they were pushed.

Within hours of the Kremlin meeting, Putin had demoted three senior admirals and sacked another eleven senior naval officers. Admiral Popov, Vice-Admiral Motsak and Vice-Admiral Burtsev, head of the Northern Fleet's 1st Submarine Flotilla, were demoted. Rear-Admiral Verich, head of the Russian Navy's Search and Rescue Department, was sacked, as was Captain Alexander Teslenko, head of the Northern Fleet's rescue service. Other heads to roll were Flotilla Chief of Staff Rear-Admiral Valery Filatov, Divisional Commander Rear-Admiral Mikhail Kuznetsov, Deputy Divisional Commander Captain Victor Kobelev, Vice-Admiral Nicolai Mikheyev, Rear-Admiral Valery Panferov, Vice-Admiral Yury Boyarkin, Rear-Admiral Vladimir Khandobin, Rear-Admiral Farit Zinnatullin and Captain Ruben Karakhanov. It was quite a list, and gave the navy an unmistakable broadside from the Kremlin. Vice-Admiral Vladimir Dobroskochenko, a deputy to Popov with thirty years' command experience, was ordered to temporarily take over as commander of the Northern Fleet. For Popov, it was the end of his active naval career. However, following his effective sacking, the head of Murmansk Regional Duma, Pavel Sazhinov, offered Popov the opportunity to represent the region in the Federation Council, or upper house of parliament. Popov agreed to re-invent himself, and became a senator.

Vladimir Putin immediately issued a press statement through the Kremlin's presidential press service. The president said the investigation into the *Kursk* accident had already provided enough evidence to 'draw a rather definite conclusion on the quality of preparations for and organisation of military exercises and the organisation of search-and-rescue operations'. Although the investigation continued to pursue all theories, the president admitted that the suggestion that the sinking was caused by a foreign submarine was looking decidedly shaky. 'It should be admitted that, despite the large amount of work done, no objective evidence proving this theory has been received up to now,' Putin stated.

A grim-faced Admiral Kuroyedov appeared on Russian television to explain the sackings and demotions. Kuroyedov was lucky to escape the axe himself. The commander-in-chief told the media that the prosecutor-general's interim report had discovered serious flaws in the Northern Fleet's combat training. On 3 December, Chief of the General Staff Anatoly Kvashnin went further and claimed the purge had nothing to do with the Barents Sea accident itself. He said the dismissals and demotions were simply due to serious failings in the organisation of the fleet's training activities. Few believed him. Kvashnin did reveal that the High Command had been investigating routine work and combat training in the Northern Fleet for the past eighteen months, even before the *Kursk* sinking.

Alexander Golts, a well-regarded independent defence analyst in Moscow, scoffed at claims that the high-ranking sackings were unconnected to the *Kursk* disaster. 'Putin had to punish these people,' Golts told Reuters. The link between the dismissals and the sinking was clear. The navy had failed to explain why its rescue operation had only begun twelve hours after the explosions had been picked up, he added. On the same day, 3 December, the newspaper *Izvestia* reported that the explanation of the Northern Fleet's twelve hours of inaction lay in the fact that it was so used to constantly malfunctioning equipment. Losing radio contact with the *Kursk* for half a day was not regarded as anything out of the ordinary. 'The state of affairs being what it is, it is only natural that any fleet exercises become a gamble with death,' *Izvestia* wrote.

'Between 1990 and 2000, the Russian Navy's ships were effectively berthed, and it was naïve at best to demand accident-free operation from sailors who had been without practice for years. There is no national programme envisaging the navy's development.' Under these circumstances, the newspaper continued, it was sensible to listen to certain naval officers who were saying that 'the heads of the General Staff are cleansing the navy of figures capable of opposing plans to reform the army and navy. One of the reform concepts has it that Russia does not need the oceanic fleet, which even the Soviet Union financed at one-third of the required amount.'

The sackings were a complete contrast to the warm congratulations bestowed on the salvage teams a few days before. More than a hundred of those involved in the salvage operation were invited to the Kremlin and given bravery awards, including two Russian divers who had spent 870 hours over a hundred metres below the surface of the Barents Sea. Franz van Seumeren, president of the Mammoet salvage consortium, was among those present, and was moved by the 'warm and sincere way' the Russian president thanked all those who had taken part. Praising the 'fantastic and unbelievable' work that had been done, Putin proudly pointed out that of the 200-odd submarines on the bottom of the world's oceans, the *Kursk* was the first nuclear sub ever to be retrieved. The project was 'an example of unique international co-operation' the president said, raising 'great human expectations'. Putin reminded everyone that the lifting operation had initially encountered a lot of opposition. 'Navy officers tried to dissuade me. Members of the commission can remember the meeting where not one person was in favour of it,' he recalled. The cost, seemingly insurmountable technical problems, and the navy tradition of viewing wrecks as sea graves, had led many to counsel against the project. Putin's message was clear: I was right to insist the *Kursk* should be raised and everyone else was wrong. The fact that Putin's gamble had paid off gave the president more confidence in his own political judgement. Putin was at last becoming a true leader.

Concluding the Kremlin reception, Putin pledged his government would learn the 'necessary conclusions' from the catastrophe. 'We need to ensure safe conditions for sailors and establish a reliable search-and-rescue service,' the president said. New and more exacting standards were needed for future ship construction. Russia, the president declared, must 'renew and refurbish' its navy and submarine fleet. The sackings of the admirals and senior captains came four days after the back-slapping reception – some people had not done such a wonderful job after all. But the president still refused to issue a definitive statement on who should be blamed for the *Kursk* disaster.

President Putin also needed to do something urgently to restore morale in the navy. On Tuesday 4 December, three days after the naval purge, he found the perfect photo-opportunity. Putin attended the launch of Russia's latest nuclear submarine, the *Gepard* ('Cheetah'), in the Sevmash shipyard in Severodvinsk on the White Sea, the same shipyard which had launched the *Kursk* seven years earlier. Putin told his Cabinet the day before that military spending would be next year's priority, as the government embarked on a 'serious and ambitious programme of military reform'. Arriving in Severodvinsk, the president met the crew aboard the new submarine, which entered service flying St Andrew's blue and white Russian fleet flag. 'I congratulate you on the launch of your submarine, the navy has received a ship it can be proud of,' Putin told the assembled submariners. Admiral

Kuroyedov and Chief of the General Staff Anatoly Kvashnin also attended the ceremony.

The multi-purpose *Gepard* is one of the quietest and fastest submarines in the world. The new sub was hailed as 'Russia's first nuclear-powered submarine of the twenty-first century', and Western experts believe the *Gepard* could be as quiet and fast as America's best Los Angeles-class submarines. The Russian sub could dive deeper and had greater firepower than the US boats.

Named after a First World War boat, the 110-metre-long *Gepard* displaces 12,270 tonnes, can dive to a depth of 600 metres, and can reach 35 knots submerged. The submarine's armament includes twenty-four nuclear-capable Granit cruise missiles and a Strela (Arrow) anti-aircraft weapons system. The Granits have a range of over 1,800 miles. The boat has a crew of sixty-three, and although it is smaller than the *Kursk*, the *Gepard* is regarded as the most formidable and up-to-date submarine in the Russian fleet. Admiral Kuroyedov said it was 'symbolic for the lost boat to be replaced by a new submarine'. Russia, he added, was building a new fleet which 'will be a tribute to the sailors who died on the *Kursk*'. The whole ceremony symbolised the regeneration of the Russian Navy. The *Kursk* was gone, but in its place was a more powerful, sleeker and capable nuclear submarine. It was as if the Russian Navy was being reincarnated in a new, more dynamic form. Russia was trying to restore its lost pride, and bury its disastrous recent past. The message was clear: look to the future, not the past. Russia is still a world power to be reckoned with.

In January 2002, the Russian authorities finally admitted that the *Kursk* sinking had not been caused by a collision with a foreign submarine. Deputy PM Klebanov swallowed his pride and acknowledged that experts examining the *Kursk* had ruled out his pet collision theory. In an interview with Interfax, reported on 22 January, Klebanov said that close examination of the hull showed that no collision had taken place. Instead, he now believed that the accident was the result of the deterioration of the Russian armed forces through the 1990s. Klebanov hoped the exact cause of the disaster would be known later in the year. His days as deputy prime minister were becoming numbered.

Russian Prosecutor-General Vladimir Ustinov came out with a blistering attack on the country's military culture in general and the navy's in particular. On 11 February Ustinov said the *Kursk's* sinking highlighted the sloppiness of the country's military. He ordered a wide-ranging investigation into senior naval officers' compliance with rules and regulations. Pointing the finger at the navy's High Command, Ustinov suggested there had been violations of combat training regulations and irresponsibility by senior officers bordering on criminal negligence. The navy's top brass became increasingly nervous as Ustinov's criminal investigation focused on their incompetence and indifference. Any hope that the navy's senior officers could hide behind allegations of a collision with a NATO sub or even a faulty torpedo were looking increasingly like wishful thinking. Arriving in Murmansk on 18 February, Ustinov categorically denied the allegation that a foreign submarine was involved in the *Kursk* sinking.

For Ilya Klebanov, the game was now up. He was sacked as deputy prime minister the same day Ustinov arrived in Murmansk. As a face-saver Klebanov kept his second post as minister for industry, science and technology. Just as the fourteen admirals and senior officers had served as useful military scapegoats, Klebanov played the role of the political sacrificial lamb. His narrow-minded adherence to the collision theory, pushed by the navy's High Command and the secret services, had not helped his political career. Once it was universally proved to be tosh, his position became untenable. His Commission of Inquiry had discovered nothing, proved nothing, and promoted far-fetched theories designed to save the navy's tarnished reputation. Ustinov and his team of investigators, on the other hand, enhanced their reputations and gained in public and political esteem.

Putin only demoted Klebanov, rather than sacking him outright from the government, on the grounds that he was not personally responsible for any of the failures which led to the *Kursk's* demise. Klebanov's failings were that he had mishandled the public relations side of the commission, and some observers had cast serious doubt on his own competence. Sacking Klebanov completely from the government would have been overly harsh from Putin's point of view. Under-achieving politicians are demoted the world over, and in Putin's case his displeasure with Klebanov reflected public dissatisfaction with the deputy prime minister's role in the *Kursk* tragedy.

Back in Murmansk Admiral Kuroyedov admitted for the first time the *Kursk* may have sunk after a practice torpedo using unstable fuel exploded onboard. He stopped short of categorically blaming the torpedo for the tragedy, but confessed the Russian Navy had 'placed unfounded trust' in the weapon, which was propelled by highly volatile hydrogen peroxide. Kuroyedov said hydrogen peroxide was 'highly unstable and its contact with certain metals may cause unpredictable consequences'. Kuroyedov told the assembled press he had ordered the weapon removed from other Russian submarines.

In a revelation that undermined several versions of the *Kursk* disaster, Russian officials said the submarine's practice torpedo contained an experimental battery, but was in all other respects standard. There had been no testing of fancy or new torpedoes aboard the *Kursk*. It was simply the old type of torpedo traditionally used by the Russian Navy, which had blown up after an internal leak followed by an explosive chemical reaction. Russian officials denied claims by some of the submariners' relatives and the media that the crew had reported problems with the torpedo to their superiors.

With the prosecutor-general sitting next to him, Admiral Kuroyedov insisted investigators were still considering a collision or hitting a mine as possible reasons for the disaster. Ustinov refused to play the navy's game and flatly contradicted Kuroyedov by telling journalists that investigators had found no evidence of any vessel in the *Kursk*'s vicinity at the time of the accident. Instead the prosecutor-general singled out 'serious violations by both Northern Fleet chiefs and the *Kursk* crew'. In Ustinov's opinion, it was 'traditional negligence' which was the main cause of the disaster. With his investigation all but complete, there were 'practically no more mysteries about what had happened aboard the submarine'. The prosecutor-general's accusation of negligence was partly based on his assertion that the *Kursk* had gone to sea with both its emergency antenna and buoy incapacitated. The previous October, Ustinov had specifically ruled out the possibility that the crew had been to blame for the explosions which sank the boat. On that occasion he had told RTR television that if there had been a problem with the torpedo, it must have been technical rather than human error. 'The human factor is absent,' he said then, because the crew had no contact with torpedoes except when executing an automatic command to fire them. The negligence Ustinov referred to on 18 February related to the poor organisation of the Barents Sea naval exercises and the state of seaworthiness of the *Kursk* itself.

As well as sacking his admirals and demoting Klebanov, President Putin had other scores to settle. He had not forgotten the drubbing he had received at the hands of the media over the *Kursk*. Putin was determined to crush his opponents and curtail the power of the media controlled by his oligarch adversaries. The president knew this would be a long process, but it was all part of his strategy to centralise power in the hands of the head of state. Yeltsin had allowed the oligarchs to grow too powerful, so much so that they were in a position to almost make or break the president. Putin wanted to re-assert the power of the presidency, and create the conditions for his smooth re-election in 2004. His whole life had taught him that the strength of the state depended on the strength of its leader.

Vladimir Vladimirich Putin was born into a relatively poor working-class family on 7 October 1952 in the Okhta district of north-east Leningrad, now renamed St Petersburg. Putin was born into a city a shadow of its imperial self, in the dying months of Stalin's dictatorship. Stalin had let Peter the Great's city and its 3,000 palaces rot, as he focused his attention on transforming Moscow into a showpiece workers' capital. Over seventy years after the Bolshevik revolution, St Petersburg is just starting to recover from decades of communist neglect. For Putin, life in Peter's 'Window on the West', or the former 'Venice of the North', meant living in a communal flat with several other families, with no hot water and no bathroom. Twenty-five people can often find themselves sharing one bathroom and one toilet in an average communal flat, even today. In his autobiography, *First Person*, Putin describes chasing rats on his staircase. 'Once I spotted a huge rat and pursued it down the hall until I drove it into a corner. Suddenly it lashed out and threw itself at me. It jumped down the landing and down the stairs.'

Vladimir Putin was known as Vovka as a child, and is still called Volodya by his close friends and family. Putin's parents married when they were both seventeen. His father, Vladimir Spirodonovich, served in the Soviet submarine fleet and was assigned to the NKVD, the KGB's precursor, during the Second World War. Fighting behind enemy lines in Estonia, Vladimir senior was badly wounded by a grenade, and left with a permanent limp, but counted himself lucky to be one of only four survivors of his twenty-eight-man unit. Despite his injury, the elder Vladimir was luckier than his wife. Maria Ivanovna was left behind in Leningrad during the infamous Nazi siege of the city, when Leningraders were dying at the rate of 5,000 a day at the height of the blockade. Over 600,000 people died in the siege, most from starvation. Putin's mother only survived because her brother was keeping her alive with his navy rations. 'Then the brother was ordered away somewhere,' Putin recalled, 'and she was on the brink of death. That's no exaggeration. Mama passed out from hunger. They thought she was dead and they even put her with the deceased. She was lucky she came to just in time and groaned. It was a miracle she stayed alive.'

Young Vladimir was his mother's third and only surviving child. Maria had given birth to two boys within a year of each other in the 1930s. One child died in infancy, only a few months old, and another died of diphtheria during the 900-day siege. Vladimir junior was born when his mother was already in her early forties. His mother had a succession of jobs as a laboratory cleaner, working in a bakery and as a janitor. Putin's father was a communist party member and after the war worked as a foreman in a factory making subway trains. The future president's paternal grandfather had been a cook to both Lenin and Stalin in Moscow. Putin remained proud of the fact that his grandfather had survived his close encounter with Uncle Joe. 'Few of those who were with Stalin all the time survived intact. But my grandfather did,' he later boasted.

Small for his age, Volodya was a much-loved late child, although his father was not the demonstrative type. At school, Putin was remembered as a clever but self-contained boy. He was not top of his class, and one schoolmate, Sergei Kudrov, said he was never the centre of attention. 'He preferred to influence events from the distance, a sort of "grey cardinal" as the saying goes . . . He's an introvert,' Kudrov concluded. Throughout his whole life, Putin preferred to remain in the shadows, which probably explains why when the *Kursk* crisis occurred early in his presidency, he wasn't prepared to lead from the front and instinctively avoided the spotlight. While those were admirable qualities for the spy he was to become, it was not what was required of a president at a time of national crisis.

Putin excelled at sport, especially judo, becoming a black belt and the city's judo champion in 1976. Earlier in his life, he had wanted to be a seaman or a pilot. But his ambitions seemed to change after he saw the Russian film *The Sword and the Shield*, about a Russian double-agent in wartime Germany. He started borrowing espionage books from his teachers. Around the time the Red Army crushed the Prague Spring in 1968, the sixteen-year-old Volodya asked to join the KGB. His approach was rebuffed. The KGB recruited the brightest directly from schools themselves, and were suspicious of being approached. A few years later, Putin tried again, this time through a friend whose father was a lieutenant-colonel in the KGB. His patience finally paid off. The KGB advised him to study law at Leningrad University, where he was formally recruited in 1975 after finishing his degree, aged twenty-two.

Putin's first assignment was spent working as an intelligence officer in Leningrad, where he met his future wife, Lydmilla. Lydmilla was then an air hostess, living in her native Kaliningrad. Valery Golubev, a former KGB officer who shared an office with Putin for three years, recalled his colleague was an 'expert in human psychology'. Putin looked for people's weaknesses and was 'very sensitive to what people felt and thought and would pay great attention to details about their troubles', Golubev recalled. The future president was learning the vital listening skills and awareness of others' needs that would be so invaluable to him at the court of tsar Boris Yeltsin. Putin's training as a secret agent would help him in later life to become a consummate courtier.

Putin married Lydmilla in 1983, and the couple were posted to Dresden in East Germany three years later. A posting to East Germany was not what an intelligence officer's dreams were made of. A high-flyer would hope and expect a posting to the West, perhaps Washington, Bonn, London or Paris. Oleg Kalugin, former head of Soviet counter-intelligence, is brutal about Putin's career path in the KGB. 'Any assignment to eastern Europe,' Kalugin said, 'East Germany included, was a sign of someone's failing or lack of abilities which would provide for him an opportunity to travel westwards. His record in the KGB is zero. He is a nonentity in the KGB.'

Putin's days in Dresden were spent recruiting Stasi and East German policemen. His official job was deputy director of the Society of German–Soviet Friendship, based in Dresden and Leipzig. Putin was a capable but not outstanding spy. He didn't see the fall of the Berlin Wall coming, and had to walk around with secret papers stuffed inside his clothing. By early 1990, his family (he now had two daughters) was packing up to return to Leningrad. After he left East Germany, one of his agents exposed one of his networks of fifteen spies working for Moscow. Usually, a foreign intelligence officer would expect promotion on his return to Russia. Instead, Putin languished at the middle rank of lieutenant-colonel. Coming back to Leningrad, he moved back into his parents' flat in Okhta. He took up a minor post as vice-rector of Leningrad University, and did some driving as a chauffeur for Galina Staravoitova, a reformist politician who was later assassinated. Putin remained on the KGB's payroll.

As luck would have it, he was recruited to work for Anatoly Sobchak, the reformist mayor who had been elected in May 1990. Sobchak had trawled through his old students' rolls in the law faculty at Leningrad University, where he had previously lectured. The mayor was looking for political and administrative assistants. Sticking close to Sobchak's coat-tails, Putin rose to be deputy mayor in 1991, an unelected position. During the hardline coup against Gorbachev in 1991, Putin was conveniently on leave. He didn't go near the pro-democracy defence headquarters set up by the city Duma. Characteristically, Putin waited to see which way the wind was blowing. When the putsch failed, he finally quit the KGB, although he retained his communist party membership card until the party was banned by President Boris Yeltsin in November 1992. Putin later admitted he had a lot of respect for the KGB boss and coup leader, Vladimir Kryuchkov. The plotters' aims were 'noble', according to Putin, as they sought to prevent the disintegration of the USSR. He also admitted he was uneasy about the direction of the democracy movement at the time: 'I was from the democrats' milieu. But it got worrying. Remember what kind of situation the security organs were in then. [The democrats] wanted to destroy, to break, to lacerate them, they called for the agency's lists to be opened up, for the secrets to be revealed.' At heart, as we have seen, Putin was a KGB man. His instincts were on the side of the security services, and for the preservation of the 'secret state'. During the *Kursk* tragedy, he sided with the navy's desire to protect the nuclear sub's military secrets. Individual liberty, life itself, was secondary to the need to protect the state. This was the KGB's code, and it remained Putin's for the rest of his life.

Putin ran Anatoly Sobchak's re-election campaign in 1996, but the latter was trounced by Vladimir Yakovlev. Sobchak's city administration had become mired in allegations of corruption and criminality. Sobchak fled criminal investigation and went into self-imposed exile in Paris, as the authorities looked into allegations that he had procured expensive city-owned flats for his relatives. Sobchak attempted a political comeback in the 1999 Duma elections, but failed to be elected in his old stamping-ground of St Petersburg. Nevertheless, he told me he remained proud of Vladimir Putin, his protégé, and backed his bid for the presidency.

Once more out of a job, Putin found himself at a loss. However, once again connections helped him. Anatoly Chubais, a deputy prime minister under President Boris Yeltsin and architect of the voucher privatisation system, found Putin a job in the Kremlin. It was no coincidence that Chubais was also from St Petersburg, and had worked with Putin in the city's administration. Putin's move to the Kremlin was assisted by Pavel Borodin, who was in charge of the Kremlin's property department. The Swiss authorities later issued an international warrant against Borodin for money laundering, and he was arrested at JFK airport in New York in January 2001 and extradited to

Switzerland. His arrest led to a formal diplomatic protest from the Russian government, who paid his bail. Putin's inexorable rise continued in a series of administrative posts in the Kremlin, including deputy head of the property department, deputy head of management in the presidential administration, head of the FSB, secretary of the Security Council and finally prime minister in August 1999.

'Putin's great talent is knowing how to please his bosses and getting noticed and trusted by them,' said Dmitri Travnin, a St Petersburg analyst and veteran Putin-watcher. 'He managed that with Sobchak and then with Yeltsin. He accomplishes it quietly by performing competently, efficiently, practically. He's the ultimate pragmatist.' By all accounts he was noticed by Tatyana Dyachenko first, Yeltsin's influential daughter, then Yeltsin himself.

Before being appointed prime minister, Putin's Kremlin career had seemed largely unremarkable. As the Federal Security Bureau's seventh boss in eight years, Putin instituted no major reforms or changes. However, while installed in the Lubyanka he had carried out one outstanding operation. The FSB had videotaped the then prosecutor-general, Yury Skuratov, or at least a close lookalike, in bed with two prostitutes. Putin ensured the tapes were leaked to the press, torpedoing Skuratov's investigation into up to 800 allegedly corrupt government officials. The trail led up to the highest reaches of the Kremlin, including President Boris Yeltsin and his 'family' of cronies. By destroying Skuratov's credibility and his career, Putin earned the Yeltsin family's gratitude and proved his unquestioning loyalty. To everyone's general surprise, in August 1999, Yeltsin sacked Sergei Stephasin and appointed the virtually unknown Vladimir Putin as his fifth prime minister in seventeen months. Yeltsin went further, astonishing the media, by announcing Putin as his preferred successor. On the back of re-invading Chechnya that September, Putin's approval rating went up from 2 per cent to over 70 per cent by the time of the presidential election the following March.

Putin, described by one analyst as a 'nobody from nowhere', was given Russia's presidency on a plate. Unlike Russia's other leading political figures, Putin had never before been elected to a single post or public office. His lack of political and leadership experience was painfully obvious in the immediate aftermath of the *Kursk* tragedy. However, Yeltsin had at last found a prime minister he felt he could trust. Following Yeltsin's dramatic resignation on New Year's Eve 1999, and the announcement of Vladimir Putin as acting president, the new leader's very first act was to sign a decree granting Yeltsin and his family immunity. Boris Yeltsin had chosen his successor well. The ailing former president was awarded a generous pension, state security protection, medical care for him and his family, and allowed to keep hold of his state *dacha*. The cost to the Russian taxpayer of looking after the Yeltsin family is over $1.4 million per year.

Yeltsin's early resignation brought the presidential election forward from the summer to late March. Most of the media backed Putin's campaign, including Berezovsky's ORT television. Parties aligned with Putin, such as the 'Unity' election bloc, spectacularly triumphed in the Duma elections, giving the Kremlin an effective majority in the lower house. Vladimir Gusinsky and NTV, which backed the opposition, were soon to face the Kremlin's wrath. Yevgeny Kiselyov, general director of NTV, said Kremlin officials had threatened Media Most's managers and editors a year before the presidential campaign. 'They made it clear that we either support the candidate that the Kremlin was going to choose or we have trouble,' Kiselyov recalled. NTV opted for trouble. Putin won the presidential election on the first ballot on 26 March, easily beating off a challenge from communist leader Gennady Zyuganov. The speed of Putin's ascent evidently surprised the ex-KGB agent. It positively astounded everyone else, including his wife.

Vladimir Putin, then aged forty-seven, was not really trained or ready to run the country in March 2000. He had been plucked from obscurity, and had only held a political post for seven months before being elected president. It was no wonder he made a hash of the first week of the *Kursk* disaster. His background had hardly prepared him for the rigours of political life. Like the rest of the military and security establishment, brought up in the old Soviet ways, his first reaction was supreme indifference. Putin was genuinely and unpleasantly shocked by the ensuing public and media outrage. He had learned some hard lessons then. One of the lessons was to bring the Russian media to heel.

As president, Putin felt he epitomised the strength and vitality of the state. He wanted to re-create a 'Great Russia' with a revitalised state apparatus. Even before the *Kursk* crisis there were moves afoot to strengthen the power of the government and specifically the institution of the presidency. During the presidential election campaign, Putin had caused some observers to fear a return to authoritarianism. 'From the very start,' Putin had said, 'Russia was created as a super-centralised state. This is part of its genetic code, traditions and people's mentality.' Familiar pledges to uphold a liberal economy, the free market, human rights, and respect for neighbours and Russia's global partners, were taken with a big pinch of salt. Putin had also spoken darkly of imposing a 'dictatorship of the law'. On 28 December 1999, three days before being anointed acting president by Boris Yeltsin, he talked to American television about the need for strong government to crush widespread lawlessness and corruption. He told his CNN audience: 'We don't need a weakened government but a strong government that would take responsibility for the rights of the individual and care for society as a whole.' Russia, he concluded, had only one ambition, to 'enjoy respect from other nations'.

Putin soon put his ideas into action. After granting Boris Yeltsin immunity, one of his first acts was to sack Yeltsin's daughter and one-time ally Tatyana Dyachenko from the Kremlin. Dyachenko had installed herself in the Kremlin as an 'adviser' to her father and the administration. Perhaps even more shockingly, Putin moved against the oligarchs in a populist gesture designed to bolster his image as his own man. Embezzlement charges were once again levelled against Boris Berezovsky, whose media interests had played an important role in getting Putin elected president. Swiss authorities alleged Berezovsky had embezzled over $970 million from Aeroflot's revenue and ticket sales in the mid-1990s. Berezovsky had previously faced such allegations under the premiership of Yevgeny Primakov in late 1998, but these had not been pursued. Primakov had ended up being sacked. By the summer of 2000, five of the country's leading oligarchs found themselves under investigation from government prosecutors and tax police.

Vladimir Gusinsky and his Media Most media empire also found himself under attack. Gusinsky was arrested for embezzlement and immediately sent to Moscow's notorious Butyrskaya prison in June 2000. He was charged with embezzling $10 million of state funds during the takeover of a St Petersburg television company in 1997. The media mogul claimed his arrest was a heavy-handed attempt to intimidate him and silence his critical TV, radio and newspapers. President Putin claimed not to be involved in Gusinsky's arrest, but showed an intimate knowledge of Media Most's affairs and the allegations against the oligarch when quizzed by journalists in Madrid, where he was on a state visit. According to Gusinsky, the Russian government offered to drop the charges and release him if he sold his controlling stake in his Media Most empire. Following an international outcry, Gusinsky was released, but not before he had (by his account) signed a promise under duress to sell off his media empire. By the winter, both Gusinsky (who had fled Russia once before under Yeltsin) and Berezovsky had left the country under threat of arrest. Insult was added to injury when Gusinsky, who holds joint Russian and Israeli nationality and is head of the Russian branch of the World Jewish Congress, had his house in Moscow seized by Russian prosecutors. It was the second time in six months that Gusinsky's house in Moscow's Chegasovo suburb had been impounded by the prosecutor's office. The charge sheet against Gusinsky grew exponentially. The Russian prosecutor-general's office now accused him of 'deceit and abuse of trust' in securing more than $300 million in loans from gas monopoly Gazprom, for a group of companies that were insolvent. Gazprom, incidentally, was 38 per cent state-owned and heavily influenced by the Kremlin.

Putin's blistering attack on the power of the oligarch-owned media continued. He had already installed Oleg Dobrodeye, an NTV founder and government supporter, as head of Russia's second state channel, RTR. In January 2001, Berezovsky, now facing mounting legal pressure from Russian prosecutors, conceded defeat and offered to sell his 49 per cent stake in ORT television. The move failed to deter the Russian prosecutor's office, which prepared an international warrant for Berezovsky's arrest. In April 2001, government supporters in the state-controlled gas monopoly, Gazprom, moved to take over NTV television. Gazprom owned 46 per cent of NTV's shares and board-room changes ensured the gas monopoly was dominated by Putin's supporters. A protest lock-in by NTV's journalists ended when most defected to TV6, a small television channel owned by Berezovsky. Even this escape was relatively short-lived, as TV6 was shut down by another state-controlled monopoly, the oil company Lukoil in January 2002. Lukoil closed down TV6 on a legal technicality, claiming its losses in 1998–2000 justified its liquidation. TV6 resisted the bank-ruptcy proceedings on the grounds that it was currently profitable. The move meant that all four television channels with national cov-erage had fallen under government control. Seventeen months after President Putin had first brought his guns to bear against the oligarch-controlled media at the time of the *Kursk* disaster, Russia's independent television channels had been extinguished.

Russia's political and intellectual elite knew that the takeover of NTV and the closure of TV6 had been politically inspired. Boris Nemtsov, leader of the Duma's right-wing Union of Right Forces and a former deputy prime minister, said the decision to close TV6 was 'dictated exclusively by political motive'. From exile in London, Berezovsky called the move 'pure politics'. Even the US State Department waded in with an unusually strongly-worded statement. 'There's a strong appearance of political pressure in the judicial process against the independent media,' said Richard Boucher, a State Department spokesman. 'Press freedom and the rule of law can be best served by keeping TV6 on the air.' Ironically, Russia had changed the law on 1 January 2002, so that minority shareholders could no longer make an application for a company to be declared bankrupt. It was held not to apply in the TV6 case.

Putin's victory over the media moguls was almost complete. In addi-tion to taking over or closing NTV, ORT and TV6, Gusinsky lost control of his Sem Dnei publishing house. The newspaper *Sevodnya* was closed on 16 April 2001. The next day the editor of *Itogi* and all the editorial staff were replaced by the new regime. To all intents and purposes, the opposition media had been closed down, with the excep-tion of a handful of independent newspapers and the radio station

Ekho Moskvy. Russia's president would never again face the barrage of criticism he had experienced at the time of the *Kursk* sinking.

Vladimir Putin's presidency has been primarily about centralisation and the accretion of power. He inherited a weak state where often Moscow's writ didn't seem to run beyond the city's ring-road. One of Russia's eighty-nine 'subjects', Chechnya, had to all intents and purposes seceded, and other parts of the Russian Federation seemed like they might follow suit. Vladivostock and the Primorski region operated like the governor's personal fiefdom. Crime, corruption and poverty were grinding the people down. Putin's answer was to strengthen the state, beginning at the centre. He appointed seven federal super-governors to impose the president's will in the regions. Laws were introduced so the president could suspend incompetent or corrupt governors. He issued decrees demanding that the regions of Bashkortostan, Ingushetia and Amur bring their laws into line with federal legislation. Regional governors lost their right to sit in the Federation Council, or upper house of parliament. Previously, the Federation Council house had occasionally opposed his predecessor, Boris Yeltsin. It would not dare defy President Putin. Alexander Rutskoi, the governor of Kursk who had rashly criticised the president over the submarine tragedy, was barred from standing for re-election.

Putin supporters were placed in control of the massive gas monopoly Gazprom and the Central Bank. The conservative and anti-reformist Victor Gerashchenko, head of the Central Bank, was replaced by Sergei Ignatiev, a deputy finance minister and a former deputy head of the bank. Alexei Miller, aged thirty-nine, an old friend from Putin's days working for St Petersburg's city administration, was appointed chief executive of the multi-billion-dollar gas giant. Putin promised an extra 50 per cent spending on defence, and embarked on reforms to streamline the military, including phasing out conscription. Russia's president planned to reduce the number of men under arms to below 1.2 million, and introduced a system of contracts to supplement the ranks of conscripts with professional troops. Some 365,000 defence ministry forces were to be axed, together with another 235,000 civilian and other military personnel. As a gesture to the past, military training was re-introduced into schools, and the Soviet anthem brought back, albeit with new lyrics. Addressing an old-style parade in Red Square in his first year as president, some Soviet veterans had to pinch themselves to remember it was almost ten years since the end of the USSR. Commemorating the fifty-fifth anniversary of the end of the Second World War, Putin said: 'We defended our great Soviet motherland . . . and kept our independence. We are used to winning. It is in our blood. It is not just the way to win wars. In peacetime it will also help us. Hurrah!'

Nevertheless, the military remained chronically underfunded. Putin had upbraided his own Security Council following the *Kursk* disaster in August 2000. 'The current structure of the armed forces is hardly optimal,' he said on that occasion. 'How can it be considered optimal if training is not conducted in many units, pilots hardly ever fly and sailors hardly ever put to sea? The structure of the armed forces must precisely correspond to the threats Russia faces now and will face in the future,' he concluded. Progress was slow, and Putin found that effective implementation was a lot more difficult than policy pronouncements. In June 2001 he bitterly castigated his Cabinet for requesting delays in bringing military pay into line with civil servants' salaries. Unusually, the Kremlin published Putin's frustrated outburst in full. 'We are speaking about the fate of millions of people – the military and their family members,' the exasperated president told his Cabinet colleagues. 'The government must take measures . . . to ensure that the military's material conditions actually improve.' Most of the Russian armed forces are still waiting.

Putin reinvigorated the KGB's successor agencies the FSB and the SVR. Many of his appointments were either old KGB colleagues, friends from St Petersburg, or both. Signalling the final rehabilitation of the KGB, in May 2002 Russia marked the anniversary of Josef Stalin's secret police by issuing a set of postage stamps bearing the portraits of six of Stalin's agents. Ironically, five were executed by Stalin. No one in Russia's secret service seemed to understand there was a moral in there somewhere. At the same time, Putin showed some signs of liberalism by keeping his team of free-market economic advisers in place, and appointing Sergei Ivanov as Russia's first civilian defence minister. German Gref, Putin's 35-year-old top economic adviser, was typical of the young pro-market economists who joined the new administration. Both Ivanov and Gref knew Putin from his St Petersburg days, and came from the city.

Politically, Putin reinforced his power in parliament when the pro- and former anti-Kremlin factions Unity and Fatherland-All Russia combined to form a single bloc in the Duma. Fatherland's regional bosses had found that opposing the president could be bad for their political health. Yury Luzhkov, Mayor of Moscow, and former prime minister Yevgeny Primakov decided to kiss and make up with the Kremlin. The Russia Regions Party and the Peoples' Deputy Party were soon queuing up to form a majority pro-Putin alliance in the Duma. The new party, the centrist Union of Unity and Fatherland and its allies, came to exert control over both houses of parliament. The opposition communists soon found themselves marginalised, together with other liberal and centre-right groupings. The Duma, which had caused Yeltsin so much trouble in the past, had now been tamed. President Putin now had no effective opposition in either parliament or the media.

In Putin's autobiography, *First Person*, the word 'democracy' hardly features at all. In an online webcast in March 2001, Putin did however use the dreaded 'D' word. Law and order and democracy are insepara- ble, he told his inquisitors. 'As long as I remain president I see no other alternative to democratic development and the market economy,' the president added. It is perhaps not the ringing endorsement of demo- cratic values that many in the West would like to see, but it is probably the best Vladimir Putin will venture. Putin believes in a 'managed democracy': one which does not threaten the state or the embodiment of the state, the president himself. The lesson for Putin from the *Kursk* crisis was that just as the media could make a president, it could break a president.

The Kremlin's cowing of the media after the *Kursk* tragedy res- onated with Putin's own view, held since his KGB days, of the state's supremacy over individual liberty. Anything which threatens the state or the president's personal position must be neutered, be it the media, the oligarchs, the military High Command, Chechen rebels, regional governors, the Federation Council or the political opposition. As Lilia Shetsova of the Moscow Carnegie Centre observed: 'This is an appointed monarchy. The successor was appointed and we, ordinary people, were also appointed to be his electorate.' Rather like choosing the colour of Ford's Model T, the Russian electorate will be given the choice to elect any president in 2004, provided it is Vladimir Putin. An opinion poll conducted by the All-Russia Centre for Public Opinion Studies named Putin as 'Man of the Year' in 2001. With his opinion-poll rating back in the comfortable 70s following his earlier setback during the *Kursk* crisis, Putin's re-election looks a racing certainty.

# 7

# Myth-Making and Fact-Finding

There have been many theories about why the *Kursk* sank. Some have been bizarre, like the claim the *Kursk* was attacked by a UFO or initial accounts that the crew had gone on strike over non-payment of wages, and deliberately let the sub lie on the bottom of the Barents Sea. Only slightly less outlandish were the accusations that a NATO submarine had targeted the *Kursk* with a torpedo, or the claim by the far-right leader Vladimir Zhirinovsky that a Norwegian sub had sunk the Russian boat. One theory suggested the submarine had been sunk by Islamic terrorists. Some gullible journalists in Russia and the West circulated speculative versions claiming the *Kursk* was sunk by a 'super-torpedo' exploding onboard, or by a missile fired by one of Russia's own warships. RTR television journalist Arkady Mamontov reported that the crew of the cruiser *Pyotr Veliky* had discovered a foreign buoy in the vicinity of the *Kursk* accident site. The supposed sighting of a green and white NATO emergency buoy seemingly added weight to the allegation that a Western submarine had collided with the *Kursk*. It was later reported that the suspected buoy was either a floating cabbage or a jellyfish.

Every retired Russian admiral or submarine commander has been keen to feed the media with their own 'truth' about the *Kursk*'s demise. In the frenzy to fill up newspaper and magazine space and reveal the 'real reason' behind the disaster, many writers have come to hasty conclusions in their attempt to give the 'final version' of the *Kursk* tragedy. Almost two years after the accident, much more is known about how and why the *Kursk* sank. It is possible to piece together the most probable chain of events in order to explain what really happened.

The Russian authorities themselves were responsible for stimulating speculation and spreading disinformation. As we have seen, Deputy Prime Minister Ilya Klebanov and the government-appointed Commission of Inquiry initially investigated twelve separate versions of the disaster, and decided not to rule out three – collision with a 'large underwater object', a euphemism for a NATO sub; a torpedo malfunction and explosion; or a collision with a Second World War mine. The latter was always regarded as the least plausible and most commentators immediately ruled it out. A submarine designed to survive a direct hit with a modern torpedo was hardly likely to have been sunk by a 50-year-old mine. Klebanov and the Russian Navy stubbornly refused to abandon the submarine collision theory until the end of 2001 or even early 2002. By this time no serious expert or commentator without an axe to grind gave any credence whatsoever to the collision theory.

Christine Toomey, writing in the *Sunday Times* magazine on 4 March 2001, repeated the version whereby the *Kursk* had sunk due to a missile going astray after being fired from the *Pyotr Veliky*. Toomey's account was based on a report published in the German *Berlin Zeitung* newspaper the previous September, and a second-hand rumour from a retired Russian admiral. The original German story said a Granit-type missile had travelled twelve and a half miles, hitting the water near the *Kursk*, causing a small explosion later followed by a larger one which sank the boat. Supposedly based on eyewitness accounts aboard the cruiser *Pyotr Veliky*, the story turned out to be completely false. A whole industry had developed around the *Kursk* accident, with journalists waving large wads of cash for personal accounts, letters and videos. The media circus helped create a feverish market for conspiracy theories and half-baked rumours. Russians love a good conspiracy theory at the best of times, and need little encouragement to speculate. The country's press was at the forefront of fanning the debate, often based on the flimsiest of rumours. Retrospectively, the missile theory seemed credible, especially when in October 2001 the Ukrainian military downed a civilian airliner above the Black Sea with an S-200 missile. In typically Soviet fashion, the Ukrainian armed forces had at first categorically denied that the missile had gone astray, killing all seventy-eight on board the Sibir airlines passenger jet. Nevertheless, the Russian government and missile experts disdainfully dismissed the *Berlin Zeitung/Sunday Times* Granit missile theory. First, Granits are designed to be long-range missiles, and were unlikely to fall so short, even if one had been fired at the time, which it had not. Apart from the alleged 'eyewitness' account, there was no evidence that a missile had been fired from the *Pyotr Veliky* and hit the sea in the vicinity of the *Kursk*. The US and Norwegians, who were monitoring the manoeuvres, reject this version. Scientific evidence from the Blacknest seismological research centre in the UK and NORSAR in Norway prove conclusively that it is nonsense. Both explosions occurred *aboard* the *Kursk*, and were not caused by any external impact.

A number of reporters faithfully described the Russians' heroic struggle against the elements using their diving bells in the week before the arrival of Norwegian and British rescue teams, working tirelessly to link up with a badly listing *Kursk*. The British and Norwegian rescue teams later told me this too is totally false. The weather was calm, the current was moderate and the *Kursk* wasn't listing at all by the time of their arrival. As Jonathan Steele also reported in the *Guardian* on 21 August 2000, the Russians didn't have any diving bells. Anyone who watched the daily television coverage on RTR from the accident site, as I did, could see that the Russians relied entirely on two obsolete mini-subs. However, Steele was incorrect to suggest that the lack of Russian divers able to go below 100 metres seriously hampered the mini-subs' rescue work. As the British LR5 submersible team told me when I visited their operational HQ in

Renfrew, Scotland, no rescue submersible in the world requires divers to assist with 'mating' operations, or attaching themselves to escape hatches. Modern rescue subs are designed to operate at depths that no diver could survive.

Ramsay Flynn's October 2001 article in the *Independent on Sunday* is another account which repeats the Russian line that they were working to save the *Kursk*'s crew with their non-existent diving bells. More seriously, Flynn makes the accusation that the *Kursk* crew knowingly loaded three potentially lethal leaking missiles, two of which were new, electrically-driven prototypes. Again, this is based on second-hand hearsay evidence. Interviewing a number of Russian nuclear submarine commanders and officers who actually commanded torpedo compartments, several points became clear. Loading leaking and dangerous torpedoes into a torpedo magazine would not be accepted by the officers in charge of the operation. It implies a level of negligence and a cavalier attitude which is grossly unfair to *Kursk* commander Captain Lyachin and his crew. Second, even if regulations were overridden, several Russian commanders on similar class nuclear submarines said that the *Kursk* had a device (a 'sleeve') to drain off fuel and any leakages from any torpedo aboard. Third, a number of relatives have said the crew were only concerned about one torpedo, a 'Fat' practice torpedo. There were no new experimental torpedoes on board, a fact confirmed by the subsequent investigation carried out by the formally independent Russian prosecutor's office.

Flynn also suggests that the first explosion occurred during the test firing, after the torpedo had been loaded and its firing chamber flooded, with its bow door open to the sea. Four of the UK's top torpedo experts and a Russian torpedo specialist told me this was not a credible scenario. If the torpedo had exploded inside its tube on the point of firing, with the bow door open, the ensuing flood of seawater would have extinguished the fire which undoubtedly followed. It would have been impossible for the fire to spread inside the submarine and cook off the other torpedoes in the compartment. The reason for this is quite simple. An explosion inside the closed torpedo tube would have blown out towards the sea, causing the compartment to flood with thousands of gallons of seawater. The other torpedoes needed over two minutes of extreme temperature caused by a confined fire to explode. The only possible explanation is that the torpedo exploded before the torpedo tube's inner door was made secure, and as it was being prepared for firing. This explains why the fireball blew back into the compartment, but was not dowsed by seawater. Scientists at Blacknest seismological research centre are able to prove that the two explosions were entirely contained aboard the *Kursk*. If the first explosion had taken place at the time of actually launching and firing the torpedo, the force of the explosion would have been projected into the surrounding water. Recordings prove that this was not the case.

A BBC *Horizon* television documentary, first shown in August 2001 and repeated in May 2002, continued the trend of sensational coverage. In accordance with the BBC's new apparent policy of 'dumbing down', scientists told me they were asked to say the second explosion was rated 4 on the Richter Scale. The BBC had told them that the public 'couldn't understand fractions', so it was better not to give the real figure of 3.5. The latter figure had been calculated by NORSAR in Norway, and it was this figure which was analysed by the seismologists at Blacknest. Maurice Stradling, a retired torpedo expert, was right to identify hydrogen peroxide, used as an oxidant for the Russian 'Fat' torpedo, as a major contributor to the disaster. Stradling recalled that the *Kursk* tragedy partly mirrored the explosion aboard HMS *Sidon* in 1955. Stradling was wrong, however, to suggest that the *Kursk*'s crew had somehow started the torpedo's motor running while still aboard the *Kursk*, which led to overheating and a subsequent explosion. Several other UK torpedo experts used to modern British and Russian torpedoes told me about the use of 'interlocks', which are now fitted to today's torpedoes. These devices make it impossible to 'accidentally' start a torpedo running when it is out of the water. Russian experts also suggested that crew members aboard the *Kursk* would have to set out deliberately to override safety systems to try to start the torpedo's engine running before firing. Firing torpedoes is now fully automated, even on Russian submarines. To imply negligence against the *Kursk* crew on the grounds that they somehow accidentally started the torpedo running inside the submarine is therefore unjustified. Expert opinion instead now suggests that there was an internal breakdown of components inside the old 'Fat' practice torpedo, which led to a chemical reaction and the torpedo casing blowing up.

Many of the earlier accounts have been discredited as the official investigation into the *Kursk* disaster has continued. Following the lack of transparency shown during the rescue phase, the Russians became a great deal more open in the later salvage and recovery operation. The increasing independence and assertiveness of the Russian prosecutor's office, and the eclipsing of Klebanov and his navy-dominated Commission of Inquiry, led to unparalleled official *glasnost*. The Russians stopped just short of putting the official blame for the disaster on the 'Fat' practice torpedo aboard the *Kursk*. Even so, when Prosecutor-General Ustinov and Navy Commander-in-Chief Kuroyedov announced preliminary findings to the press on 19 February 2002, it was clear that the hydrogen peroxide-propelled 'Fat' torpedo was the main culprit behind the catastrophe. Russian officials also confirmed for the first time that the old torpedo had had an experimental battery fitted. This account confirmed the version which had been given to me by some of the crew's relatives. It also explains why there were only two relatively junior test engineers on board from the Dagdiesel torpedo manufacturing plant at the time of the explosion, and just five staff officers from the Northern Fleet's 1st Submarine Flotilla.

If a major new torpedo system were being tested, there would have been more senior test engineers on board the *Kursk*, and many more senior visiting staff officers from the Northern Fleet. Russian Admiral Georgy Kostev has suggested the *Kursk* sinking was due to a VA-111 Shkval torpedo exploding. He claimed there were an extra thirty-six officers on board to witness the inaugural firing. That many guest officers aboard would indeed have indicated a major new system was being tested. However, the published crew list shows Kostev was mistaken. The *Kursk* only had seven extra people on board during the naval exercises of 12 August 2000. Following the February press conference by Ustinov and Kuroyedov, the navy admitted its confidence in hydrogen peroxide-propelled torpedoes had been misplaced, and the offending torpedoes were withdrawn from the submarine fleet's service.

Virtually all commentators now accept that the 'Fat' hydrogen per-oxide-propelled torpedo was responsible for the first explosion aboard the *Kursk*. The Shkval is a solid rocket-propelled torpedo and so does not have the same propensity to self-detonate. In any event, it seems pretty clear that there were no Shkval rocket torpedoes on the *Kursk*. One BBC documentary-maker has apparently been told by another veteran Russian submariner that the torpedo which caused the explo-sion aboard the *Kursk* was a Type 65-71 TEST torpedo. An upgraded Type 53 (TEST-71) 533 mm torpedo has been produced by Russia's Dvigitel manufacturing plant. They are to be used on Project 877 EKM and Project 636 submarines to replace earlier Type 53–65 tor-pedoes. These do not include Oscar II-class boats like the *Kursk*. The TEST-71 ME NK torpedoes are electric remote-controlled homing torpedoes, powered by a silver-zinc single-use ampoule battery. A prac-tice version is available for training and test-firing. However, this type of torpedo can be ruled out because it only has a diameter of 533 mm. The Russian Navy, investigators, prosecutors and relatives are all united in blaming the 650 mm 'Fat' torpedo. It is also significant that the two test engineers aboard the ill-fated *Kursk* were from the Dagdiesel plant, not the Dvigitel factory which makes the TEST-71 torpedoes.

The most likely culprit identified is the SS-N-16 (NATO designa-tion 'Stallion') torpedo, which is a 650 mm-calibre anti-ship cruise missile capable of being fitted with a 10–20 kiloton warhead or a Type 40 (RU-100 Veder) torpedo. The Veder has a 90–100 kg high explosive warhead and a range of up to seventy-five miles. The system consists of a missile launched from the sub's torpedo tubes. Once fired from the submarine, it clears the surface and flies to the target area where it ejects the torpedo payload. A parachute is deployed to reduce its speed and let the weapon enter the water at the right angle. When it hits the water, the torpedo is automatically activated and begins a search-and-track pattern. The fuel used is liquid oxygen plus a hydrogen peroxide oxidant. Each Russian sub-marine is believed to carry up to four Veder torpedo systems, and about 400–600 have been produced for the navy. However, the one discrepancy here is that the SS-N-16 Stallion was only deployed from between 1978 and 1981, whereas versions of the Soviet 'Fat' torpedo have been around since the late 1950s. With the regular recycling of test torpedoes carried out by all the world's navies, it is possible the 'Fat' torpedo responsible for the *Kursk* disaster was over thirty years old. This would rule out the more modern SS-N-16 being responsible for the *Kursk* accident.

The Russians initially pushed the collision theory very hard. Websites started appearing full of material alleging Western involvement in the *Kursk* disaster. A typical example was a four-page piece on the *www.murman.ru* website, written by 'Dmitry' on 23 November 2000, claiming that a British submarine collided with the *Kursk*. On the same website another article claimed a US Los Angeles-class boat had caused the accident. The Russian government's own official website on the *Kursk* tragedy was one of the worst offenders, giving enormous prominence to the collision theory involving a Western submarine. In particular, the official site promoted the views of Captain Vladimir Shigin, a staff writer for the Russian-language *Marine Journal*. As late as 16 September 2001, the official website published a piece entitled: ' "Murder will out" says author probing foreign sub ramming theory.' Based on Shigin's ideas, the website proclaimed that a head-on ramming with a foreign submarine was being 'aired anew as a convincing theory of how [the] *Kursk* died'. It continued: 'And the finger points this week to whether a British or US boat crashed into the Russian vessel's forward combat compartment, detonating its torpedo arsenal.' The whole collision myth was a rehash of the *Versiya* newspaper story which had been planted in the press by Russian intelligence in September 2000. The only surprising thing about Shigin's fanciful account was that he had the temerity to repeat the collision myth over a year later, contrary to all the available evidence.

The British and Americans did their best to stamp out the resurgent collision story, once more denying its veracity. Two days after the Shigin article, a naval British diplomatic source in Moscow told the *Kursk.strana.ru* website that the UK did not have a submarine 'within 1,000 miles of the *Kursk*' at the time of the accident. The same source told me the same thing. Normally the Royal Navy and the British government does not comment on operational matters relating to its submarine fleet, but the official said that 'given the exceptional circumstances, we told the Russians there were no British submarines within a thousand miles of the Barents Sea when the *Kursk* sank'. The day before, a US spokesman had issued a similar but less categorical denial. He said no one had brought forth 'a shred of evidence' implicating a US submarine, and added that operational issues were not subject to comment.

The US response was thought less than convincing by Russia's multitudinous conspiracy theorists. The Americans had hardly helped their own image when the USS *Grenville* collided with a Japanese trawler, the *Ehine Maru*, leaving nine fishermen dead off Hawaii. The US sub had sixteen civilian visitors in the control room at the time of the accident on 9 February 2001. The boat was supposedly carrying out a high-speed emergency drill, surfacing rapidly right under the Japanese vessel and sinking it. Russian submariners accused the US submarine commander of recklessness, and showing off to his visitors. In Russian, the manoeuvre carried out by the USS *Grenville* is called *Pryzhok Kasatki*, 'a whale jumping out of the water'. Some Russian commentators saw the *Ehine Maru* accident as further evidence that the US had a cavalier attitude towards underwater safety and was perfectly capable of colliding with the *Kursk*.

There were two factors which comprehensively demolished the collision theory. The first were the results of the investigation carried out by Russia's own prosecutors. They eventually discovered that the Russian Navy's cherished collision version was not supported by any evidence found aboard or near the *Kursk*. Second, there was overwhelming scientific evidence to disprove the collision theory and a whole host of other versions cooked up by those with a conspiratorial bent. The key to understanding the cause of the *Kursk* accident was work done by the NORSAR seismological group in Norway, and the Blacknest seismic research centre in Berkshire, England. Blacknest is part of the UK's Atomic Weapons Establishment, Aldermaston, which is operated by AWE Management on behalf of the Ministry of Defence. Situated in an old country house in Brimpton on the

Berkshire/Hampshire border nearly fifty miles west of London, AWE Blacknest had been researching techniques for over thirty-five years to distinguish seismic signals caused by nuclear explosions from those generated by earthquakes.

NORSAR recorded two seismic events on 12 August in the Barents Sea, the first timed at 7:28:27 A.M. GMT and the second 135 seconds later. In summer, allowing for daylight saving time, local and Moscow time is four hours ahead of GMT. The first explosion therefore took place at 11:28 A.M. local time in the Barents Sea, although some accounts still mistakenly put the time of the accident at 10:28 A.M. Dr David Bowers, a senior scientist at Blacknest, has produced a scientific paper on the *Kursk* disaster entitled 'AWE's Analysis of Seismic Signals Associated With the Sinking of the *Kursk* Submarine'. Dr Bowers' paper is based on an analysis of the seismic signals recorded by NORSAR's seismometer array at ARCES in Northern Norway. Bowers' research proved that the second explosion took place at about 100 metres, just above the Barents seabed, with a yield of about 5 tons of TNT (in the range of 2–8 tons). The seismic wave-forms or shock-waves recorded by ARCES for both seismic events were remarkably similar, suggesting the first disturbance was also an underwater explosion, not a collision. If a collision had occurred, the seismic wave-forms recorded by the seismometer array would have looked very different. David Bowers concluded the relative magnitude of the first explosion would produce an explosive yield of about 40 kg (in the range 2–80 kg), at a depth of plus or minus forty metres. Critically, Bowers found no evidence of a 'bubble pulse' in the case of the initial seismic event, suggesting the first explosion had not breached the hull. If the first explosion was fully contained within the submarine, the seismic signals would probably have been muffled or decoupled by air within the boat.

The absence of a 'bubble pulse' suggests very strongly that the first explosion was contained within the *Kursk*. When an explosion occurs underwater a bubble containing hot gases and steam rapidly expands, until the expansion is halted by hydrostatic pressure, after which contraction sets in. During contraction pressure and heat increases within the bubble, the contraction ends and expansion starts once again.

The cycle continues until the bubble reaches the surface, gradually reducing in size through energy loss and eventually escaping into the atmosphere. The lack of any signs of a bubble pulse suggests there was no collision, and it also implies that when the torpedo detonated, the torpedo's bow door was shut. Instead of exploding outwards, towards the sea, the thrust of the explosion was inwards, and contained within the first torpedo compartment. Visiting Blacknest and talking to Dr David Bowers and Dr Peter Marshall (Head of Group) about their research, I found their conclusions compelling evidence that no outside impact was involved in the loss of the *Kursk*.

Dr Bowers' work also proved several other interesting facts about the *Kursk* tragedy. Allowing for the size of the *Kursk* submarine, the location of the explosion in the first compartment and a reasonable range for scientific modelling, the evidence suggests the *Kursk* was at periscope depth when it sank. Second, the boat was sinking between the two explosions, not rising, which gives an indication that the surviving crew members did not manage to get the *Kursk* nearer to the surface after the first explosion. If everyone in the Central Command Post had survived the first explosion, as several accounts attest, they would have been able to blow the main ballast tanks and get the *Kursk* to rise. The fact that the *Kursk* was going down at the time of the second explosion implies that most or all crew in the CCP were killed or put out of action by the first explosion. This would also explain the mystery of why the *Kursk* sent no distress signal in the two minutes following the first blast. The spread of the smoke and fire from the torpedo compartment directly into the CCP is explained by the fact that submarine crews often left the hatch open between the first and second compartments during a torpedo firing. Although against regulations, a number of Russian submariners told me this was regularly done to reduce pressure and to protect the torpedomen's eardrums. Officers overlooked the practice.

Norway's NORSAR seismological observatory conducted their own research on the *Kursk* data, which broadly agreed with Blacknest's analysis. Dr Frode Ringdal, NORSAR's Scientific Director, told me the results of their work. According to Dr Ringdal:

While it is difficult to calculate the exact yields of the two explosions, we have estimated that the first explosion was at least a hundred times smaller than the second explosion. This estimate is based on the seismic recordings, which give Richter magnitudes of 1.5 for the first explosion and 3.5 for the second explosion. The 'absolute' yield estimates (1–2 tons for the largest explosion and correspondingly less for the smaller explosion) are based upon comparisons to observed data from underwater explosions of known yields (e.g. explosions used in seismic profiling).

Ringdal added that NORSAR estimated the first explosion was probably around 100–200 kilograms of explosive material, and confirmed that the second explosion was 'certainly consistent with one or (more likely) several torpedoes exploding simultaneously'. The discovery of 400 tonnes of ammunition fragments and munitions aboard the *Kursk* wreck proves that not all the torpedoes on the sub detonated. Although NORSAR's statistics on the explosive yield of the two explosions differ from Blacknest's calculations, the figures are in the same range of magnitude. Certainly Dr Bowers' analysis indicates that the first explosion could not have been caused by a torpedo's warhead detonating. A warhead would have an explosive force far more than the 40 kilograms posited by his study. It is therefore more likely that the first explosion was due to a smaller detonation, matching the explosive force of the casing on a dummy practice torpedo blowing apart.

Investigations by the teams which entered the *Kursk*'s wreck in Roslyakovo dockyard provided more evidence on how the submarine and her crew had met their end. Postmortems on the twenty-three submariners' bodies in the stern of the boat showed that they had not survived beyond the first day of the accident. Doctors and forensic scientists were able to put the time of death at between 7 and 8 P.M. on Saturday 12 August. They also calculated that the submarine had taken no more than eight hours to flood with water. Talk of some of the submariners surviving for several days and tapping out messages on the hull were fanciful. American intelligence sources confirmed that

US submarines monitoring the Barents Sea exercises heard no sound from the *Kursk* after the second huge explosion.

Examination of the bodies of those found in compartment nine showed signs of a localised fire, which accounted for several badly burned torsos. Olga Kolesnikova had the traumatic task of identifying her husband Dmitri's body, and was shocked to discover how badly burned it was. Evidence of the fire was also provided by the Anglo-Norwegian divers responsible for opening the aft escape hatch. Air samples examined by the Norwegians showed that the divers were right to assume the dark bubbles escaping from inside the sub were the result of a local fire. A postmortem showed that Dmitri Kolesnikov had died of carbon monoxide poisoning, and not by drowning. Again, this pointed to the cause of death being a lack of oxygen, exacerbated and hastened by the fire in the ninth compartment. It seems most likely that the cause of the fire in the compartment were the regeneration plates used in the sub's oxygen regeneration unit, which react violently with water and oil. In their narcosis-induced condition, it is fairly reasonable to assume that the survivors in the compartment could easily have let the regeneration plates come into contact with water. Given the partly flooded conditions inside the compartment at the time, and the poor design of the plates, it was almost impossible for the crew to keep the regeneration plates clean and dry while changing them.

The fact that only a handful of the crew in the ninth compartment had burns to their upper body suggests that not all the crew were directly affected by the ensuing fire. Only those men fitting the new regeneration plates, and those next to the regeneration unit, would have been affected. It is possible that some of the crew, like Dmitri Kolesnikov, tried to shelter their colleagues from the flash fire. In any event, as previously described, any fire would quickly exhaust reserves of oxygen in the compartment. One way or another, once the survivors discovered they could not get out of the badly-designed Russian escape chamber, they knew they were almost certainly doomed.

Much of the coverage of the *Kursk* crisis was influenced by stories in the Russian press and on the Internet. Although some of the Russian press is of a high standard, many of the newspapers have a tendency to repeat unsubstantiated rumours and lean towards sensationalist stories, rather like the British tabloid press. Parts of the Russian media are notorious for ignoring the facts in the search for a good conspiracy, making even some of the British tabloids look heavyweight by comparison. Those accounts of the *Kursk* tragedy which have relied more than is prudent on Russian media coverage and Internet sites are shot through with inaccuracies and official disinformation. Russian newspapers published an alleged account of a conversation between President Bill Clinton and President Vladimir Putin in August 2000, for example, claiming the US leader admitted an American sub collided with the *Kursk*. Clinton supposedly promised to cancel the proposed National Missile Defence shield to hush up the affair. At the same time, the CIA's director, George Tenet, reportedly went to Moscow to smooth over the incident. These stories were all bunkum.

Sometimes all this conjecture may seem harmless enough. Yet in other ways some of the versions which have appeared have tended to be grossly offensive to the crew and the relatives they left behind. Claims of stupidity or negligence laid against the *Kursk*'s crew are an insult to the memory of a brave and honourable group of men, who despite the odds served their country with distinction and courage.

In the many versions I have read of the sinking of the *Kursk*, I remember particularly the story of Mamed Gadjiev, a civilian engineer aboard the submarine when it went down. Early stories in the Russian press suggested the *Kursk* might have been sunk by Islamic terrorists, either from Chechnya or in support of the Chechen separatists. The press reported that two of the crew came from Dagestan on the Chechen border, and one of them was Gadjiev. When Admiral Vladimir Kuroyedov went to Kaspiesk on the Caspian Sea in Dagestan, Gadjiev's mother begged the admiral to tell everyone her son was not responsible for the disaster. She feared he would be blamed because he was a Dagestani, from a mainly Muslim republic of the Russian Federation, and because he was a torpedo expert. Press coverage had in effect criminalised Gadjiev because of his ethnic background, and his mother was left alone to salvage her dead son's reputation.

The *Kursk* disaster happened for many reasons. It happened because the Russian Navy relied on antiquated practice torpedoes propelled by the volatile and unstable hydrogen peroxide, abandoned by most Western navies in the 1950s following the explosion aboard the British submarine HMS *Sidon*. It happened because of repeated and severe cuts in the navy's budget for weaponry, training, maintenance and rescue services. The blinkered attitude of the navy's High Command, and indifference from the president down, initially hampered rescue efforts and attempts to explain the tragedy. Russia's delusional leaders hung on to the belief that the country could still aspire to its former superpower status, despite the lack of funds to support its 'Great Power' aspirations. Nowhere could this be seen more than in Russia's desperate efforts to maintain its Northern Fleet's nuclear submarine capability. Design failures, especially the design of the aft escape chamber, played their part in sealing the fate of the *Kursk*'s surviving crew. But all these failings, grave as they are, cannot be laid at the feet of Mamed Gadjiev, Captain Gennady Lyachin, Dmitri Kolesnikov and the rest of the crew. These were decent men, doing a difficult job in a modern nuclear submarine deprived of the necessary resources to make it safe. President Putin has promised to put most of these things right, starting with the poor pay, a complete overhaul of the rescue services and a thorough reform of Russia's armed forces. Let us hope he succeeds, although two years after the disaster precious little seems to have changed for Russia's benighted navy. After all the froth and all the theories, there is only one version of the *Kursk* tragedy that counts. One hundred and eighteen submariners died serving aboard the vessel. Russia let them down, but to the very end, they refused to let down their country or the families they left behind.

# Epilogue:
# Russia's Lost Pride

In August 2000, President Vladimir Putin lamented the state of his country. 'This emergency,' he said, 'highlights the condition of our vital facilities as well as of the entire nation. Only economic development will enable us to prevent such calamities in the future.' The Russian president wasn't referring to the *Kursk* tragedy, but the devastating fire which wrecked the 540-metre Ostankino television tower in Moscow's northern suburbs. The year 2000 was truly Russia's *annus horribilis*. The *Kursk* disaster was followed less than two weeks later by the Ostankino fire, while around the same time the ageing Mir space station suffered a series of breakdowns, leading to the decision to scrap the station completely. For Russians, August 2000 symbolised the disintegration of the fabric of the state and a loss of national pride. Of the three disasters, the *Kursk* was the most poignant metaphor for the state of post-Soviet Russia.

President Putin came to power in March 2000 seeking to re-create Russia as a Great Power almost a decade after the collapse of communism. Instead, he found himself managing the decline of a country which had not come to terms with its collective identity crisis following the break-up of the Soviet Union. Over 20 million Russians found themselves stranded in the newly independent states which had formed part of the USSR. The sinking of the *Kursk* shattered any illusions that Putin and the Russian military had that Russia could quickly regain its former Great Power status, let alone its standing as a superpower. Despite the continued Great Power rhetoric, President Putin's pragmatic international policies show that he understands Russia can aspire to no more than medium-power status. Russia's policy of opposition to NATO enlargement, the US's National Missile Defence shield and abrogation of the Anti-Ballistic Missile Treaty is undimmed. What has changed is Russia's acceptance that it no longer has the international clout to stop these developments. It can only hope to be allowed limited influence in future Western (primarily American) policy formulation.

On one level the *Kursk* crisis showed how attitudes at the top in post-USSR Russia have remained little changed since the communist era. The overwhelming impression in the early days of the tragedy was one of indifference. Indifference shown by the president and the Russian Navy towards the families of the crew, and towards the very survival of the submariners aboard the *Kursk*. Avoiding responsibility and blame, and protecting naval secrets, seemed more important than the lives of the 118 crew. The Russian Navy made it clear from the beginning that the crew were expendable, and the president probably felt the same. After all, in Russia today more than 1,000 servicemen die every year in peacetime accidents. Thousands have died and continue to die in Chechnya. Protecting the *Kursk* from espionage was regarded as far more important than letting Western rescue teams anywhere near the stricken boat. Putin and the naval High Command had failed to take into account the reaction from the independent sections of the Russian media. While the state-controlled media muted its criticism, the independent media tore into the president and the military for their handling of the disaster. The loss of the *Kursk* was seen as a blow to already diminished self-confidence and national pride. The international media took up the hue and cry.

Putin learned valuable lessons from his drubbing at the hands of the Russian media. He needed to improve his PR skills, which he later admitted he got wrong during the *Kursk* crisis. 'I probably should have returned to Moscow,' he told journalists at the Kremlin in July 2001, 'but nothing would have changed. I had the same level of communication both in Sochi and in Moscow, but from a PR point of view I could have demonstrated some special eagerness to return.' If he had gone to Vidyayevo and Severomorsk, he might also have figured out that the navy was pulling the wool over his eyes when it assured him it had the resources to save the crew without Western help.

The other big lesson Putin learned from the *Kursk* disaster was that if he were to secure his own power-base, he needed to exert full control over Russia's major independent media. Especially important here was the control of TV, which most Russians rely on for their information since many newspapers are a relative luxury for the average person. Within eighteen months of the *Kursk* crisis, the Kremlin effectively controlled all three major television stations and had engineered the closure of a fourth. Although Putin's centralising tendencies had been present before the *Kursk* disaster, the submarine accident and its fallout accelerated the president's desire to create a strong centralised presidency. The oligarchs, politicians, the military and the media all suffered from Kremlin-inspired 'purges', involving arrests, sackings, mergers and takeovers. Putin has achieved his post-*Kursk* objective of a 'managed democracy' and the accretion of power. The opposition is crushed, cowed or supine. For the Russian people, at least Putin offers the hope of order, economic reform and stability. He may not have delivered on all these just yet, but he seems a marked improvement on the sick and incompetent last days of Boris Yeltsin.

As Putin manages Russia's decline from superpower to 'Great Power' to medium European power status, the *Kursk* disaster can be seen as a watershed in the country's development. The *Kursk* was a metaphor for Russia's overblown desire to be a Great Power. Its sinking showed that although the country had the ability to put the state-of-the-art boat to sea, it could not afford to maintain and equip it properly. Its sinking represented the sinking of Russia's hopes that the country could once more be a Great Power on the world stage, militarily or politically. The tragedy was a watershed because it vindicated Putin's pragmatic policy of accepting Russia's limitations, and his strategy of working with, rather than against, the West. An old adage runs that if you can't beat them, you must try to join them. The only caveat to Putin's current pro-Western strategy is that many in Russia do not believe it will work. They see many fundamental differences in strategic interests between Russia and the West, particularly between Moscow and Washington.

For the current generation of military leaders, NATO remains more of a potential threat than an ally, especially as former republics of the Soviet Union like the Baltic States join its ranks. Interests between Russia and the US diverge in the Middle East, Iraq, Iran, North Korea and China. For evidence of the deep-seated distrust at the heart of the Russian political and military establishment, it is necessary to look no further than the unrelenting spying game, which continues unabated by all sides despite the end of the Cold War. While many changed attitudes were revealed by the *Kursk* disaster in Russia, particularly the Russian people's desire for truth and honesty from their leaders, other attitudes remain steeped in the ways of the Soviet Union. President Putin and his military commanders are creatures of their time and upbringing, in the president's case his sixteen years in the KGB. Russia's pro-Western phase may be just that, another phase in the ongoing love–hate relationship the country has had with the West since the days of Peter the Great.

# Note on Sources

## 1: Interviews

A list of those people I interviewed who did not object to their names being mentioned can be found in the Preface at the beginning of the book. These included politicians, diplomats, defence and intelligence experts, military personnel, submariners (both active and retired), relatives of the *Kursk's* crew, torpedo and weapons experts, scientists, seismologists, rescue experts, divers and submarine escape specialists.

## 2: Newspapers

Newspapers and journals consulted include: (in Russian) *Chas Pik*, *Itogi*, *Izvestia*, *Kommersant*, *Komsomolskaya Pravda*, *Novaya Gazeta*, *Obshchaya Gazeta*, *Rossiskaya Gazeta*, *Segodnya*, *Vremiya MN* and *Zhizn*; (in English) *Daily Telegraph*, *Financial Times*, *Guardian*, *Independent*, *Independent on Sunday*, *International Herald Tribune*, *Moscow Times*, *New York Times*, *Observer*, *St Petersburg Times*, *Sunday*

*Telegraph, Sunday Times, The Times, USA Today* and the *Wall Street Journal.*


### 3: Internet

There are very many Internet sites with varying degrees of relevance to the *Kursk* tragedy; here are some of them:

www.kursk141.org / www.kursk.strana.ru

www.cnn.com

www.murman.ru/kurskmem

www.janes.com

www.fas.org

www.newsmax.com

www.aeronautics.ru

www.popularmechanics.com

www.defenselink

www.therussianissues.com

www.bellona.no

www.warships.com

www.militarism.navy.ru

www.norsar.no

www.blacknest.gov.uk

www.milparade.com

www.chinfo.navy.mil

www.fco.gov.uk

www.mod.gov.uk

www.rnsubmus.co.uk

www.kurskfoundation.org

www.kursk.com

www.russianobserver.com

www.rumic.co.uk

www.subrescue.navy.mil

www.reuters.com

www.russiatoday.com

www.museum.navy.ru

*www.en.rian.ru*
*www.britemb.msk*
*www.naval-technology.com*
*www.users.bigpond.com*
*www.kursksalvage.com*
*www.dailynews.yahoo.com*
*www.museum.navy.ru*
*www.csis.org*
*www.itar-tass.com*
*www.interfax-news.com*


## 4: Books

There are precious few books published which are relevant to the *Kursk* tragedy. Of those published, the best are Nicolai Cherkashin's *Unesyonnye Bezdnoi*, 'Drawn into the Bottomless Pit' (Moscow: Top Secret Collection, 2001), followed by M. U. Korushin's *Podvodnaya Lodka Kyrsk*, 'Submarine Kursk' (Moscow: Olimp, 2000). In English, Clyde Burleson's *Kursk Down* (New York: Warner Books, 2002) contains many factual inaccuracies and has largely been superseded by revelations and events since the original research was undertaken. In general terms, *Blind Man's Bluff: The Untold Story of Cold War Espionage* by Sherry Sontag *et al.* (New York: HarperCollins, 1998) remains the outstanding book in its field. For background reading on submarines I would recommend: Commander F. W. Lipscomb, *The British Submarine* (London: Conway Maritime Press, 1975); Edwyn Gray, *Few Survived: A Comprehensive Survey of Submarine Accidents and Disasters* (London: Cooper, 1986); Peter Huchthausen *et al.*, *Hostile Waters* (London, 1998); Peter Maas, *The Terrible Hours* (London: Hutchinson, 1997); and C. Warren and J. Benson, *Thetis: Disaster in Liverpool Bay* (The Wirral: Avid, 1997). Don Camsell's book *Black Water: My Secret Life in the Special Boat Service* (London: Virgin, 2000) records some of the SBS's secret operations. On the military/strategic balance, the International Institute for Strategic Studies' *Strategic Survey* and *Military Balance* series remain a valuable resource, as do

*Jane's Fighting Ships* and *Jane's Naval Forces News Briefs*. For post-Soviet domestic and foreign policy, I would refer readers to my own *Russia First: Breaking With the West* (London: I. B. Tauris, 1997). On the voyages of Willem Barents, there is Gerrit de Veer's *The Three Voyages of William Barents to the Arctic Regions* (New York, 1876) and the more recent Rayner Unwin's *A Winter Away from Home: William Barents and the North-east Passage* (London: Seafarer, 1995).

## 5: Other

I am grateful to Dr David Bowers, of AWE Blacknest's Division of Forensic Seismology (DFS) in the UK, for supplying me with a copy of his paper 'AWE's Analysis of Seismic Signals Associated With the Sinking of the Kursk Submarine' (AWE Report 632/01, December 2001). The Russian Embassy in London kindly supplied me with a copy of 'The Foreign Policy Concept of the Russian Federation', approved by President Vladimir Putin on 28 June 2000. Special mention should also be made of the Norwegian environmental group Bellona's excellent report 'The Russian Northern Fleet' (1996), which is available on their website, *www.bellona.no*.